The Select Series:
Microsoft® Visual Basic .NET

Harry Fisher
Ray Schweighofer

Pamela R. Toliver
Series Editor

Prentice
Hall

Upper Saddle River, New Jersey

LIBRARY OF CONGRESS CATALOGING-IN-PUBLICATION DATA

Fisher, Harry (Harry Rayner)
     The select series. Microsoft Visual Basic .NET / Harry Fisher and Ray Schweighofer.
       p. cm.
     ISBN 0-13-060177-2
       1. Microsoft Visual BASIC. 2. BASIC (Computer program language) 3. Microsoft .NET.
I. Title: Microsoft Visual Basic .NET. II. Schweighofer, Ray. III. Title.

   QA76.73.B3 F54 2002
   005.2'768—dc21   2002013526

Publisher and Vice President: Natalie E. Anderson
Executive Acquisitions Editor: Jodi McPherson
Senior Editorial Project Manager: Thomas Park
Assistant Editor: Melissa Edwards
Editorial Assistant: Jasmine Slowik
Developmental Editor: Samantha Penrod
Media Project Manager: Cathleen Profitko
Marketing Manager: Emily Williams Knight
Production Manager: Gail Steier De Acevedo
Project Manager, Production: Tim Tate
Associate Director, Manufacturing: Vincent Scelta
Manufacturing Buyer: Natacha St. Hill Moore
Design Manager: Maria Lange
Interior Design: Lorraine Castellano and Proof Positive/Farrowlyne Associates, Inc.
Cover Design: Lorraine Castellano
Full-Service Composition: Black Dot Group/An AGT Company
Printer/Binder: Banta Book Group, Menasha

10 9 8 7 6 5 4 3 2 1
ISBN 0-13-060177-2

THE SELECT SERIES: MICROSOFT® OFFICE XP

Series Authors

Pamela R. Toliver and Yvonne Johnson

Volume I

Volume II

Brief

Getting Started

Volume I

Volume II

Comprehensive

Brief

Dedication

This book is dedicated to my wife, Rosanna, who provided support and encouragement during the writing of this book. She understands the effort required for such a significant task and was always there for me.

This book is also dedicated to my children, Amanda and Michael. Thanks for understanding and patience as this book was written.

Harry

This book is dedicated to my wife, Karen, who has carried my compass and always pointed me in the right direction when faced with the inevitable crossroads that life always brings. Without her support and unselfish willingness to carry the burden of managing our household and the four children who reside in it, this book and the career experiences necessary to write it would not be possible.

Ray

Acknowledgments

Learning has always been an exciting journey for me. I always dream of what can be done and take whatever action is required to move forward. This fine textbook could not have been accomplished without the cooperation and support of many other individuals from Prentice Hall, Penn State Great Valley, friends, my coauthor Ray, and my family.

To the Prentice Hall team, many thanks to Jodi McPherson for her confidence in my ability and faith in my determination and gung-ho attitude. For the many hours of careful coding review, our thanks go to Chris Panell. He followed every line of programming code to ensure it was clear and meaningful. Thanks to Caryl Wenzel for allowing her gifted copyeditor Amy Schneider to have the time she needed to perform her "copy magic." Our book is remarkably better as a result. To Scott Patterson for his comprehensive attention to details in researching our consulting and other background information. Special thanks also to Pam Toliver for her kind encouragement and direction. Having a mentor like Pam really made a big difference for us. She provided a guiding light to help navigate the way and was always available.

To the Penn State Great Valley team, I would like to thank Jay Polakoff, Peggie Finan, Jean Calazzo, Sharon Kauffman, and Lillian Mina for their never-ending inquiries about our progress on the writing task. Most importantly, I would like to thank Lee Dougherty for offering me the invitation to leap from the realm of teaching and consulting into the exciting world of publishing. Read Wickham and Lee Dougherty presented the challenge to me, and it has been quite a ride ever since.

To my friend Kiran Raval, many thanks for your conscientious efforts in providing insights from the perspective of a student. Your strong faith and vision have always been refreshing.

To Ray Schweighofer, you have proven to be a man of your word and a thoughtful and significant writing partner. I look forward to many more years of writing pleasure with you.

To my family: Rosanna, my wife of over 15 years, thank you for your faith and confidence in my abilities. To my children, Amanda and Michael, whom I hold so precious in my heart, thanks for your understanding and joy as we celebrate this accomplishment together.

Finally, I would like to thank my parents, Gloria and Harry, for their wisdom to help build a strong foundation for me. My father in heaven is surely proud that his determination and perseverance have helped me to achieve this lifelong dream.

Harry

One of my mantras is, "The whole is greater than the sum of the parts," and the writing of this book has served to accentuate the concept of a "team." I would like to thank Jodi McPherson, who was willing to give both Harry and I the opportunity to write our first book. Significant thanks go to Harry Fisher, who has demonstrated the true value of partnership and the need for complementary skills. Many thanks and appreciation go to Chris Panell, for his technical editing and positive words of encouragement, and also to Pam Toliver, who helped show us the publishing ropes and was always available when we needed her.

I would also like to take the time to acknowledge Jay Polakoff of Penn State Great Valley for his endless energy, support, and commitment in making the Accelerated Certificate Programs the best they can be for all students.

Thanks also to my friends at Wyeth, where I have found a professional family and a place where I can pursue my passion for excellence in application architecture and programming.

Immeasurable respect and appreciation goes to my wife, Karen, who has been my partner in life for 21 years and given me four beautiful, healthy, and intelligent children who are the pride of my life and represent my life's most significant achievements.

Finally, I would like to recognize the contribution of my parents, Nancy and Ray, who gave me the foundation necessary to succeed in a very demanding field that requires a lifelong commitment to learning. A special note to my mother who passed away this year after a 6-year-long battle with cancer: "All those hours forcing me to read and study was really worth it... Thanks!"

Ray

Preface

About this Series

The Select Series uses a class-tested, highly visual, project-based approach that teaches students through tasks using step-by-step instructions. You will find extensive full-color figures and screen captures that guide learners through the basic skills and procedures necessary to demonstrate proficiency in their use of each software application.

The Select Series introduces an all-new design for Microsoft Office XP. The easy-to-follow design now has larger screen shots with steps listed on the left side of the accompanying screen. This unique design program, along with the use of bold color, helps reduce distraction and keeps students focused and interested as they work. In addition, selectively placed Tip boxes and Other Ways boxes enhance student learning by explaining various ways to complete a task.

Our approach to learning is designed to provide the necessary visual guidance in a project-oriented setting. Each project concludes with a review section that includes a Summary, Key Terms & Skills, Study Questions, Guided Exercises, and On Your Own Exercises. This extensive end-of-project section provides students with the opportunity to practice and gain further experience with the tasks covered in each project.

What's New in the Select Series for Office XP

The entire Select Series has been revised to include the new features found in the Office XP suite, which contains Word 2002, Excel 2002, Access 2002, PowerPoint 2002, Publisher 2002, FrontPage 2002, and Outlook 2002.

The Select Series provides students with clear, concise instruction supported by its new design, which includes bigger screen captures. Steps are now located in the margin for ease of use and readability. This instruction is further enhanced by graded exercises in the end-of-project material.

Another exciting update is that every project begins with a Running Case from Selections, Inc., a department store that has opened shop online as e-Selections.com. Students are put in an e-commerce–based business environment so that they can relate what they are learning in Office XP to a real world situation. Everything is within a scenario that puts them in the department store where they perform tasks that relate to a particular division of the store or Web site.

About the Book

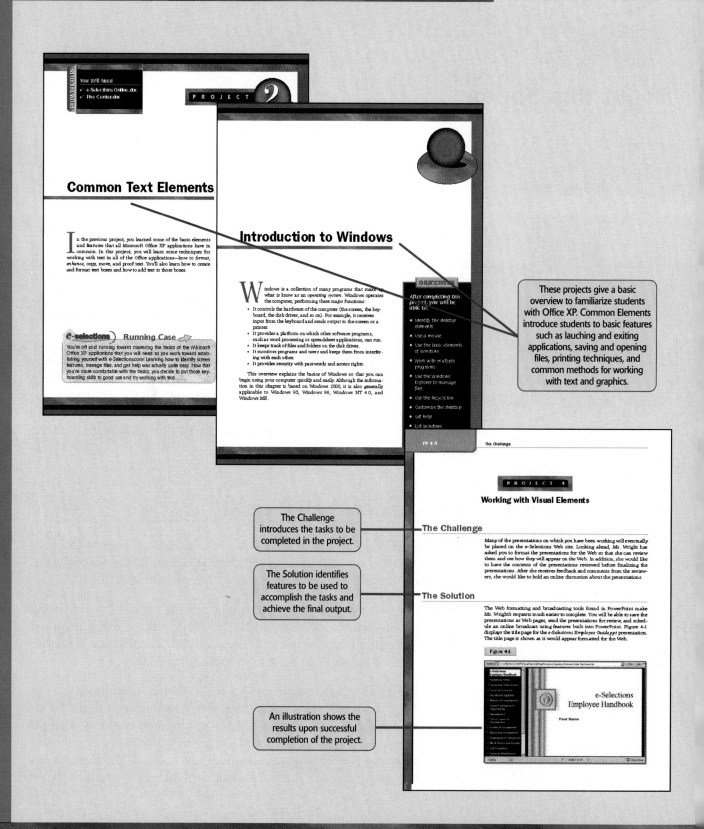

These projects give a basic overview to familiarize students with Office XP. Common Elements introduce students to basic features such as lauching and exiting applications, saving and opening files, printing techniques, and common methods for working with text and graphics.

The Challenge introduces the tasks to be completed in the project.

The Solution identifies features to be used to accomplish the tasks and achieve the final output.

An illustration shows the results upon successful completion of the project.

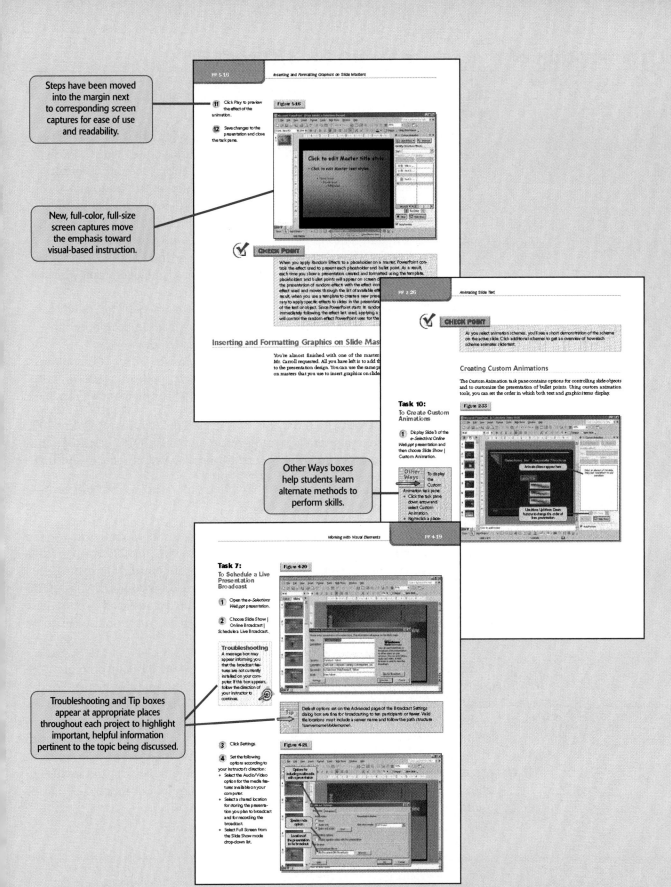

Steps have been moved into the margin next to corresponding screen captures for ease of use and readability.

New, full-color, full-size screen captures move the emphasis toward visual-based instruction.

Other Ways boxes help students learn alternate methods to perform skills.

Troubleshooting and Tip boxes appear at appropriate places throughout each project to highlight important, helpful information pertinent to the topic being discussed.

Organization of the Select Series for Office XP

The new Select Series for Office XP includes four combined Office XP texts from which to choose:

- **Microsoft Office XP Volume I** is MOUS certified at the Core level in each of the major applications in the Office suite (Word, Excel, Access, and PowerPoint). Four additional supplementary modules (Introduction to Internet Explorer, Introduction to Windows, Introduction to Outlook, and Common Elements) are also included. In addition, three integrated projects are included which integrate files and data among Word, Excel, Access, and PowerPoint.
- **Microsoft Office XP Volume II,** MOUS certified at the Expert level, picks up where Volume I leaves off, covering advanced topics for the individual applications.
- **Microsoft Office XP Brief** provides less coverage of the individual applications than Volume I (a total of four projects as opposed to six). The supplementary modules are also included.
- A new volume, **Getting Started with Microsoft Office XP,** contains the Introduction and first chapter from each application (Word, Excel, Access, and PowerPoint) plus the four supplementary modules.

Individual texts for Word 2002, Excel 2002, Access 2002, and PowerPoint 2002 provide complete coverage of each application and are MOUS certified. They are available in Volume I and Volume II texts and also as Comprehensive texts.

This series of books has been approved by Microsoft to be used in preparation for Microsoft Office User Specialist exams.

APPROVED COURSEWARE

The Microsoft Office User Specialist (MOUS) program is globally recognized as the standard for demonstrating desktop skills with the Microsoft Office suite of business productivity applications (Microsoft Word, Microsoft Excel, Microsoft PowerPoint, Microsoft Access, and Microsoft Outlook). With MOUS certification, thousands of people have demonstrated increased productivity and have proved their ability to utilize the advanced functionality of these Microsoft applications.

Customize the Select Series with Prentice Hall's Custom Binding program. The Select Series is part of the Custom Binding Program, enabling instructors to create their own texts by selecting projects from Office XP to suit the needs of a specific course. An instructor could, for example, create a custom text consisting of the specific projects that he or she would like to cover from the entire suite of products. The Select Series is part of PHit's Value Pack program in which multiple books can be shrink-wrapped together at substantial savings to the student. A value pack is ideal in courses that require complete coverage of multiple applications.

Instructor and Student Resources

Instructor's Resource CD-ROM

The **Instructor's Resource CD-ROM** that is available with the Select Office XP Series contains:

- Student data files
- Solutions to all exercises and problems
- PowerPoint lectures
- Instructor's manuals in Word format that enable the instructor to annotate portions of the instructor manual for distribution to the class
- A Windows-based test manager and the associated test bank in Word format

Companion Website www.prenhall.com/select

This text is accompanied by a companion Website at *www.prenhall.com/select*.

Features of this new site include the ability for you to customize your homepage with real-time news headlines, current events, exercises, an interactive study guide, student data files, and downloadable supplements. This site is designed to take learning Microsoft Office XP with the Select Series to the next level.

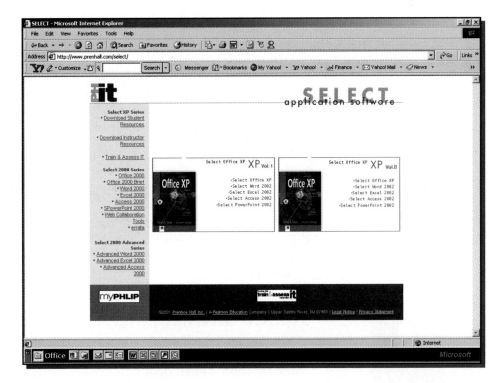

Now you have the freedom to personalize your own online course materials! Prentice Hall provides the content and support you need to create and manage your own online course in WebCT, Blackboard, or Prentice Hall's own Course Compass. Choose "Standard" content to enhance the material from this text or "Premium" content, which provides you with even more lecture material, interactive exercises, and projects.

Training and Assessment www.prenhall.com/phit

Prentice Hall offers Performance Based Training and Assessment in one product, Train&Assess IT. The Training component offers computer-based training that a student can use to preview, learn, and review Microsoft Office application skills. Web- or CD-ROM delivered, Train IT offers interactive, multimedia, computer-based training to augment classroom learning. Built-in prescriptive testing suggests a study path based not only on student test results but also on the specific textbook chosen for the course.

The Assessment component offers computer-based testing that shares the same user interface as Train IT and is used to evaluate a student's knowledge about specific topics in Word, Excel, Access, PowerPoint, Windows, Outlook, and the Internet. It does this in a task-oriented environment to demonstrate proficiency as well as comprehension of the topics by the students. More extensive than the testing in Train IT, Assess IT offers more administrative features for the instructor and additional questions for the student.

Assess IT also allows professors to test students out of a course, place students in appropriate courses, and evaluate skill sets.

CourseCompass www.coursecompass.com

CourseCompass is a dynamic, interactive online course-management tool powered exclusively for Pearson Education by Blackboard. This exciting product allows you to teach market-leading Pearson Education content in an easy-to-use, customizable format.

BlackBoard www.prenhall.com/blackboard

Prentice Hall's abundant online content, combined with Blackboard's popular tools and interface, result in robust Web-based courses that are easy to implement, manage, and use—taking your courses to new heights in student interaction and learning.

WebCT www.prenhall.com/webct

Course-management tools within WebCT include page tracking, progress tracking, class and student management, gradebook, communication, calendar, reporting tools, and more. GOLD LEVEL CUSTOMER SUPPORT, available exclusively to adopters of Prentice Hall courses, is provided free-of-charge upon adoption and provides you with priority assistance, training discounts, and dedicated technical support.

Brief Table of Contents

Table of Contents

Introducing Visual Basic .NET

V isual Basic .NET is a Microsoft application designed to make writing computer programs easier. Using Visual Basic .NET, programmers can create complex programs designed to operate on many computer platforms by simply placing visual objects where they want them on a blank palette. While creating computer programs is somewhat more complex than this description might imply, Visual Basic has become extraordinarily popular among average computer users because it makes creating sophisticated programs possible without having to learn detailed program coding. Visual Basic .NET takes care of much of the tedious coding automatically as you design the program.

OBJECTIVES

After completing this project, you will be able to:

- Understand programming terminology
- Launch Visual Basic .NET
- Open an existing Visual Basic .NET project
- Recognize Visual Basic .NET screen elements
- Save project changes
- Run the project
- Exit the application

e-selections   **Running Case**

Welcome to the Information Technology Department of e-Selections! You have been assigned to work with Travis Traylor on a Visual Basic .NET project. Mr. Traylor would like you to review the new Visual Basic .NET interface and become familiar with the Login project he created for you.

An Introduction to the Unified Modeling Language (UML)

Create UML drawings before you write code and create great applications in less time with all the functionality required.

Throughout the evolution of software development, we have had contentious views on the best way to describe and visualize software that was to be built using an object-oriented language such as Visual Studio .NET.

We have evolved to a unified modeling approach, using the unified modeling language (UML).

Microsoft, IBM, Sun, Rational, and Borland are a few of the companies that have endorsed UML.

A good reason for modeling your application with UML is to communicate your design ideas. With UML, you can visually model existing and proposed business processes, application architecture, data structures, and user interactions. UML diagrams are easy to understand and help facilitate understanding what the application does and how people interact with it. As the UML diagrams are developed, you can present how the intended application works and incrementally refine the application's design.

As Internet applications become more complex, developers will need to analyze their applications before they begin to develop them.

UML is based on object-oriented concepts, with seven standard diagramming techniques to describe a complete panoramic picture of the software project.

The two most important diagrams in the UML are Use Case diagrams and Class diagrams. Use Case diagrams are most useful to identify *what* we are going to build and *who* is going to use what we build. It is a superior technique for clarifying with business users the scope of the project.

Class diagrams are used to describe how the software is constructed. In an object-oriented system, many different components all interact with each other. Class diagrams identify each of these components. Classes are the basis for object-oriented programming because they encapsulate both process and data by identifying variables (properties) and procedures (methods). Using Classes

Applications can link to businesses allowing people to work anywhere!

effectively positions your software for improve reusability and reduce maintenance and enhancement activities.

We will use these diagrams throughout this book to both describe our requirements (Use Case diagrams) and how we construct our programs (Class diagrams). Use Case diagrams are the central view of the UML. The contents of the Use Case diagram drive the entire software model and allow technical professionals to confirm with business users and customers, "Is this what you want?," so that what is in scope and what is not in scope becomes clear to everyone involved with the project. The following figure is a sample Use Case diagram with the Login form.

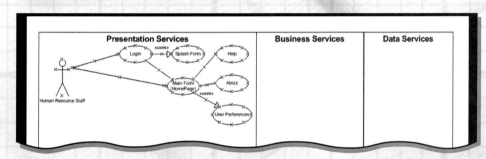

This sample Use Case diagram indicates that the system will have three sets of services: Presentation Services, Business Services, and Data Services.

Presentation Services include screens that system users will use to maintain data such as employee information.

Business Services include verifying that information provided in a maintenance screen is valid before it is placed into the database and used for processing paychecks and generating related reports.

Data Services include storing data within a database structure. This data storage may reside on external computers to help optimize performance, and may include predefined programs known as Stored Procedures that retrieve information rapidly because they are precompiled and stored in the database along with the data.

As you can see, it was much easier to read the Use Case diagram than it was to read the paragraph that described what it represented. Visual UML modeling is a very powerful concept that only becomes more apparent as our system complexity increases.

Introducing Visual Basic .NET

The Challenge

The *Login.sln* file can be found at \\vb.net_brief\ vb.net_datafiles\00\ Login.NET.

Mr. Traylor wants a login screen to appear that determines whether the user has entered a valid user name and password. A warning will appear if the login information is invalid.

An invalid login could consist of a blank or invalid password or user name. Some systems are case sensitive and may not accept a user name or password that does not exactly match the upper or lowercase format of the value initially saved.

The Solution

You will be guided through opening a login screen in an existing project. As you do so, you will learn about the Visual Basic .NET interface.

The interface consists of the screens that display information to the application user. They might include buttons, caption headings, and other controls. To most users, the interfaces, or screens, represent the entire application. As we progress with development of the Pay Transaction System you will learn about all the component parts of a real-world application.

Understanding Programming Terminology

Terminology associated with programming is quite different from terminology used in other software applications. Before starting the Visual Basic .NET program and exploring the screen features, you should recognize some of the terminology you will be using as you explore object-oriented software development (Table 0-1).

Table 0-1	Object-Oriented Software Development Terminology	
Term	**Description**	**Example**
IDE	Visual Studio .NET Interactive Development Environment	The command center console that contains the Menu, Solution Explorer, and Properties windows used to build a project.
Solution Explorer	A collection of related projects that interoperate with each other to provide a total solution.	A Solutions file contains a list of projects in a group necessary to provide the solution.
Project	A collection of related files	The *Login.vbprog* project contains a form and a little code.
Form	A collection of controls that is displayed when the program runs	The *frmLogin.vb* form contains Label, Textbox, and Button controls.
Control	A self-contained object that has properties and provides features	The Textbox control provides a data entry field.
Property	A value that is stored within a control	The Password Textbox control stores the value in the Text property.
Design mode	When the application is under construction and we can add controls and set properties	When the *Login.vbprog* project is first loaded, the program is in Design mode.
Run mode	When the application is processing code using a compiled (*.exe*) version of the program	Pressing the F5 key or choosing **Tools	Debug	Run** starts Run mode.

Launching Visual Basic .NET

As with other Microsoft applications, there are several ways to launch Visual Basic .NET:

- Double-click the Microsoft Visual Studio .NET icon on the desktop.
- Click the Launch Microsoft Visual Studio .NET button on the Quick Launch toolbar.
- Choose **Start | Programs | Microsoft Visual Studio .NET.**

Task 1:
To Launch Visual Basic .NET

1 Choose **Start | Programs.**

2 Choose **Microsoft Visual Studio .NET**.

3 Choose **Microsoft Visual Studio .NET** again.

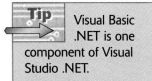

Tip Visual Basic .NET is one component of Visual Studio .NET.

4 Click the **My Profile** link and select **Visual Basic Developer**.

Figure 0-1

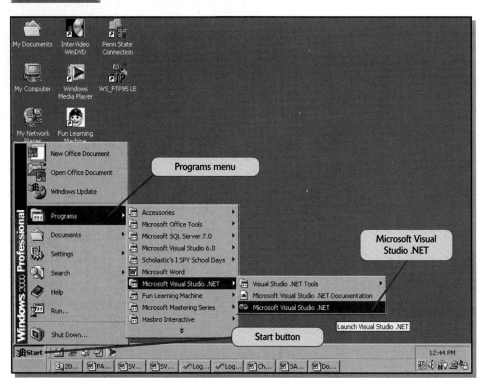

Figure 0-2

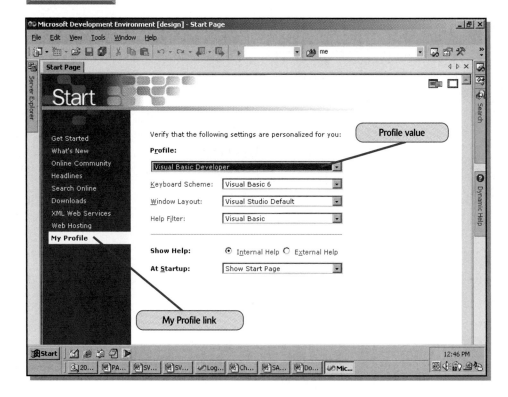

Opening an Existing Visual Basic .NET Project

Viewing an active project in Visual Basic will help you get a better perspective of the information normally contained in the Visual Basic .NET window. The procedures used to open Visual Basic .NET projects are similar to the procedures used to open files in other Office applications.

Task 2:

To Open an Existing Visual Basic .NET Project

1 Click the **Get Started** link and then click the **Open Project** button.

Figure 0-3

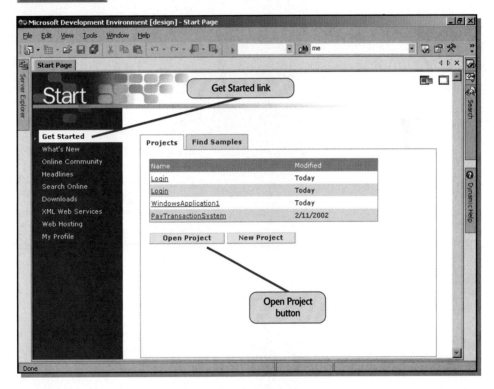

2 Select the *Login.sln* file and click the **Open** button.

Figure 0-4

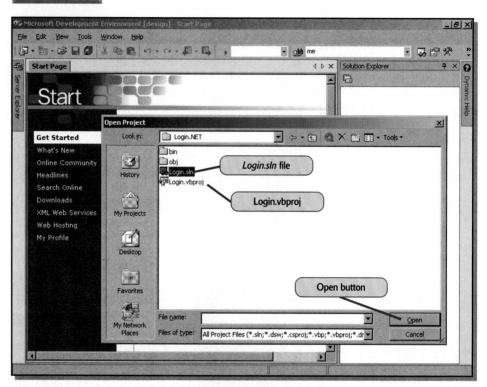

3 Choose **View | Solution Explorer.**

4 Choose **View | Properties Window.**

5 Choose **View | Toolbox.**

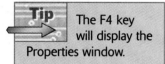
Tip The F4 key will display the Properties window.

Figure 0-5

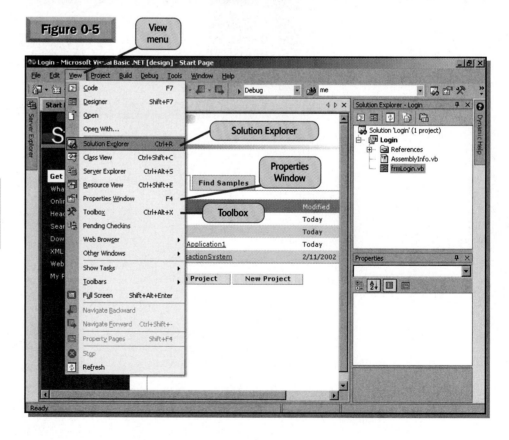

Identifying Visual Basic .NET Screen Elements

The Interactive Development Environment (IDE) displays all solution objects and provides a way to access different objects.

Task 3:
To Review Project Properties

1 Double-click the *frmLogin.vb* form object in the Solution Explorer to display the form and select it.

2 Select the **Text** property and verify that it is **Login**.

3 Select the **Start Position** property and verify that it is **Center Screen**.

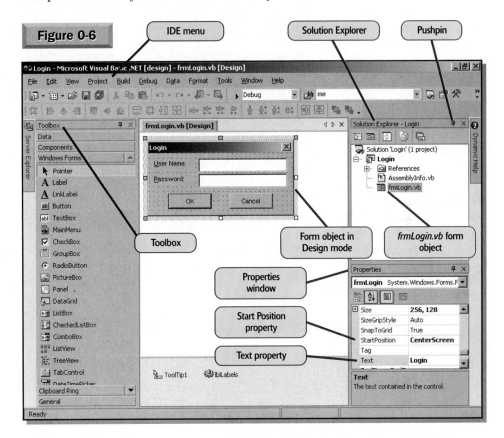

Figure 0-6

The Properties window displays the property values for the currently selected object. In step 1, we double-click the *frmLogin.vb* form object to select it, and the Properties window is automatically refreshed. Only form-related properties appear for review or modification.

Table 0-2 identifies the purpose of each screen element identified in Figure 0-6.

Table 0-2	IDE Screen Elements
Screen Element	**Purpose**
IDE menu	Provides access to commands used to perform tasks
Toolbox	Contains a collection of objects, such as user interface (UI) controls
Solution Explorer	Provides an organized view of your projects and their files as well as ready access to the commands that pertain to them
Form object	Contains the controls and code needed to present the user interface
Pushpin	Automatically hides an individual navigation window
Properties window	Views and changes the Design mode properties of selected control objects that are located in forms

4 Select the **Name** property and verify that it is **frmLogin**, verify that the **AcceptButton** property is **cmdOK**, and verify that the **CancelButton** property is **cmdCancel**.

Tip The **AcceptButton** property value determines which button will be launched when the Enter key is pressed. The **CancelButton** property value determines which button will be launched when the Esc key is pressed. The advantage of setting these two properties is that application users who prefer using the keyboard have the option of not using the mouse.

Figure 0-7

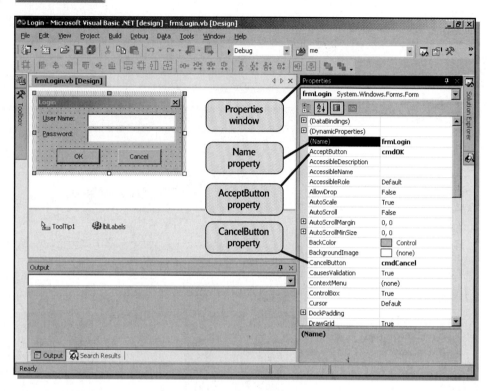

Running the Login Project

The purpose of the project you just opened is to run the Login dialog. After verifying the values and exploring the project panes, you can run the project to see what happens and test the project to ensure that it is functioning as expected. To run a project that is open in the Visual Basic .NET window, use the Debug menu.

Task 4:
To Run and Test the Login Project

1 Choose **Debug | Start | Run**.

2 Type Tester in the **User Name** field, type bad password in the **Password** field, and click **OK**.

3 Type password in the **Password** field and click **OK**.

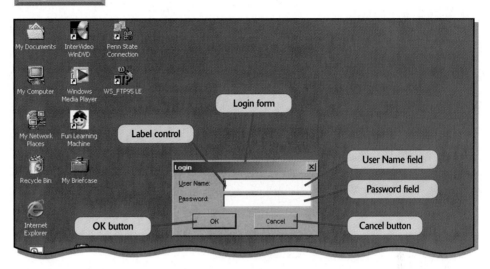

Figure 0-8

Login form

Label control

User Name field

Password field

OK button

Cancel button

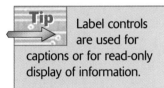

Tip Label controls are used for captions or for read-only display of information.

Tip A warning message will appear asking you to verify the password. The message window has an OK button. Click OK to acknowledge that you read the warning message. The blinking cursor will reappear in the **Password** field in preparation for you to retype another password.

Saving Project Changes

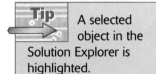

Tip A selected object in the Solution Explorer is highlighted.

Saving your project, a very important fundamental task, ensures that your programming efforts are protected. There are several ways to save your project, as described in Table 0-3.

Table 0-3	Methods for Saving Project Files	
Location	**Method**	**Description**
Toolbar	Save *frmLogin.vb*	Saves the currently selected object in the Solution Explorer. For example, if *frmLogin.vb* is selected, this button saves only the file named *frmLogin.vb*.
Toolbar	Save All	Saves every object in the Solution Explorer. This is the preferred method for saving objects, ensuring that all programming or development changes are safely protected. The files will be stored in the project location defined when the project was created.
Menu	File | Save *frmLogin.vb*	Saves the currently selected object in the Solution Explorer. For example, if *frmLogin.vb* is selected, this button saves only the file named *frmLogin.vb*.
Menu	File | Save *frmLogin.vb* as	Same as the Save option, except this option provides a file save dialog in case you want to save the file with a different name or in a different location.
Menu	File | Save All	Saves every object in the Solution Explorer. This is the preferred method for saving objects, ensuring that all programming or development changes are safely protected. The files will be stored in the project location defined when the project was created.

Task 5:
To Save a Visual Basic .NET Project

1 Use one of the following procedures to save a Visual Basic .NET project:

- Click the **Save All** button on the Standard toolbar.
- Choose **File | Save All**.

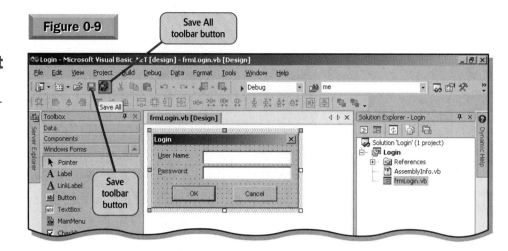

Figure 0-9

Save All toolbar button

Save toolbar button

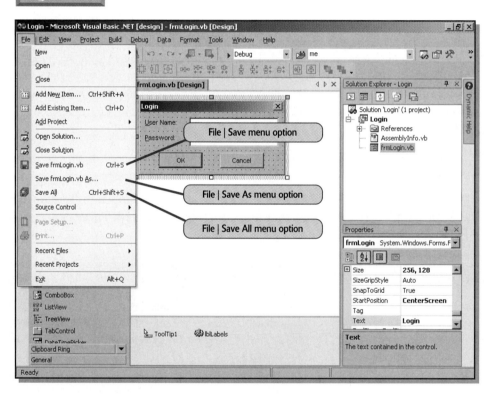

Figure 0-10

File | Save menu option

File | Save As menu option

File | Save All menu option

Exiting Visual Basic .NET

Before you exit Visual Basic .NET, you should save your work and close the files you have open. If you exit the application without saving changes to your open files, Visual Basic .NET prompts you to save changes. Be sure to read these prompts carefully to ensure that you take the action you intend and avoid unnecessary loss of data.

Task 6:
To Exit Visual Basic .NET

1 Use one of the following procedures to exit Visual Basic .NET:

- Click the Close **X** button.
- Choose **File | Exit**. If multiple files are open in the application, all files close as you exit the application.
- Click the application control icon at the left end of the title bar and choose **Close**.
- Press [Alt] + [F4].
- Right-click the application button on the Windows taskbar and choose **Close**.

Figure 0-11

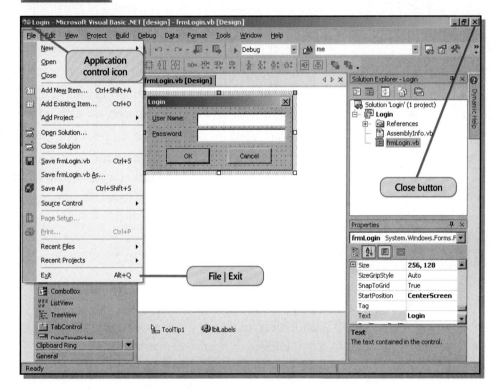

SUMMARY AND EXERCISES

SUMMARY

- Microsoft Visual Basic .NET is a tool that organizes your programming components, classes, and modules.
- A project consists of one or more components such as forms.
- Forms display a user interface for users to interact with.
- One or more controls can be added to a form to provide functionality, such as buttons and textbox controls for data entry.
- Labels are used for captions and for read-only display of information.
- Pushpins permit you to toggle windows to automatically move aside and recall the window to maximize your visible work area.
- Save all files before exiting Microsoft Visual Basic .NET.

KEY TERMS & SKILLS

KEY TERMS

control (p. 5)	IDE menu (p. 9)	Properties window (p. 9)
Design mode (p. 5)	project (p. 5)	Run mode (p. 5)
form object (p. 9)	property (p. 5)	Solution Explorer (p. 5)
form (p. 5)	pushpin (p. 9)	Toolbox (p. 9)
IDE (p. 5)		

SKILLS

Exit Visual Basic .NET (p. 13)	Review project properties (p. 9)
Launch Visual Basic .NET (p. 6)	Run and test the Login project (p. 11)
Open an existing Visual Basic .NET project (p. 7)	Save a Visual Basic .NET project (p. 12)

STUDY QUESTIONS

MULTIPLE CHOICE

1. Which Microsoft Visual Basic .NET object provides a means to add controls to a form?
a. Solution Explorer
b. Project Explorer
c. Properties window
d. Toolbox

2. What Textbox property stores the password entered in the Login form?
a. Name
b. Value
c. Text
d. Caption

3. What part of the IDE provides a means of setting values within controls?
a. Solution Explorer
b. Toolbox
c. Properties window
d. none of the above

4. Which property is changed to center a form on the screen?
a. Startup Position
b. Alignment
c. Left
d. Top

5. Project-related objects are easily accessible using the
a. Solution Explorer.
b. Project Explorer.
c. Property window.
d. IDE menu.

6. After you have planned your application, the object that must be created first is a
a. project.
b. form.
c. control.
d. none of the above.

7. Which control object allows users to enter, edit, and view data in an easy-to-use format?
a. label
b. button
c. textbox
d. caption

8. What UML symbol is a straight line?
a. Generalization
b. Association
c. Use Case
d. Actor

9. Which of the following Use Cases were used in the Sample UML diagram?
a. Login
b. User Preferences
c. Main Form
d. all of the above

10. Which of the following features makes Visual Basic .NET a great tool?
a. Makes writing computer programs easier.
b. Can create complex programs designed to work on multiple platforms.
c. Provides programming assistance, extensive helps, and sample code.
d. all of the above

SHORT ANSWER

1. What is the Solution Explorer?
2. What are three UML chart symbols?
3. What does IDE stand for?
4. What control is most commonly used as a data entry field?
5. What type of object did we add the controls to in this project?
6. What three-letter prefix is used when naming a form object?
7. Which menu is used to start running a program?
8. The Save All option is available on which menu?
9. What are two ways to exit Visual Basic .NET?
10. When would you use a login form?

FILL IN THE BLANK

1. A _____ type form provides security for an application to ensure that only valid users can use it.
2. The _____ _____ contains a collection of related projects.
3. A _____ contains setting values for a control.
4. When the application is in _____ mode, we are using a compiled (.*exe*) version of the program.
5. When the application is in _____ mode, we add controls.
6. The _____ link on the IDE was used to set the Visual Basic Developer mode.
7. The _____ _____ link on the IDE provided the Open Project and New Project options.
8. The _____ feature is used to make the windows of the IDE disappear when the mouse moves away from them, to maximize the work area.
9. A _____ control is used for captions or read-only display of information.
10. The _____ _____ language is the standard approach to modeling software development using object-oriented diagrams.

FOR DISCUSSION

1. How would UML be helpful in planning an application?
2. Explain how the Actor, Use Case, and Association symbols are used.
3. Why is planning your application important?
4. How do the Label and Textbox controls differ?
5. Give an example of when a login screen would be needed.

Creating a Program in Visual Basic .NET

Our first project will create a Windows Application type project that enables users to set default colors for the foreground and background in our application. This will be the first of many user preferences that we will add to our system; all additional forms within our project will inherit these preference properties to control the look, feel, and behavior of our application.

Tip The *Wrench.ico* file can be found at C:\Program Files\ Microsoft Visual Studio.NET\Common7\Graphics\Icons\ Industry\Wrench.ico.

OBJECTIVES

After completing this project, you will be able to:

- Understand form controls and properties

- Create the Pay Transaction System project

- Create the User Preferences form

- Add data to ComboBox controls

- Run the Pay Transaction System project

e-selections **Running Case**

Mr. Traylor needs to create a common way of setting screen and text colors within the application. This usability-related feature will enable users to decide what colors are best for their needs. Some individuals are color-blind and need to change the screen colors to help them use the application most effectively. Colors are often used to provide a visual indication that something is not quite right.

Introducing the Pay Transaction Project

Create three sections of programming components and then assemble them to build a real-world application.

In this book, we will build the presentation services for a real-world application that is comprised of three parts: **Presentation Services, Business Services, and Data Services**. The Objective for this training is to focus on the presentation services while recognizing that most enterprise applications have business and data services that you will need to integrate with.

This application will include a Microsoft Access database file that contains all the tables needed to manage the data.

Each project provides details about the construction of the necessary presentation service components.

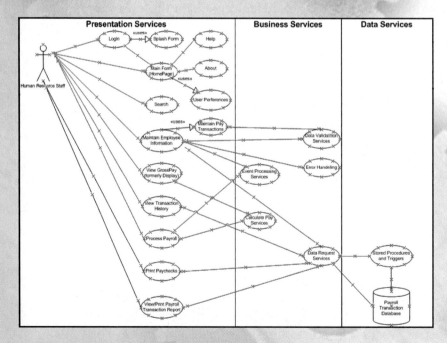

The Presentation Services section of the application provides the visual aspect of the project. It consists of screens, reports, and a few processes. To many computer software users, this graphical user interface represents the entire application. As we construct this application, you will create many powerful components. Most are not visible to the typical user, but to a developer, they are very significant.

You will learn as we build this application that many components combine to build a robust application.

In addition to displaying information in screens, the Presentation Services section will provide reporting and other processes that validate data entry. It will also provide a menu and status bar to help users navigate within the application conveniently.

The Business Services section performs common functions that validate information before storing it into the database. It manages messages that could notify the user that it may need more information before it can compute a paycheck, such as a number of hours worked greater than zero.

The Business Services section performs mathematical calculations based on formulas and business rules provided to the programmer. Once all the elements of a formula are available, the system can quickly calculate net pay.

Data Services provides a single place for maintaining programming code needed to interact with a database. This provides a means to change or relocate computer equipment or database type programs with a minimal impact on system maintenance. Database-related changes protect users by ensuring that critical data is never lost and allow the system to remain available to users without interruption.

Computerized applications have increased the speed of working with information!

PROJECT 1

Creating a Program in Visual Basic .NET

The Challenge

The User Preferences form will be created to enable a user to select background and foreground colors from a predefined list. This application will need a few new controls, including the ComboBox and a GroupBox.

The Solution

A Windows Application type project will be created that contains a GroupBox for the Text/Foreground color and Background color ComboBox controls will be filled with a list of color name values to enable users to make a quick selection and eliminate any potential risk of human error related to typing an invalid or misspelled color.

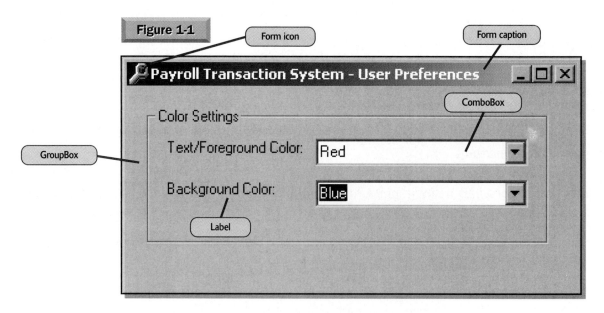

Figure 1-1

Understanding Form Controls and Properties

As we progress through the projects, new terms will be introduced. Table 1-1 presents the terms that are included in this project.

Table 1-1 Form Controls and Properties Terminology	
Term	**Description**
BackColor property	Returns or sets the background color of an object. For example, a form could have a background color of blue and all controls would appear on top of a blue background. Gray is the default background color.
Executable	A compiled version of a project. A Windows-based application that can run outside the development environment. An executable file has an *.exe* extension.
ForeColor property	Returns or sets the foreground color of an object. For example, the foreground color of a label is usually black to create a contrast to the gray background. You might set the foreground color to red to draw attention to a message. For example, if a required field is not filled in, you could create a label with red letters in a central location on a form, with the message text dynamically set—for example, "Employee Last Name is required."
GroupBox control	Displays a frame around a group of controls with or without a caption. Use a GroupBox control to logically group a collection of controls on a form.
Icon	An image associated with the application and displayed in the taskbar, or an application control at the left end of the title bar of a form. This is set in the project properties.
Intrinsic controls	Tools you can use to develop a form. The intrinsic controls include PictureBox, Label, TextBox, GroupBox (Frame), CheckBox, RadioButton, ComboBox, ListBox, HScroll Bar, VScrollBar, Timer, DriveListBox, DirListBox, FileListBox, Shape, Line, Image, and Data Control.
Label control	A Label control is a graphical control you can use to display text that a user cannot change directly.
Syntax error	An error that occurs when you enter a line of code that Visual Basic .NET does not recognize.
Syntax checking	A feature that checks your code for correct syntax. If the Syntax checking feature is enabled, a message is displayed when you enter code that contains a syntax error and the suspect code is highlighted.
TextBox control	A TextBox control, sometimes called an edit field or edit control, displays information entered in Run mode.
Windows Application project	A project template designed to create applications using the user interface common to all Windows operating systems.

Creating the Pay Transaction System Project with Visual Basic .NET

The Pay Transaction System project is the foundation on which additional forms and many common processes will be built.

Task 1:

To Create the Pay Transaction System Windows Application Project

1 Choose **File | New | Project**.

Tip In this section, we will deal with the **New Project** dialog box. It is extremely important that we make settings in the **New Project** dialog box very carefully.

Figure 1-2

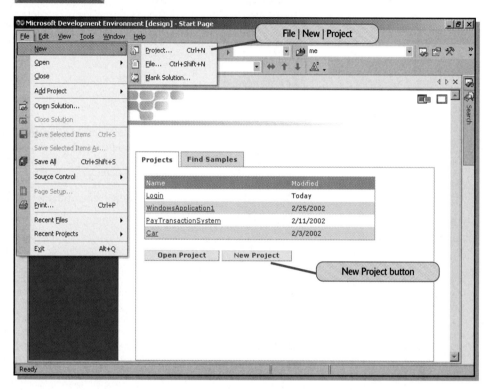

2 Select **Visual Basic Projects** then **Windows Application**.

3 Type **PayTransactionSystem** in the **Name** field.

4 Type **c:\public\ vbNetClass\ Students\HR** in the **Location** field and click **OK**.

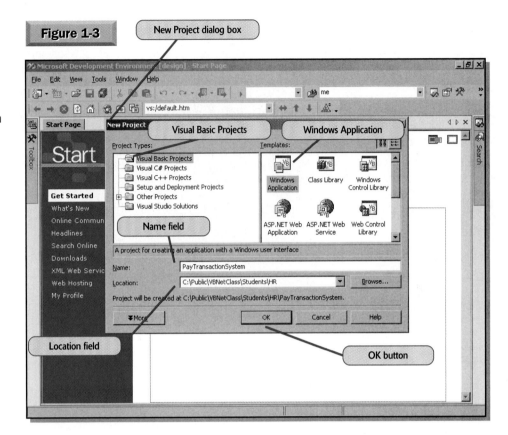

Figure 1-3

In a production application, team-oriented development environment you place source code, or programming code, in version control systems that keep a copy of your programs in a network computer that is backed up regularly. Version control systems retain a copy of the program, a copy of changes made to the programs, and usually some maintenance history log files. Team members must check out a file before it can be modified. This is very much like borrowing a book from the library. Only one individual can have a single book at a time. Version control protects a developer from losing work and helps identify the latest programming code when enhancements are needed. Visual SourceSafe comes with Visual Studio .NET and is an excellent source code control utility.

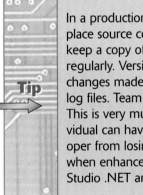

Creating the User Preferences Form

Several steps are required to complete the User Preferences form. They include setting form properties, adding a group box, adding a label, adding two *ComboBox controls*, and populating the ComboBox controls with color values.

Setting Form Properties

When you create a new Visual Basic .NET project, a form named *form1.vb* is added to the project. We are going to rename the form to *frmUserPreferences.vb*, add controls, and then set properties.

Task 2:

To Create the User Preferences Screen

1 Click the *Form1.vb* file in the Solution Explorer.

2 Type **UserPreferences** for the **Name** property and press Enter.

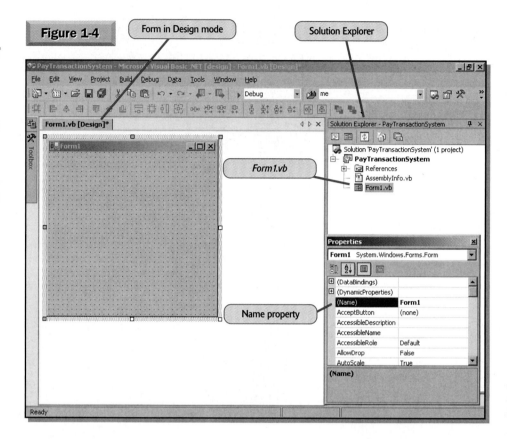

Figure 1-4

Form in Design mode

Solution Explorer

Form1.vb

Name property

3 Type Payroll Transaction System - User Preferences for the **Text** property and press Enter.

4 Choose **Center Screen** for the StartPosition property.

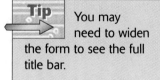

Tip You may need to widen the form to see the full title bar.

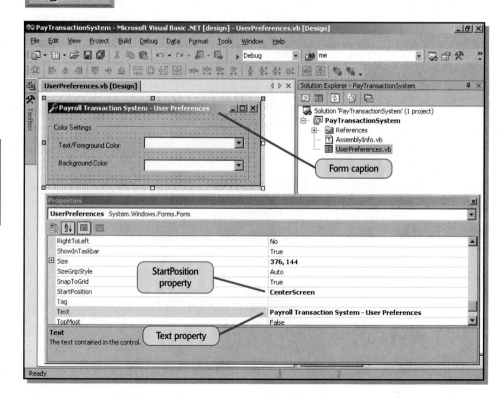

Figure 1-5

Form caption

StartPosition property

Text property

5 Type **376** for the **Width** property and type **144** for the **Height** property.

Troubleshooting
Click the plus sign next to the **Size** property if you cannot find the **Width** property in the Properties window. The width for the User Preferences form is 376 and the height is 144.

Figure 1-6

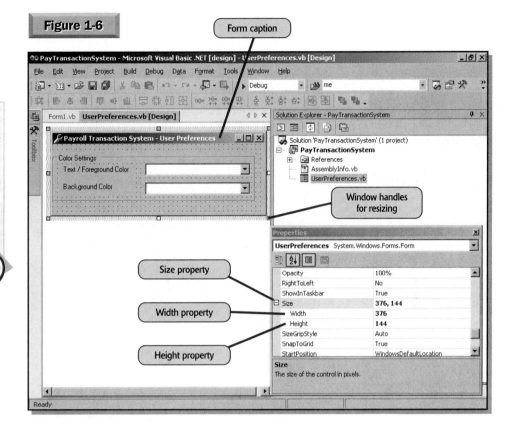

Form caption

Window handles for resizing

Size property

Width property

Height property

6 Click the **Ellipse** button for the **Icon** property.

7 Choose *Wrench.ico* and click OK.

Figure 1-7

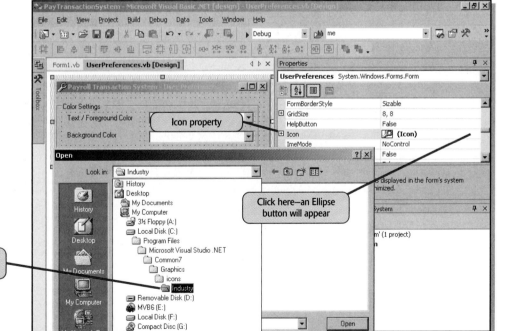

Icon property

Click here—an Ellipse button will appear

Location of Icon image files

Adding a GroupBox Control

A GroupBox control creates a frame on the form where you can group various objects together that are related. In this task we will create a Color Settings GroupBox where we will group all color related User Preferences for the Payroll Transaction System application.

Task 3:
To Add a GroupBox Control

1 Choose **View | Toolbox**; then double-click the **GroupBox** control.

2 Resize the GroupBox control using the sizing handles of the control.

3 Type **gbxColorSettings** the **Name** property.

4 Type **Color Settings** for the **Text** property.

Figure 1-8

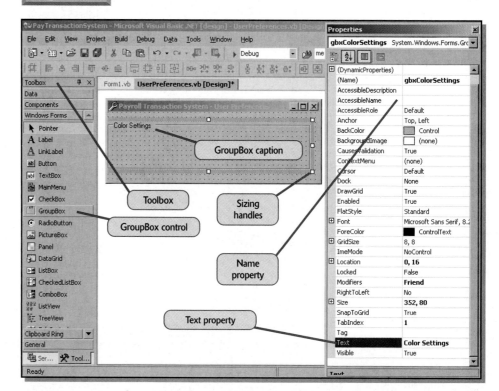

Tip

To move the GroupBox, scroll over the edge of the GroupBox control, between the sizing handles, so that the mouse pointer takes the form of four arrows. Then hold down the left mouse button to position the GroupBox control.

The easiest approach to sizing the Group Box control is to click and hold down the left mouse button while selecting the lower right sizing handle and slowly drag the mouse until the GroupBox control is about 3 inches wide. Release the mouse to complete the resizing.

Adding a Label Control for the ComboBox Captions

A Label control provides a caption that is used as a read-only display of information where you choose not to permit a user to alter the data.

Task 4:
To Add a Label Control

1 Click to select the Label control in the Toolbox.

2 Draw one label on the form.

3 Choose **Edit | Copy**, then **Edit | Paste**, and answer **No** to the control array prompt. This creates another label the same size as the first label.

4 Align the labels.

5 Click the top label, type **lblFgrdColor** for the **Name** property, and type **Text/Foreground Color** for the **Text** property.

6 Click the bottom label, type **lblBackgroundColor** for the **Name** property, and type **Background Color** for the **Text** property.

Figure 1-9

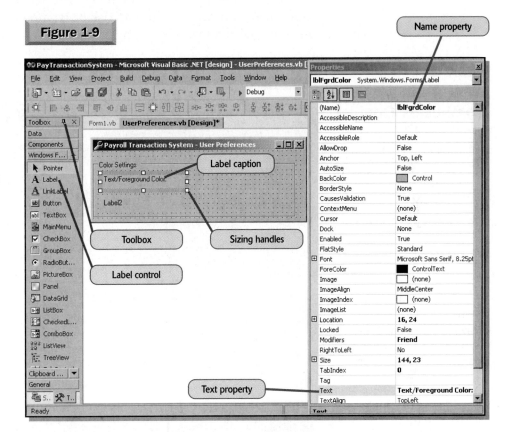

Tip As an alternative, you can add a control (user interface object) to a form by double-clicking the object in the Toolbox. The object will appear centered in the form and you can drag it to the desired location. You can also click the object in the Toolbox; the cursor will change to a plus sign and you can draw the object on the form. When drawing the control, click in the form where you want the object to start, hold the left mouse button down, and drag until the object is the desired size.

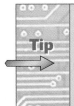

Tip *Inheritance* enables you to write and debug a *class* once, and then reuse that code over and over as the basis of new classes. Classes are templates that have methods and attributes names and type information, but no actual values. They are an abstract representation of something. Classes are made of properties, methods, and events.

Adding ComboBox Controls for the Foreground and Background Color

A ComboBox control provides valid choices for selecting values. This is a very convenient way to eliminate the risk of typing incorrect values. It also eliminates the need for the user to memorize different values.

Task 5:
To Add a ComboBox Control

1 Click to select the ComboBox control in the Toolbox.

2 Draw one ComboBox control on the form.

3 Choose **Edit | Copy**, then **Edit | Paste**, and answer **No** to the control array prompt. This creates another ComboBox the same size as the first.

4 Align the ComboBox controls.

5 Click the top ComboBox control, type **cboForegroundColor** for the **Name** property, and type **Text/Foreground Color** for the **Text** property.

6 Click the bottom ComboBox control, type **cboBackgroundColor** for the **Name** property, and type **BackGround Color** for the **Text** property.

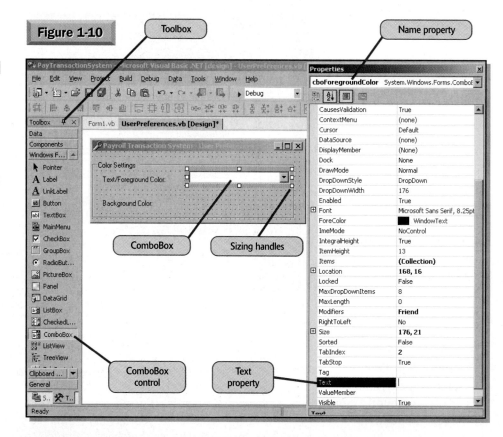

Figure 1-10

 Tip To align two identical controls, select each control by holding down the (Shift) key and selecting format/align from the menu.

Adding Data to ComboBox Controls

There are two ways to add values to a ComboBox control. The first approach will manually set the items. The second is to use programming code and load the item's property dynamically at runtime. A collection is a special type of property that contains a set or list of information in a predefined order.

Task 6:
To Add Data to ComboBox Controls

1 Click the **cboForegroundColor** ComboBox control to select it.

2 Click the **Items** property to make the **Ellipse** button appear.

3 Click the **Ellipse** button to display the **String Collection Editor** dialog box.

4 Type Black, Red, Lime, Yellow, Blue, Magenta, Cyan, and White. Press Enter after each color value, then click **OK**.

5 Repeat steps 1–4 for the cboBackgroundColor Combo Box.

Figure 1-11

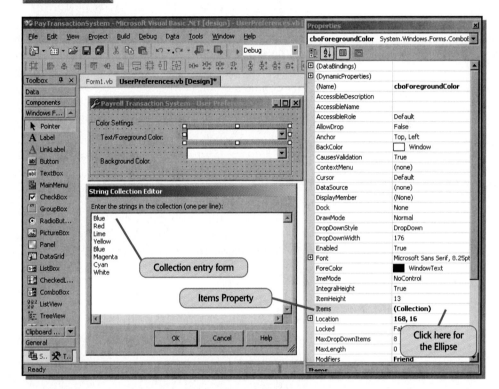

Other Ways

To add items to a collection dynamically through Visual Basic .NET programming you would enter syntax similar to the example below. We will get involved in programming and modifying code a little later. Do not type in the sample code at this time.

CboForegroundColor.Items.AddRange(New Object (7) _

{"Black","Red","Lime","Yellow","Blue","Magenta","Cyan","White"})

Running the Project

At this point we have not written any programming syntax but we can still run and test the project. We run (test) the program periodically to evaluate our progress and make sure the program behaves the way we expect. Visual Basic .NET lets you run the program within the Interactive Development Environment (IDE) quickly and easily without creating an executable (a Windows *.exe* file). Visual Basic .NET has a sophisticated debugger that helps developers improve productivity by performing a variety of debugging tasks, which will be covered in more detail in the next project.

Each control should display all the colors that were typed in to the collection. Since we have not added code to the User Preferences form, you will not notice any changes when colors are selected.

Tip

Since the form named **form1** was renamed to **frmUserPreferences** after the form was first added, Visual Basic .NET needs to know what form to display when the project starts. To set the startup object right-click the **PayTransactionSystem** project in the Solution Explorer and choose **Properties**. The Project Property dialog box appears. Select **UserPreferences.vb** for the **Startup Object**, and then click **OK**. If you skip this step, you will receive a message when the project starts requesting the name of the startup object.

Task 7:
To Run the Pay Transaction System Project

 Choose **Debug | Start**.

Figure 1-12

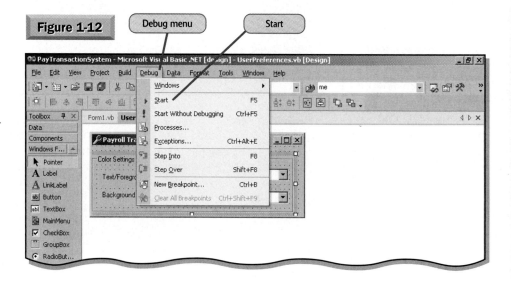

2 Click the **cboForegroundColor** Combo Box and verify that color data appears.

3 Click the **cboBackgroundColor** Combo Box and verify that color data appears.

4 Choose **Debug | End**.

5 Choose **File | Save All**.

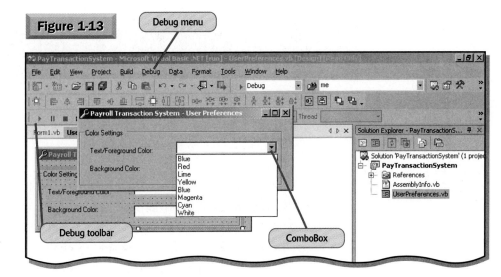

Figure 1-13

The Debug toolbar can be used to stop or start a project.

SUMMARY AND EXERCISES

SUMMARY

- A greater understanding of form controls and properties was obtained.
- The Pay Transaction System project was created as a foundation for the rest of the presentation services you will develop in this book.
- The User Preferences form was created to enable users to conveniently set colors so that they can use the application based on their own color preferences.
- The ComboBox controls were manually populated although we also learned they can be dynamically populated using programming code.
- Within the Pay Transaction System project, users can choose color values to eliminate potential human errors. ComboBox controls provide a more convenient way to identify colors—no need to memorize color codes, just select a color from the list.

KEY TERMS & SKILLS

KEY TERMS

BackColor property (p. 1-5)
class (p. 1-11)
ComboBox control (p. 1-7)
executable (p. 1-5)
ForeColor property (p. 1-5)
GroupBox control (p. 1-5)
icon (p. 1-5)

inheritance (p. 1-11)
intrinsic controls (p. 1-5)
Label control (p. 1-5)
syntax error (p. 1-5)
syntax checking (p. 1-5)
TextBox control (p. 1-5)
Windows Application project (p. 1-5)

SKILLS

Add a ComboBox control (p. 1-12)
Add a GroupBox control (p. 1-10)
Add a Label control (p. 1-11)
Add data to ComboBox controls
  (p. 1-13)
Create the Pay Transaction System
  Windows Application project (p. 1-6)

Create the User Preferences Screen
  (p. 1-8)
Run the Pay Transaction System
  project (p. 1-14)

STUDY QUESTIONS

MULTIPLE CHOICE

1. A GroupBox control is used to
   a. organize related controls.
   b. permit single selection of RadioButton controls.
   c. display a rectangular frame that can have a caption.
   d. all of the above.

2. What property is set to change the color of characters in a label control?
   a. Text
   b. Caption
   c. ForeColor
   d. BackColor

3. What type of control, when clicked, drops down and allows users to type a search value and find a value choice on a list?
   a. Label
   b. ComboBox
   c. Form
   d. TextBox

4. What type of control is used to present information in a read-only format?
   a. GroupBox
   b. Icon
   c. TextBox
   d. Label

5. Color highlighting is used to identify
   a. mandatory fields on a data entry screen that have not been filled in.
   b. data that is provided that does not match acceptable formats, such as dates.
   c. where information should be entered.
   d. all of the above

6. What type of file has an *.exe* file name extension?
   a. executable
   b. design-time
   c. text
   d. module

7. An example of an intrinsic control is a
   a. TextBox.
   b. Label.
   c. CheckBox.
   d. all of the above

8. What property is NOT included within the Size property category?
   a. Length
   b. Height
   c. Width

9. Which of the following is/are Services of the Pay Transaction Application?
   a. Data Services
   b. Business Services
   c. Presentation Services
   d. all of the above

10. Which of the following forms is NOT included in the Presentation Services?
   a. Main
   b. Maintain Pay Transactions
   c. Maintain Reports
   d. Search

SHORT ANSWER

1. What is the feature called that checks your code for correct values, displays a message, and highlights suspect code?
2. What is the most common control used for user data entry?
3. How is an Icon image used in a Visual Basic .NET application?
4. What Microsoft Version Control tool is commonly used to manage versions of programming files?
5. What property is changed when setting the caption that appears at the top of a form?
6. What form property would you use to center the form on the screen?
7. When changing the Width or Height property of a form, what property category do you have to open if the Width or Height property is not visible?
8. When changing the form icon, what is the name of the little button inside the Icon property that must be clicked to display the Icon Image Selection dialog box?
9. What is the name of the little square boxes that appear when the GroupBox or other controls are added or selected on a form and used to resize the control?
10. What three-letter prefix is used as a naming convention for a label control?

FILL IN THE BLANK

1. A _____ error occurs when you enter a line of code that Visual Basic .NET does not recognize.
2. A _____ _____ project template is designed to create applications using the user interface common to all Windows operating systems.
3. A good approach to protecting valuable programming code is to use the Microsoft Visual SourceSafe tool. This tool is used for _____ _____.
4. You can provide valid choices for users and eliminate human error relating to mistyped values by adding a _____ control to a form.
5. The _____ property is changed when you want a blue colored appearance behind the controls on the form.
6. The _____ property is changed when you want black colored characters as the text of a label.
7. The _____ property is the most important property to set to ensure uniqueness and clear understanding, and also to associate code with controls.
8. _____ setting of properties is when the properties are set at runtime, during the running of a program, rather than during design time. The data may vary especially when it is provided by a database.
9. The _____ _____ Editor is used to append a list of valid choices to a ComboBox control during design time manually using the Properties window.
10. Debugging is used to improve the _____ of developers.

FOR DISCUSSION

1. Why would you use version control?
2. When are ComboBox controls used?
3. Explain how to organize related controls on a form.
4. Why is a color preferences selection screen important to users?
5. Where would you use a Label control?

GUIDED EXERCISES

TO CREATE A LOGIN FORM

1 Launch **Visual Basic .NET**, choose **Get Started**, and click **New Project**.

2 Name the project **LoginGuidedExercise** and save the project in a new folder named **LoginGuidedExercise**. Using the Toolbox, add the controls in Table 1-2 to the form.

Table 1-2	Controls and Properties
Control	**Property Values**
Form	Name = frmLogin.vb Text = Login
Label	Name = lblUserName Text = User Name:
Label	Name = lblPassword Text = Password:
TextBox	Name = txtUserName Text = Leave blank (select Textbox1, then backspace to delete this default value)
TextBox	Name = txtPassword Text = Leave blank (select Textbox1, then backspace to delete this default value)
Button	Name = cmdOK Text = &OK Default = True
Button	Name = cmdCancel Text = &Cancel

3 Double-click OK to display the code view.

Tip The code in Figure 1-14 includes the statement **Public LoginSucceeded As Boolean**. **LoginSucceeded** represents a **Boolean** (T/F) variable that can only have a value of **True** or **False**. Variables will be covered in more detail later in the book. The statement **System.Windows.Forms. SendKeys.Send("(Home)|(End)")** instructs Visual Basic .NET to highlight the contents of the **Password** text box starting with the value on the left (home) and continuing to the right (end) until the end of the contents is reached.

4 Type the code presented in Figure 1-14.

Figure 1-14

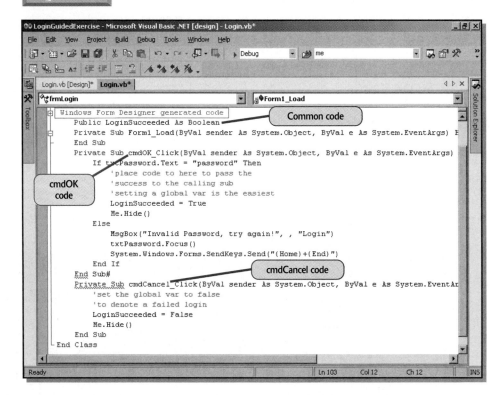

5 Choose **Build | Build Solution**, then choose **Debug | Start** to run the project. Type **Tester** in the **User Name** field and type **Bad Password** for an invalid password. Click **OK** to display an invalid password warning message.

6 Type **Password** for a valid password, and click **OK**. You will not see a warning—success!

7 Choose **Debug | Stop Debugging** to stop the project; choose **File | Save All** to save all files, then choose **File | Exit** to exit the application.

 Tip   You will have to change your project startup object in order to test the frmLogin.vb form.

PROJECT 2

Enhancing Our First Project with Programming Syntax

At this point, our project contains only code that was generated by Visual Basic .NET through the process of adding forms and User Interface controls from the Toolbox to the form. Now we need to add logic so users can see the visual impact of their preference selections by changing the color of the labels based on the selection made from the Text/Foreground Color combo box.

 Tip   The *PayTransactionSystem.sln* file can be found at \\vb.net_brief\vb.net_datafiles\02\PayTransactionSystem.

OBJECTIVES

After completing this project, you will be able to:

- Identify programming terminology relating to dialog boxes
- Add the Color dialog box
- Add data and code to the Color dialog box controls
- Set defaults
- Test the software

e-selections **Running Case**

Mr. Traylor needs to enhance the User Preferences form to add code and common Windows color features. You will need to know basic programming code as you prepare to add new forms and eventually integrate them with a database.

The Software Development Life Cycle

Learn about the five phases of the Software Development Life Cycle (SDLC)

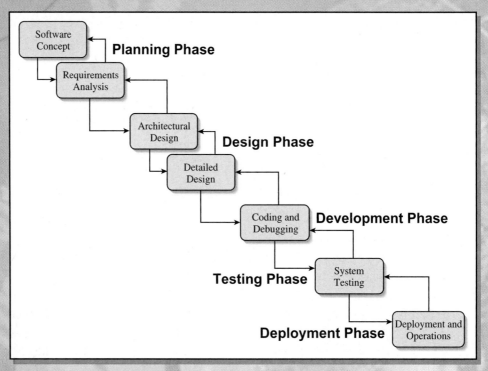

The major phases of the SDLC are composed of many activities that can be summarized as follows: Planning, Design, Programming, Testing, and Deployment and Operations. The following table provides an overview of the five phases of the SDLC.

Phases of the Software Development Life Cycle

Phase	Overview
Planning	The Planning phase is where a project begins and is the start of the development life cycle.
	Typical outputs from this phase:
	■ Vision/Scope document (contains the project idea, time frame, constraints, and resources)
	■ The requirements document contains a description of the high-level business requirements for the application.
	■ The functional specification contains a detailed description of how the requirements will manifest in the application; it may include screen shots, process flows, and other resources to assist in communicating the expected behavior of the application.
	■ The project plan contains the detailed work items, resources, relationships, and timeline for building the application.

Phase	Overview
Design	In the Design phase, the requirements are used to create a detailed architecture and specification for building the application. The output of this phase can be thought of as a detailed blueprint and road map for the application. Some of the activities in this phase are creating logical architecture specifications, as well as detailed physical design specifications. *Typical outputs from this phase*: Conceptual and logical design
Development	In the Development phase of the application life cycle, the application is constructed. Construction refers to the writing of code that executes the logic of the application, displays the user interface, updates data, and responds to user direction. The outputs from this phase include items such as compiled objects in the form of *.dll*s or *.exe*s. The construction of database scripts, including stored procedures, also occurs during this phase. Developers, who have the key role in this phase, usually perform unit testing of their code. Unit testing is the act of exercising individual tests on a component and ensures that the methods behave as the developer intends. At a minimum, the tools that developers typically use in this phase include an integrated development environment, language compilers, and automated testing tools. *Typical outputs from this phase*: ■ The application, consisting of many potential components, data, scripts, and test files. ■ Unit tests can include a "harness" and scripts for easy reproduction of unit tests.
Testing	During the Testing phase, the application is verified against the requirements. This typically involves integration testing on functions, performance and scaleability. Ideally, the testing phase overlaps part of development—meaning that as soon as portions of the application become functional, they can also be tested in a more formalized way than the unit testing done by developers. The concept of a "daily build" comes into play here, where the development team will create periodic builds of the application (periodic can be daily, weekly, and so forth) that are then formally tested. This enables an application to evolve through an iterative process in which the decision to ship is based on features and stability at any given point. *Typical outputs from this phase*: ■ Test plan ■ Test cases ■ Automated test scripts
Deployment and Operations	In the Deployment and Operations phase of the life cycle, the completed and verified application is placed into a production environment for usage. The activities in this phase involve creating an operations plan that covers tasks such as expected availability, backups, updates, and disaster recovery. This is also when the product support team will begin to support the application. The operations team monitors production applications for overall health and, along with product support, may submit change requests back to the development team to fix issues that were not uncovered during the test phase. *Typical outputs from this phase*: Operations plan

Enhancing Our First Project with Programming Syntax

The Challenge

You will enhance the User Preferences form to integrate the Color dialog box and the code required to implement color changes when a user selects a color.

The Solution

After the enhancements to the User Preferences form are completed, a new Color dialog box will appear, enabling the user to select additional colors if the standard colors are not desired.

Figure 2-1

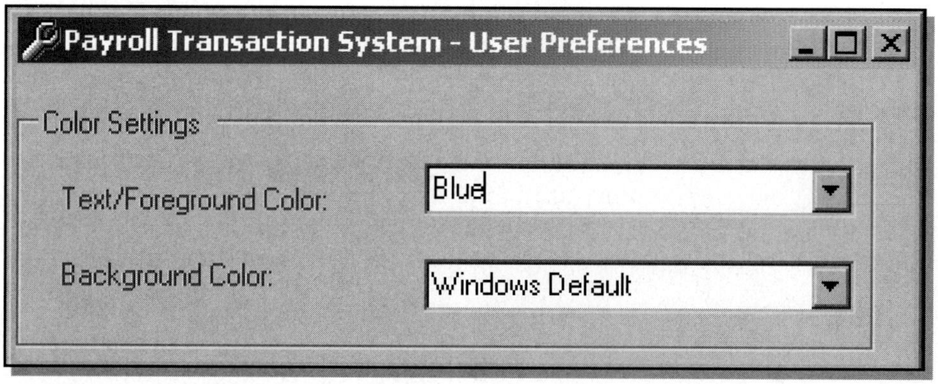

> **⚙ Payroll Transaction System – User Preferences** — ▢ ✕
>
> ┌─ Color Settings ─────────────────────────────┐
> │   │
> │ Text/Foreground Color: | Blue   ▼ | │
> │   │
> │ Background Color: | Windows Default ▼ | │
> │   │
> └───┘

Identifying Programming Terminology Relating to Dialog Boxes

We begin by learning some basic programming-oriented terms to become more familiar with them as the emphasis of the projects moves into a more code-based format (Table 2-1).

Table 2-1   Programming-Oriented Terminology

Term	Description
Case statement	Executes one of several groups of statements depending on the value of an expression
Code view	Displays the code window so you can write and edit code associated with the selected item
Color dialog box	Enables the user to specify the desired color if one of the default values will not do
Condition	Can be any valid expression recognized by the debugger. It is usually evaluated as either True or False.
Custom colors	Within the Color dialog box, the user can choose to create a custom color. Once a custom color is created, the user can select it from the bottom of the Color dialog box and click OK to set the Color property.
Default item	The selected item in the combo box. The ComboBox control appears in two parts. The top part is a text box that enables the user to type a list item; the bottom part is a list box that displays a list from which the user can select one item.
Define Custom Colors button	Within the Color dialog box, the user can create a custom color. Click the Define Custom Color button and then click in the Color Selection area to update the Hue, Sat, and Lum fields. You must click in the vertical bar at the right to select the exact color desired. This will update the Red, Green, and Blue values. The RGB color codes displayed in the Color field will be inserted when you close the Color dialog box. The decimal values displayed to the right of each slider range from 0 (no color) to 255 (maximum color).
Design view	Displays the object window for the selected item—an existing form, module, ActiveX object, or user control—so you can add controls
Expression	A combination of keywords, operators, variables, and constants that yields a string, number, or object. An expression can be used to perform a calculation, manipulate characters, or assign values for example, X=2.

If statement	One of the most useful control structures; enables you to evaluate a sequence of statements if a condition is true and evaluate a different sequence of statements if it is not true. When a multiple-line If...Then...Else is encountered, the condition is Nested. If the condition is True, the statements following Then are executed. If the condition is False, each ElseIf statement is evaluated in order. When a True ElseIf condition is found, the statements immediately following the associated Then are executed. If no ElseIf condition evaluates to True, or if there are no ElseIf statements, the statements following Else are executed. After executing the statements following Then, ElseIf, or Else, execution continues with the statement following EndIf.
	
	 This example shows both the multiple- and single-line forms of the If...Then...Else statement.
	
	 Dim Number, Digits As Integer
	 Dim MyString As String
	 Number = 53 ' Initialize variable.
	 If Number < 10 Then
	   Digits = 1
	 ElseIf Number < 100 Then
	 ' Condition evaluates to True so the next statement is executed.
	   Digits = 2
	 Else
	   Digits = 3
	 End If

> **Tip** Select Case might be more useful when evaluating a single expression that has several possible values.

Table 2-1 cont.	Programming-Oriented Terminology
Term	**Description**
Inherits	Causes the current class or interface to inherit the attributes, fields, properties, methods, and events from another class or interface. For example, multiple instances of a Form class share the same code and are loaded with the same controls with which the Form class was designed. During runtime, the individual properties of controls on each instance can be set to different values.
SelectedIndexChanged event	A property provided by Visual Basic .NET when a combo box selection is made. The Selected Index property returns an integer value that corresponds to the selected list item. You can programmatically change the selected item by changing the Selected Index value in code. The corresponding item in the list will appear in the text portion of the combo box. If no item is selected, the Selected Index value is -1. If the first item in the list is selected, then the Selected Index value is 0. This indicates which item you selected from the list.
Show Dialog method	In Visual Basic .NET, the Show Dialog method is used to display a form modally; the Show method is used to display a form nonmodally. A form shown modally must be closed before any other activity can be done in the application. It is often used to present a message to the user that you want to make sure he or she sees. The user then simply clicks an OK button and the form is closed. An About box is an example of a form that is shown modally.
Statements	A syntactically complete unit that expresses one kind of action, declaration, or definition. A statement generally occupies a single line, although you can use a colon (:) to include more than one statement on a line. You can also use a line-continuation character (_) to continue a single logical line onto a second physical line.

Adding the Color Dialog Box

We will incorporate a standard Color dialog box in order to set the background color that will give us an enhanced way to change color preferences. This will require adding an instance of the Color Dialog object from the Windows Form class library.

Opening the Pay Transaction System Project

By typing just a little code, you can create a color selection dialog box. Reusing existing components saves time because you write less code. It also reduces testing effort since there is less code to test than if you wrote everything from scratch.

Task 1:
To Open the Pay Transaction System Project

1 Choose **File | Open | Project**, navigate to where the *PayTransactionSystem.sln* file is saved, select it, and click the **Open** button.

Figure 2-2

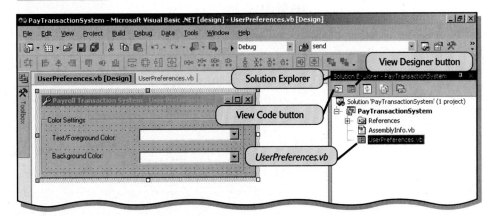

 Other Ways You can also launch Visual Basic .NET, choose **Open Project**, and then select the project we began working on in Project 1. We will continue development of this project.

2 Click the *UserPreferences.vb* file in the Solution Explorer.

3 Click the **View Code** button at the top of the Solution Explorer.

Figure 2-3

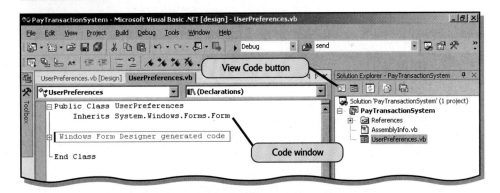

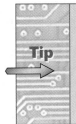 **Tip** In Code View mode you can see the Visual Basic .NET syntax that makes up the form, as seen in Figure 2-3. The Interactive Development Environment (IDE) hides some of the detail, such as the "Windows Form Designer generated code" with a plus sign (+) in front. If you click the plus sign, the code will expand to show you all the additional code generated based on the objects you added and properties you set in the form.

Adding the Color Dialog Box and Color Object Instances

For each .NET class object we want to reference in our program, we must first make sure that we inherit the appropriate class library and declare the objects from that library that we wish to use. Visual Basic .NET has added the System.Windows.Form class library by default because we have added or renamed a form object in our project.

> **Tip** Make sure that the insertion point is beneath the line of code "Inherits System.Windows.Forms.Form" before typing. In Visual Basic .NET, when you type a period character (.) the program provides a list of valid choices. This is referred to as Auto List Members. Selecting from the list inserts the member into your code.

Task 2:

To Add the Color Dialog Box and Color Object Instances

1 Type **Private bgColorDialog as** ColorDialog.

2 Type **Private CurrentBgColor as** Color.

Figure 2-4

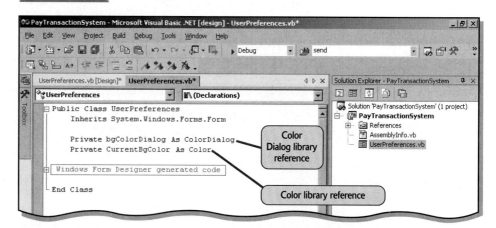

> **Tip** You declare a variable to specify its name and characteristics. The declaration statement for variables is the Dim statement. Its location and contents determine the variable's characteristics. A local variable is declared within a procedure. A module variable is declared at module level, inside the module but not within any procedure internal to that module. For example, the statement Dim strCity defines the variable **strCity** as a character string; the statement StrCity = "Middletown" assigns the character string **Middletown** to the variable **strCity**. Dim defines the variable; "str" represents a string-type value, and City is a meaningful name. A string is a data type that allows letters, numbers, and many characters.

The keyword *Inherits* indicates that our User Preferences form will be able to use all of the properties and methods available to any standard Windows form. To add the Color dialog box to our form, we must declare an instance of the Color Dialog object, as shown in the Code view declaration section below the Inherits statement in Figure 2-4. The first statement creates "bgColorDialog" as an instance of the Color Dialog object. The second statement creates "CurrentBgColor" as an instance of the Color object.

Add Data and Code to the Color ComboBox Controls

In order to enhance our ComboBox controls so they display a color selection dialog box, we need to add data to the list of colors in the color ComboBox controls, then add code that determines whether the user has chosen to display the custom color selection screen.

Adding Data to the Background Color Combo Box

To have our combo box invoke the Color dialog box, we will add two data items to the BackgroundColor ComboBox Items property collection. The new values to be added are "Windows Default" and "Change Colors."

Task 3:
To Add Data to the Background Color Combo Box

1 Double-click *UserPreferences.vb* in the Solution Explorer to display the form.

2 Click the **cboBackgroundColor** ComboBox control to set focus on it.

3 Choose **View | Properties Window**.

4 Click the **Items** property, then click the **Ellipsis** button.

5 Replace existing text, type **Windows Default**, press the [Enter] key, type **Change Colors**, and click **OK**.

Figure 2-5

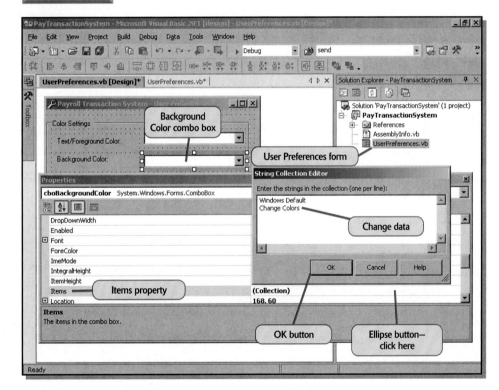

Preparing the Background Color Combo Box to Handle Events Code

Code needs to be written to determine what to do when a color is selected. To add code to a control, select the form within the Solution Explorer and then double-click the control that needs code added behind it. This displays the Code View for the control that you double-clicked.

Task 4:
To Add Event Code to the Background Color Combo Box

1 Double-click the *UserPreferences.vb* form within the Solution Explorer.

2 Double-click the **cboBackgroundColor** ComboBox control to display the Code View window. Click **X** to close the Properties window.

Figure 2-6

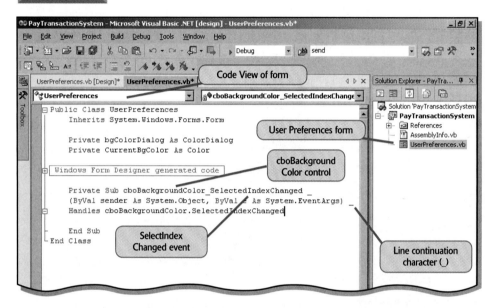

Tip

When you double-click the ComboBox control, Visual Basic .NET generates code for the SelectedIndexChanged event procedure. The first three lines starting with "Private Sub cboBackgroundColor_SelectedIndex Changed" are actually one line with an underscore (_) at the end of the first two lines. Visual Basic .NET enables you to continue long lines so that you can see all of the syntax beyond the size of the Code View window. In the next step, we will add code to the SelectedIndexChanged event.

Adding Code for the Background Color Combo Box to the Indexed Changed Event

Once you click the Background Color combo box, the program enters the SelectedIndexChanged event. To have our combo box invoke the Color dialog box, we will add the following code to the SelectedIndexChanged subprocedure.

Task 5:
To Add Code for the Background Color Combo Box

1 Type bgColorDialog = New System. Windows.Forms. ColorDialog().

2 Type bgColorDialog. AllowFullOpen = True.

3 Type bgColorDialog. AnyColor = True.

4 Type bgColorDialog. SolidColorOnly = False.

5 Type bgColorDialog. ShowHelp = True.

6 Type bgColorDialog. ShowDialog().

7 Choose **File | Save All**.

Figure 2-7

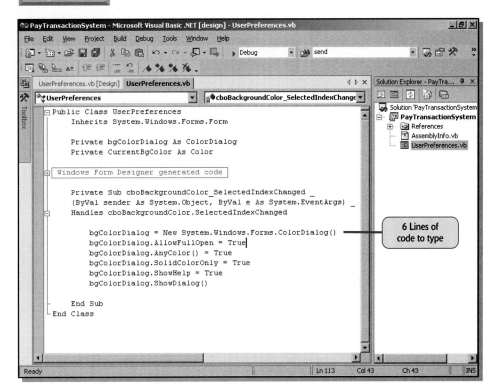

Tip

This code instantiates (creates an instance of) **bgColorDialog** as a new Windows Form Color Dialog and then sets up some default properties to allow it to open in full size, use any color available in the system palette, use color beyond solid colors, and show help if desired. Finally, the last line displays the Color dialog box through the ShowDialog() command.

Testing the Software

Before adding code to view how your preference changes look, you will pause and verify that your Color dialog box is available and works as you expect.

Task 6:
To Test the Software

1 Choose **Debug | Start**. The User Preferences form appears.

2 Click the down arrow in the **BackgroundColor** combo box and then select **Change Colors**.

3 Verify that the Color dialog box appears.

Figure 2-8

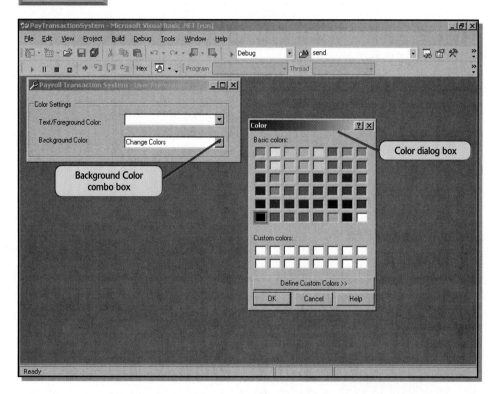

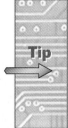
Tip

If everything goes right, you should see the Color dialog box overlay the User Preferences form. Notice that the **Help** and **Define Custom Colors** buttons are enabled. This is because we set the properties **AllowFullOpen** and **ShowHelp** to True.

If we had set them to false, the Define Custom Colors button would be disabled, and the Help button would not be visible.

4 Notice in Figure 2-9 that these two buttons appear differently.

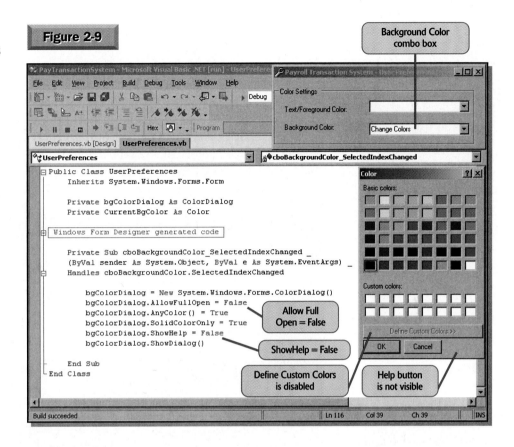

Figure 2-9

5 Click the **Define Custom Colors** button.

6 Click **OK** to close the Colors dialog box.

Tip When you click the **Define Custom Colors** button, the dialog box expands to the right. The form now enables you to pick any combination of color attributes and add the resulting color visually to the Custom Colors area on the left.

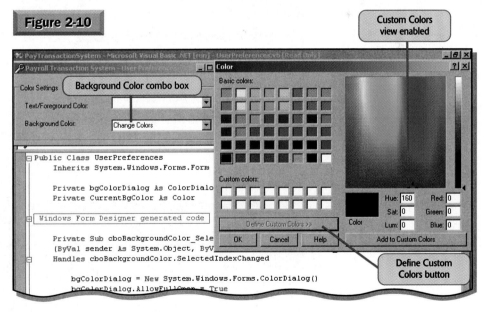

Figure 2-10

Setting Defaults

> **Tip** Object-oriented programming is very powerful; we have added a significant amount of capability with very little coding. You are now ready to use the color preferences to change how your project looks.

To finish our initial form, we will use the color preferences selected for both the foreground and background colors and change our form's appearance to match those color settings. We will accomplish this using programming logic and Visual Basic .NET code to set the default values for each combo box. Then we will place code behind each of the ComboBox control's "SelectedIndexChanged" events to set the colors of the labels and group box text as well as the form's background color whenever the color setting is changed.

Setting the Default Items for Each Combo Box

Every form has a base set of class events that are used to trigger logic to be executed whenever that event occurs. We will use the Form Load event to set the combo box default values.

Task 7:
To Set Default Items

1 Click the *UserPreferences.vb* form in the Solution Explorer.

2 Click the **View Code** button.

3 Choose **Base Class Events** from the left list box.

4 Choose the **Load** event from the right list box.

Figure 2-11

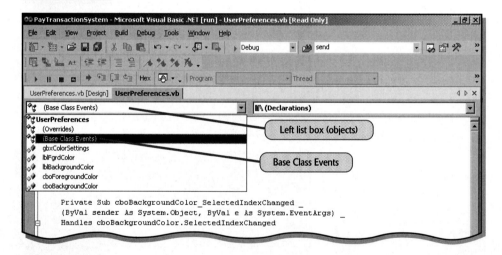

Figure 2-12

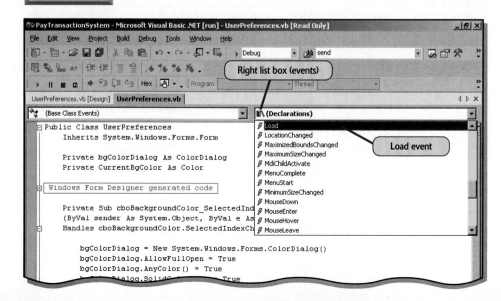

5 Type cboForegroundColor. SelectedIndex = 0 'Black.

6 Type cboBackgroundColor. SelectedIndex = 0 'Windows Default.

Figure 2-13

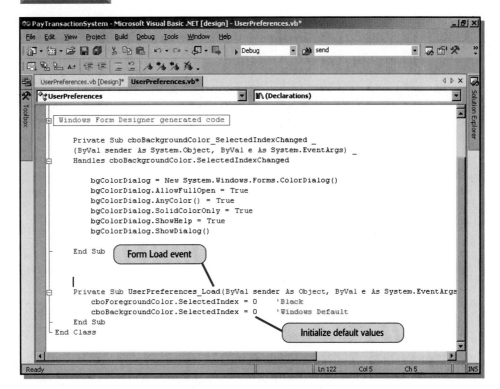

Tip

Notice the Visual Basic .NET comment above; it begins with an apostrophe ('). Visual Basic permits comments at the right end of a line of code or on a separate line. Comments are strongly encouraged because they help organize logic and can be extremely helpful for programmers who maintain the code later.

Tip

When you select the Load event, an empty subprocedure called UserPreferences_Load is created. To have the first item in each collection be the default, enter the two lines of code as shown in Figure 2-14. A default value is the value that appears in the combo box when the user first starts the program and before a selection is made. In this case you are referring to the collection index number instead of the actual value. All arrays and collections start with zero (0). For example, if you wanted the third item in the collection to be the default, then you would set the Selected Index property of the combo box to two (2).

Defining the SelectedIndexChanged Event for the Background Color Combo Box

Every time "Change Colors" is selected from the Background Color combo box, we want to set the background of the form to the color that was last selected from the Color dialog box.

Task 8:

To Define the Selected Index for the Background Color Combo Box

1 Choose **View | Code** for the User Preferences form.

2 Select **cboBackgroundColor** from the left list box.

3 Select the **SelectedIndexChanged** event from the right list box.

4 Type **If** cboBackgroundColor. Text <> "Windows Default" Then above the **bgColorDialog = New** line.

5 Type **Me.BackColor =** bgColorDialog.Color below **ShowDialog0**.

6 Type **Else** below **Me.BackColor = bgColorDialog.Color**.

7 Type **Me.BackColor =** bgColorDialog.Color. LightGray   'Windows default below **Else**.

8 Type **End If**.

9 Choose **File | Save All**.

Figure 2-14

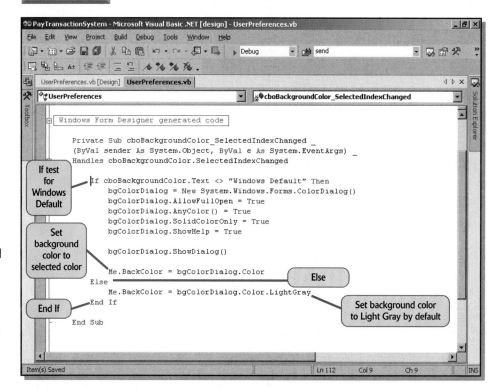

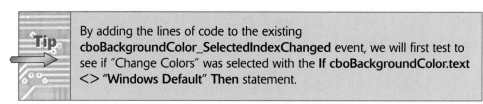

By adding the lines of code to the existing **cboBackgroundColor_SelectedIndexChanged** event, we will first test to see if "Change Colors" was selected with the **If cboBackgroundColor.text <> "Windows Default" Then** statement.

If our current selection does not equal "**Windows Default**," the program performs the logic after the Else condition. Since there are only two choices, a value of "**Change Colors**" will cause the first part of the If statement to be invoked. When this occurs, we set the form's background color to the color of our instance of the Color dialog box called **bgColorDialog**. Further explanation of If/Then statements will be provided later in the book.

The statement **Me.BackColor = bgColorDialog.Color** is translated to Me (User Preferences form). The BackColor property is the same as the **bgColorDialog.Color** property value. When you selected **item = "Windows Default,"** you set the background to Light Gray with the **Me.BackColor = bgColorDialog.Color.LightGray** statement.

Defining the SelectedIndexChanged Event for the Text/Foreground Color Combo Box

A different technique needs to be used to set the Text/Foreground color because of inconsistencies in the data type from the **cboForegroundcolor.Text**, which is a String, and the **lblTextColor.ForeColor**, which needs to be a Color Object from the System.Forms class. Variables will be covered in more detail later in the book.

Task 9:

To Define the Selected Index for the Text/Foreground Color Combo Box

Figure 2-15

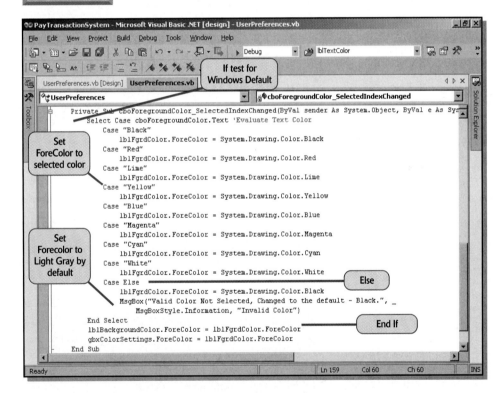

1 Choose **View | Object.**

2 Double-click the **cboForegroundColor** ComboBox control.

3 Type the code from Figure 2-15 into the **cboForegroundColor_Selec tedIndexChanged** event code window.

Tip We want to evaluate which color the Text property is set to and set the Color properties of the two labels and group box to the equivalent System.Form Class Color. In cases where there are several different conditions to evaluate, it is more efficient and convenient to use a Select Case statement as an alternative to a series of If statements.

Here we use **Select Case cboForegroundColor.text** to identify what we are going to evaluate; each of the respective Case statements identifies a specific condition that we are looking for. Thus, if the **cboForeground.Text** property is set to "**Red**," we change the **lblFgrdColor.ForeColor** property to Red.

Finally, since both the **lblBackgroundColor.ForeColor** and the **gbxColorSettings.ForeColor** need to be set to the same color, we set them to the color value of **lblFgrdColor.ForeColor**.

You may have noticed that we also added a final line to the Case statement, Case Else, that will be executed only when none of the expected conditions occur. This is good programming practice so that nothing unexpected happens to the appearance of our program event when the unexpected occurs. If the message box is ever invoked due to an invalid color being set, we set the text back to Black and display a message box that looks like Figure 2-16.

Testing the Solution

The User Preferences form is now complete and ready to be tested. During the testing a foreground color will be selected and the foreground color of the two labels will change. If a color is not selected, a warning message will appear. The message will be **Valid Color Not Selected, Changed to the Default - Black**. When the background color is selected, the color behind the labels will change.

Task 10:

To Test the User Preferences Form

1 Choose **Debug | Start**.

2 Select a **Text/Foreground Color** and verify that the label character color changes properly.

3 Select a **Background Color** and verify that the background color changes properly.

Figure 2-16

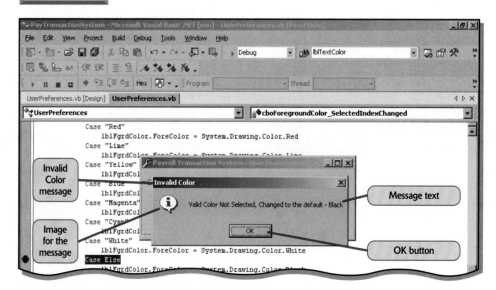

4 Select Red for the **Text/Foreground Color** and verify that the label and group text color changes to red.

5 Choose **File | Save All**.

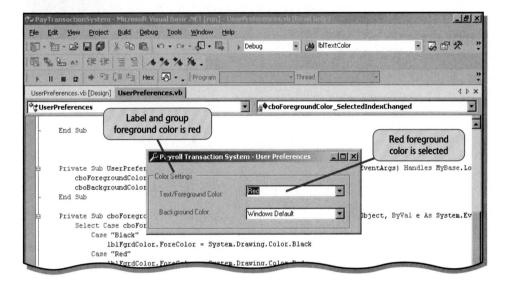

Figure 2-17

Tip In most cases, a procedure needs some information about the circumstances in which it has just been called. A procedure that performs repeated or shared tasks uses different information for each call. This information consists of variables, constants, and expressions that are passed to the procedure when it is called. Each value passed to a procedure is called an argument. The first argument is the message to be displayed ("Valid Color not…"), the second argument identifies the icon to be displayed (Information), and the last argument identifies the test for the Title Bar ("Invalid Color").

SUMMARY AND EXERCISES

SUMMARY

- Logic in the form of code needs to be added behind controls to determine how the forms will appear.
- A standard Color dialog box can be incorporated into a Visual Basic .NET project with just a couple of lines of code.
- When utilizing the Color dialog box, a reference to the Color Dialog object from the Windows Form class library is required.
- Private object variables are required to instantiate the Color Dialog and Color objects.
- The Properties window enables you to add data to a combo box by using the Ellipsis button and typing in the data you want to see when the combo box is clicked.
- Double-clicking a control displays a code view and enables you to add or modify code.
- Software testing is very important to ensure that the program functions as expected.
- Daily builds, or creating an executable (*.exe*), is a good practice to identify exceptions early before they can cause trouble. A solution and its individual projects are typically built and tested in a Debug build. Developers will compile a Debug build repeatedly, at each step in their development process. When a project or solution is fully developed and sufficiently debugged, its components are compiled in a Release build. By default, a Release build employs various optimizations.
- The Color dialog box provides many options for customizing the appearance of the application.
- Default values are a good design consideration. In this example, the colors were defaulted to the Windows Default values.
- Select Case statements are a more readable way to organize code that must select from several choices. It is preferred over If/End If statements if more than two options are available.

KEY TERMS & SKILLS

KEY TERMS

Case statement (p. 2-5)
Code view (p. 2-5)
Color dialog box
    (p. 2-5)
condition (p. 2-5)
custom colors (p. 2-5)

default items (p. 2-5)
Define Custom Colors
    button (p. 2-5)
Design view (p. 2-5)
expression (p. 2-5)
inherits (p. 2-6)

instance (p. 2-8)
SelectedIndexChanged
    event (p. 2-6)
Show Dialog method
    (p. 2-6)
statement (p. 2-6)

SKILLS

Add code for the Background Color
    combo box (p. 2-11)
Add data to the Background Color
    combo box (p. 2-9)
Add event code to the Background
    Color combo box (p. 2-10)
Add the Color dialog box and Color
    object instances (p. 2-8)
Define the Selected Index for the
    Background Color combo box
    (p. 2-16)

Define the Selected Index for the
    Text/Foreground Color combo box
    (p. 2-17)
Open the Pay Transaction System
    project (p. 2-7)
Set default items (p. 2-14)
Test the software (p. 2-12)
Test the User Preferences form
    (p. 2-18)

STUDY QUESTIONS

MULTIPLE CHOICE

1. Which of the following is NOT an expression?
a. X = 2
b. Y = 1 + myAge
c. If X = 3 Then Y = 5
d. What is my age?

2. To add a control to a form we usually change to
a. Code View mode.
b. View Designer mode.
c. Run mode.
d. Debug mode.

3. To type code we usually change to
a. Code View mode.
b. Design Time mode.
c. Run mode.
d. Debug mode.

4. When you add a control to a form, you are creating
a. an instance of the control.
b. an image of a control.
c. a uniquely named control.
d. both A and C

5. In the Color Dialog, what method is required to select a color?
a. ShowFullOpen
b. ShowHelp
c. ShowColors
d. ShowDialog

6. In Code View mode, Visual Basic .NET often hides code. To display the code,
a. click the Maximize button.
b. click the More button.
c. click the plus sign.
d. click the Start button.

7. When using code libraries, you must
   a. declare public variables.
   b. declare the objects from that library.
   c. initialize constants.
   d. make API calls.

8. When a new control is added to a form, Visual Basic .NET
   a. assigns a name to the new control.
   b. compiles code for errors.
   c. generates code.
   d. both A and C

9. The keyword *Inherits* indicates that the User Preferences form will be able to
   a. create new forms.
   b. use all of the properties and methods available to any Windows form.
   c. run precompiled programs.
   d. display messages.

10. To type code into the ComboBox control, you can:
   a. double-click the control.
   b. select the form and click the Code View button on the Solution Explorer.
   c. choose View Code from the menu.
   d. all of the above

SHORT ANSWER

1. Where do you add a reference to the Color Dialog library in code?
2. Where do you add code that initializes values within a form when a project is started?
3. What button in the Color dialog box enables you to select additional colors?
4. Name three steps needed to add data to a ComboBox control.
5. What Visual Basic .NET menu enables you to start the application?
6. When using a ComboBox control, what is the index number for the top item on the list?
7. If no item is selected from a ComboBox control, what is the value of the Index number?
8. What is the name of the event that is launched when a value is selected from a ComboBox control?
9. What is a default property?
10. What is the name of the little button on the Item property?

FILL IN THE BLANK

1. We need to add _____ for the users to see the visual impact of their preference selections by changing the color of the labels based on the selection made from the Text/Foreground Color ComboBox control.
2. We use the _____ _____ box to provide a standard method for selecting colors.
3. Click the _____ _____ _____ button in the Color dialog box to display additional custom colors.
4. _____ _____ statements are the most effective way to handle branching when multiple options are available in code. This approach is easier to read and preferred over If/End If structures when more than two options are present.

5. The various colors within the SelectedIndexChanged event were selected using _____ statements.

6. A _____ is used to evaluate if an expression is evaluated as True or False.

7. X = 2 represents a _____.

8. Visual Basic .NET provides the _____ _____ character to split a long line of code into several lines on the screen so it is more easily read and debugged.

9. The colon character allows more than one _____ on a single line of programming code.

10. When using the Select Case statement code structure, always put the _____ _____ statement at the end to complete the structure.

FOR DISCUSSION

1. Why is the Select Case statement code structure preferred over the If/End If code structure?

2. When are Msgbox controls used?

3. Why are ComboBox controls used?

4. How do you handle a condition that is unexpected within a Select Case code structure?

5. What is the ForeColor property?

P R O J E C T **3**

Building and Debugging a Visual Basic .NET Project

Once a program is ready for testing or deployment, you can build an executable for distribution so it can be run on another computer without the source code and the Visual Basic .NET Interactive Development Environment (IDE). You should first test your program thoroughly using the debugger as we discussed earlier. Once you are satisfied with the results, you are ready to create (build) an *.exe* file.

After completing this project, you will have developed, tested, and deployed your first complete program.

Tip   The *PayTransactionSystem.sln* file can be found at\\vb.net_brief\vb.net_datafiles\03\PayTransactionSystem.

***e*-selections**) **Running Case**

Other employees in the e-Selections Division of Selections, Inc. have heard about your Visual Basic .NET project and would like to see a demonstration. It is time to learn how to build and debug your project and prepare to show it to other people.

Steps in Building a Routine

Learn about the Steps in Building a Routine with the Program Design Language (PDL).

Building a routine most effectively consists of following a process that ensures consistently well-written code that contains clear comments and thoughtful logic.

We will focus on the specific steps for building an individual routine that are critical on projects of all sizes. The following are the steps for building a routine: 1) Program Design Language (PDL) to Code Process, 2) Design the Routine, 3) Check the Design, 4) Code the Routine, and 5) Check the Code.

With PDL, you write comments and then add code later in a fill-in-the-blank fashion. If you can organize your plans within comments, the coding is actually very easy to do. Table 1 is an example of PDL.

 Tip PDL is sometimes referred to as "pseudo code" meaning it is not real code. It is a very good idea to write out PDL or pseudo code before you write your Visual Basic .Net code.

Table 1

Programming Design Language Example

Present the Login Form
 - Show User Name
 - Show Password
 - Show OK button
   -- default using Enter key
 - Show Close button
   -- Esc key will affect this button
Validation
 - User Name
   -- Check length of User Name
     --- Warning message
 - Password
   -- Check length of password
 - Verify User Name & Password are valid
   -- Warning Message if invalid
   -- Display Splash if valid
   -- Database stores values
   -- Common routine to validate
 - Show Cancel button
 - End the application without warning

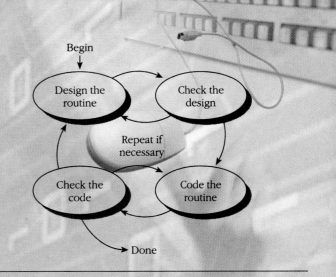

Table 2 provides an overview of building a procedure.

Table 2

How to Build a Procedure

Phase	Overview
Design the procedure	The first step in constructing a procedure is to design it.
	Make sure the procedure is well defined and fits cleanly into the overall architecture. Define the problem the procedure will solve, inputs and outputs, and how it will handle errors.
	Name the procedure with a clear, unambiguous name. Decide how to test the procedure. Think about efficiency. Research the algorithms and data structures. Write the PDL. Think about the data. Check the PDL. Iterate. Try as many ideas as you can in PDL before you start coding.
Code the routine	Once you have written the PDL and designed the data, take a minute to review the PDL you have written. Back away from it and think about how you would explain it to someone else. Begin to fill in the code below each comment.
	Write the procedure declaration. Write the procedure interface statement or function declaration. Turn the PDL into high-level comments. Fill in the code below each comment.
	Check the code informally. Mentally test each block of code as you fill it in below its comment. Make sure that all the input and output data is accounted for and that all parameters are used.
	Check for inaccurate variable names, unused data, and undeclared data. Check for off-by-one errors, infinite loops, and improper nesting. Check the procedure's documentation. Make sure the PDL translated into comments is still accurate.
Check the code	Mentally walkthrough the procedure for errors. Mentally executing a procedure is difficult, and that difficulty is one reason to keep your procedures small. Compile the procedure. Use the Visual Basic .NET debugger to check the procedure for errors by stepping through the code one line at a time. Remove errors from the procedure.

Writing good PDL calls for using understandable English, avoiding features specific to a single programming language, and describing what the design does rather than how it will do it. The PDL-to-code process is useful for detailed design and makes coding easier and less error prone.

Building and Debugging a Visual Basic .NET Project

The Challenge

Mr. Traylor is pleased with the work you have done on the e-Selections Pay Transaction System and the speed with which you have learned the fundamentals of the Visual Basic .NET IDE. Now he wants to see a compiled version of what you have done so far, so he can evaluate how the tool has helped you become even more productive. He intends to run the executable program in the next status meeting with other managers of the firm.

The Solution

Visual Basic .NET has many capabilities to ensure that your code contains the correct syntax. The IDE includes many error-handling features, and generates compiled code that is fast. Mr. Traylor wants to be certain that the demonstration goes extremely well. He wants you to carefully check your code to ensure that no errors exist, and if you find any, to correct them and create a new executable file. You will need software testing and debugging skills to verify that the code is ready. Figure 3-1 shows how the application appeared after successfully running and debugging the application code in Task 10 of Project 2.

Figure 3-1

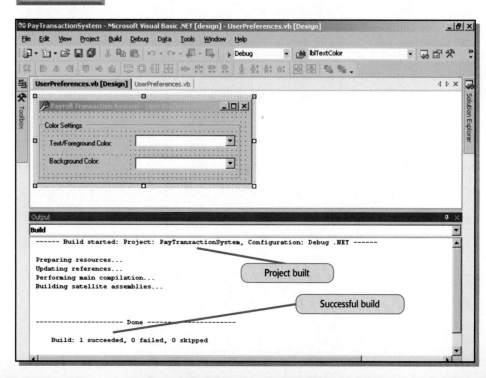

Identifying Debugging Terminology

As the project evolves we will test the application and walk through the code one line at a time. These debugging techniques will teach new skills and additional terms (Table 3-1).

Table 3-1   Debugging Terminology

Term	Description
Autos window	When you are debugging an application and stepping over a function call (F10), the Autos window displays the return value for that function and any functions that may be called by that function. To open the Autos window, you must be debugging; choose **Debug	Windows	Autos**.
Bin subdirectory	Specifies the working directory of the program being debugged. In Visual Basic .NET, the working directory is the directory the application is launched from \bin by default.
Breakpoint	A breakpoint tells the debugger that an application should break (pause execution) at a certain point or when a certain condition occurs. When a break occurs, your program and the debugger are said to be in break mode.
Build Output box	This window displays status messages for various features in the integrated development environment (IDE). These include build errors that occur when a project is compiled.
Build type	Displays the kind of project build desired and lists all of the available kinds of builds. Visual Basic .NET can create two types of executable files: one as a debug build and the other as a release build.
Configuration Manager	Use this dialog box to create and edit solution build configurations and project configurations. Any changes you make to solution build configurations are reflected on the Configuration page of the Solution Property Pages dialog box. You can access the Configuration Manager from the Build menu, from the Solution Property Pages dialog box, or from the solution configuration drop-down menu on the main toolbar.
Debugging	Once you have created your application and resolved the build errors, you must correct any logical errors that keep your application or stored procedures from running correctly. You can do this with the development environment's integrated debugging functions. These allow you to stop at procedure locations, inspect memory and register values, change variables, observe message traffic, and get a close look at how your code works or does not work. Variables will be covered in more detail later in the book.
Deployment	The primary purpose of deployment is to install files on a target computer. The deployment tools in Visual Studio enable you to control where and how those files will be installed.
Distribution	When distributing your application, you need to determine what files are needed in your setup. The files you include depend on the components used in the application, the data source used for the application, and the options you want available to end users.
Errors	Each error message topic covers a single message and provides information on possible causes and potential solutions or workarounds to solve the problem.
Executable file	A Windows-based application that can run outside the development environment. An executable file has an *.exe* file name extension. Operating system requirements for Visual Basic .NET applications are Windows 2000, Windows XP, or Windows NT 4.03.
Immediate mode	The Immediate mode of the Command window is used for debugging purposes such as evaluating expressions, executing statements, and printing variable values. It enables you to enter expressions to be evaluated or executed by the development language during debugging. In some cases, you can change the value of variables.
Run dialog box	Provides a place for you to type the location and file name of the program you want to run. If you are not sure of the program's location or file name, click **Browse**. You can make a temporary network connection by typing the path to a shared computer. You can also connect to the Internet by typing the address (uniform resource locator, URL) of the site you want to open. You can activate the Run dialog box by choosing **Start	Run**.
Scope	Defines the visibility of a variable, procedure, or object. For example, a variable declared as Public is visible to all procedures in all modules. Variables declared in procedures are visible only within the procedure and lose their value between calls unless they are declared Static.
Watch window	You can use the Watch window to evaluate variables and expressions and keep the results. You can also use the Watch window to edit the value of a variable or register. To open the Watch window, the debugger must be running or in break mode. Choose **Debug	Windows	Watch**.

Building an Executable

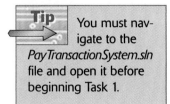

Tip You must navigate to the *PayTransactionSystem.sln* file and open it before beginning Task 1.

This process is completed when an *.exe*-named file is created. During the process, Visual Basic .NET compiles the program by checking every line of code for syntax errors. The completed file will be placed in the bin directory of the application.

Task 1:
To Build an Executable

1 Choose **Build | Build PayTransactionSystem**.

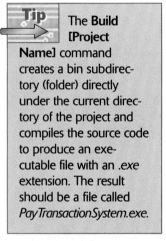

Tip The **Build [Project Name]** command creates a bin subdirectory (folder) directly under the current directory of the project and compiles the source code to produce an executable file with an *.exe* extension. The result should be a file called *PayTransactionSystem.exe*.

Figure 3-2

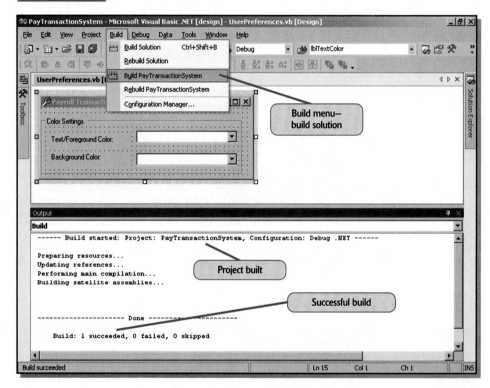

2 Choose **Start | Run | Browse**.

Tip The executable file should be located by accessing C:\Public\VBNetClass\ Students\HR\ PayTransactionSystem\ bin\PayTransaction System.exe.

Troubleshooting
For long pathnames, it is not possible to see the full directory path, and you cannot resize the Run dialog box. To see the full path, click in the list box and press Home to see the path from the far left; press End to see the path from the far right.

Figure 3-3

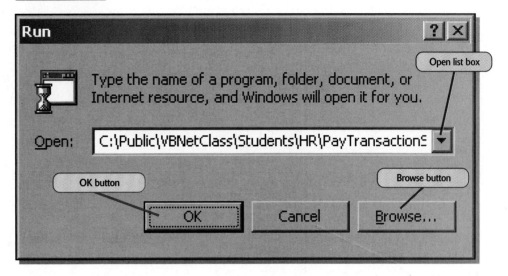

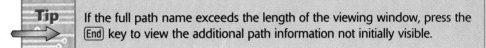

Tip If the full path name exceeds the length of the viewing window, press the End key to view the additional path information not initially visible.

3   Click **OK** to run the executable.

Figure 3-4

Tip

Visual Basic .NET can create two types of executable files: one as a debug build and the other as a release build. Debug builds are the default type; they contain debug information that make them run more slowly, while the process of producing the physical *.exe* file is performed much more quickly. When you prepare your project for production or commercial use, you should change the build type to a release build, in which unneeded debugging information is removed and the code is optimized for superior performance at runtime. The release build usually takes a little longer to produce the *.exe* file—but since you are doing this only on an occasional basis when your project reaches a significant milestone, it is worth the wait.

4 Choose **Build | Configuration Manager**.

Figure 3-5

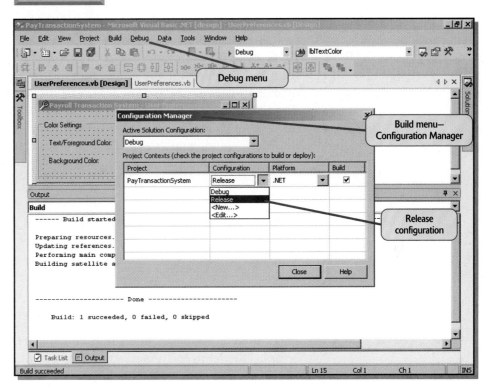

5 Choose **Build | Build PayTransactionSystem**.

Figure 3-6

6 Verify that the build was successful.

7 Choose **File | Save All**.

Tip You must change the configuration type back to Debug to complete the rest of these tasks. You will be making many more changes and enhancements to this project; it will be useful for the builds to contain the debugging information, and the compiles will perform more quickly.

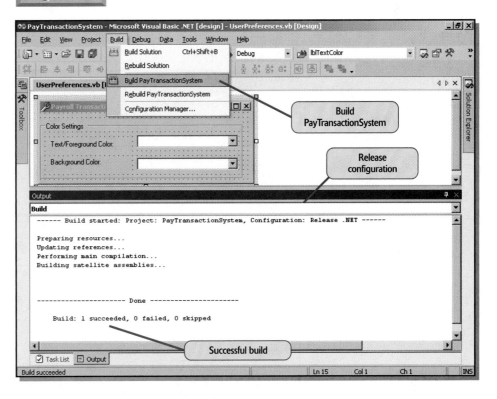

The Visual Basic .NET Debugger

When we write our programs, we have many opportunities to make mistakes (we are only human). Some of these mistakes may be syntax-related, as when we mistype the name of a keyword or variable. Sometimes the syntax is perfectly acceptable, but the code is placed in an area that is out of scope or incompatible with the type of syntax being entered. Some errors happen only during the execution of the program under certain conditions, and logical mistakes occur when the syntax is correct but the program does not perform as we intended. We refer to any of these situations as "bugs" or "defects," and they either stop the program from running or prevent it from running correctly.

Visual Basic Debugging Tools—Using the Debug Menu

Visual Basic .NET provides debugging tools to help identify faulty code and to enable you to walk through code one line at a time. The Debug toolbar will be needed in this section.

The Visual Studio .NET debugger is a powerful tool that enables you to observe the runtime behavior of your program and determine the location of semantic errors. The debugger understands features that are built into programming languages and their associated libraries. With the debugger, you can break (suspend) execution of your program to examine your code, evaluate and edit variables in your program, view registers, see the instructions created from your source code, and view the memory space used by your application.

Task 2:
To Use the Debug Menu

1 Choose **View | Toolbar | Debug**.

Figure 3-7

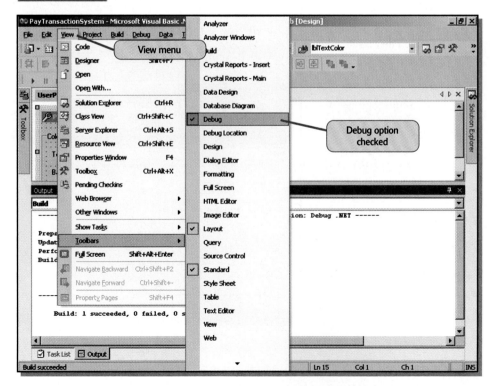

2 Review the Debug toolbar.

Figure 3-8

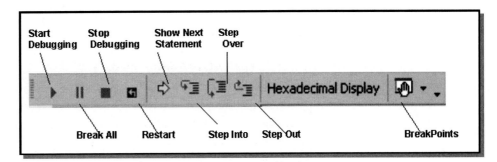

Other Ways

To display the Debug toolbar, choose **Tools | Customize**. The Customize dialog box will be displayed.

Figure 3-9

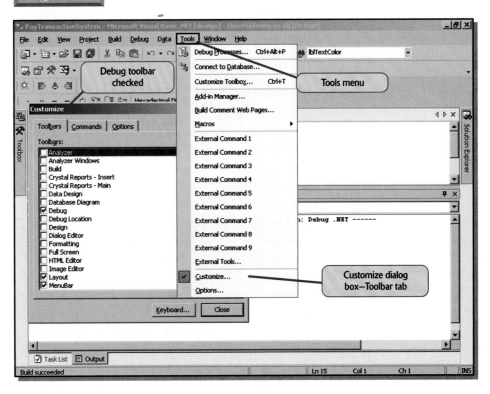

Identifying Debug Menu Options

There are numerous debugging options that will allow us to step through the code (Table 3-2).

Table 3-2	Debug Menu Options
Menu Option	**Description**
Windows	Displays breakpoints and Immediate submenu options.
Windows— Breakpoints	The Breakpoints window contains a toolbar and a list of breakpoints currently set in your program.
Windows— Immediate	The Immediate window opens in Break mode and is empty. You can type or paste a line of code and press Enter to run it, or you can copy and paste the code from the Immediate window into the Code View window, but you cannot save code in the Immediate window.
Start	Starts the Visual Studio .NET debugger tool.
Start Without Debugging	Starts the program but does not debug the code.
Processes	The Processes dialog box enables you to view and manipulate programs in a Visual Studio solution. Using this dialog box, you can debug multiple programs at the same time in a single solution.
Exceptions	The Exceptions dialog box enables you to change the way the debugger handles exceptions (errors) or categories of exceptions.
Step Into	Executes code one statement at a time. Step Into executes the statement at the current execution point. If the statement is a call to a procedure, the next statement displayed is the first statement in the procedure.
Step Over	Similar to Step Into. The difference in use occurs when the current statement contains a call to a procedure.
	Step Over executes the procedure as a unit, and then steps to the next statement in the current procedure. Therefore, the next statement displayed is the next statement in the current procedure regardless of whether the current statement is a call to another procedure. This command is available in Break mode only.
New Breakpoint	Opens the New Breakpoint dialog box, which gives you complete options for creating a new breakpoint.
Clear All Breakpoints	Removes all breakpoints that are currently set. You cannot undo this operation.
Disable All Breakpoints	Disables all breakpoints that are currently set. This retains the breakpoints in case you want to reuse them later in your testing session.

Identifying Error Terminology

As we perform testing errors will be identified. The errors will be one of the following three types (Table 3-3).

Table 3-3	Error Terminology
Term	**Description**
Logical errors	Conditions that cause the program to produce the wrong results. Logical errors are the most common and most difficult to correct; many of the debugging tools help us diagnose and correct them.
Runtime errors	Conditions that occur only after you run the program (hence "runtime"). A user may enter data out of the expected range of input, or a file may unexpectedly reach an end-of-file (EOF) condition. Runtime errors could also be misspellings, in which you incorrectly name a table or column and receive an error only when you attempt to use that table or column. The code editor cannot determine that a table or file is misspelled because it might not be created until after the program is running. To fix these types of errors, a variety of tools and techniques are at our disposal.
Syntax errors	Conditions where a keyword or variable is misspelled; the code editor points out these conditions visually by underlining the syntax in question with a jagged blue line. These errors are the easiest to spot; you cannot run the program until all syntax errors are identified and corrected. The following is an example of a syntax error where the label object "**lblFgrdColor**" is misspelled as "**lblFgrdXolor**"; if you were walking through the code, the debugger would highlight this syntax error by underlining the mistyped label name with a blue jagged line.

Key Debugging Concepts—Setting a Breakpoint

To see your code execute through the debugger, you need to set a breakpoint. A breakpoint is a bookmark in the source code to identify when you want your program to suspend normal processing and enter the debugger, where you can visually execute your program one line at a time.

 Tip   You can also debug your program from the beginning without setting a breakpoint by pressing the F8 key, or choosing Debug | Step Into to start debugging with the first line of code to be executed.

Task 3:
To Set a Breakpoint

1 Double-click the **Text/Foreground Color** combo box to enter the code editor.

2 Move the mouse pointer to the indicator bar in the left margin.

3 Click in the left margin (inside the vertical gray bar) next to the **Private Sub cboForegroundColor_ SelectedIndexChanged** statement.

Figure 3-10

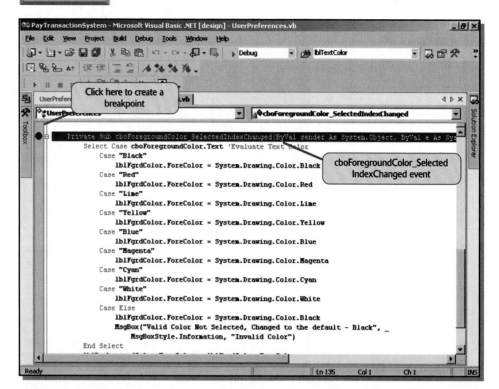

Other Ways

You can also access many features through the Debug menu.

Figure 3-11

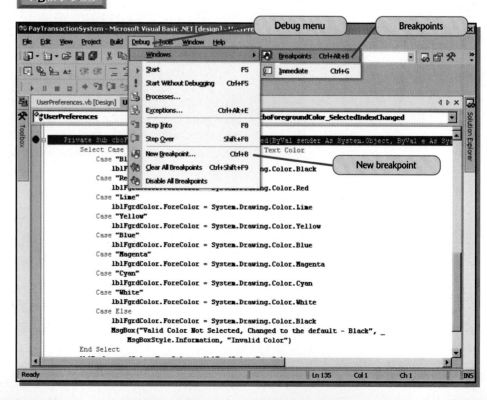

4 Choose **Debug | Start** or press F5.

Figure 3-12

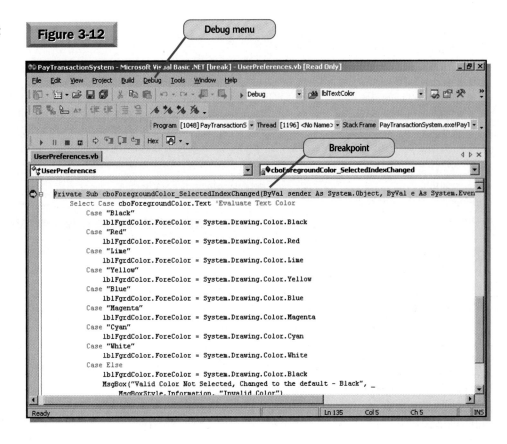

Debug menu

Breakpoint

5 Choose **Debug | Step Into** or press F8 to move one line at a time.

6 Press F8 until the **Case "Blue"** statement is highlighted.

7 Move the mouse pointer over **cboForegroundColor.Text** to obtain the current value.

8 Press F8 until the **lblfgrdColor. Forecolor = System. Drawing.Color.Blue** statement executes.

9 Press F8 and verify that the **End Select** statement runs next, then press F8 until the procedure is finished.

10 Choose **Debug | Stop Debugging**.

Figure 3-13

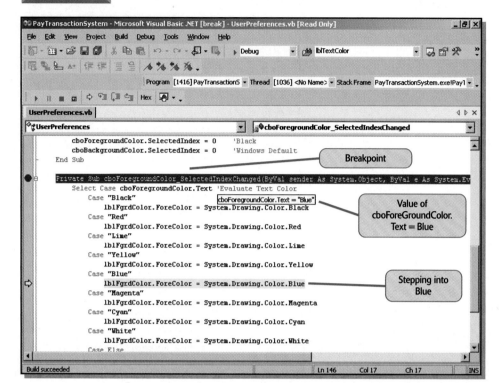

Tip When you set a breakpoint, the line of code where the breakpoint is set changes to a brownish red color. This is where execution will "break" so that you can use the Visual Basic .NET debugging tools.

Viewing the Autos Window

Visual Basic .NET displays an Autos window whenever you are stepping through code in the debugger. This window shows the state and values of properties and variables currently being used. For instance, if the Text/Foreground Color combo box value is changed from Black to Blue, the Autos window indicates the change of the cboForegroundColor.Text property.

Task 4:
To View the Autos Window

1 Choose **Debug | Start**.

2 Choose **Debug | Windows | Autos**.

3 Verify the Black color value in both the floating screen tip and the Autos window.

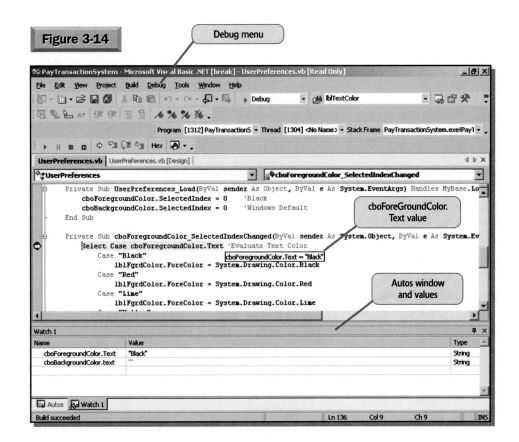

Figure 3-14

Creating Variable Watches

To view the status of variables and object properties through the entire execution of your program in debug mode, you must use a Watch window. This tool enables you to track values as they change during program execution or identify conditions to be tracked only when they occur. For instance, we could set up a condition to create a watch in both of the ComboBox controls for foreground and background color.

Task 5:
To Create a Variable Watch

1 Choose **Debug | Clear All Breakpoints**.

2 Select the **User Preferences** form from the Solution Explorer and click the **View Code** button.

3 Go to the **cboForegroundColor_SelectedIndexChanged** event in preparation for setting a breakpoint.

4 Set a breakpoint on the line of code containing **Select Case cboForegroundColor.Text**.

5 In the **SelectedIndexChanged** event for the **cboBackgroundColor** combo box, set a breakpoint on the line of code that contains **If cboBackgroundColor.text <> "Windows Default" Then**.

6 Choose **Debug | Start**. Visual Basic .NET enters Break mode at the Select Case statement.

7 Highlight **cboForegroundColor. Text**, right-click, and choose **Add Watch**.

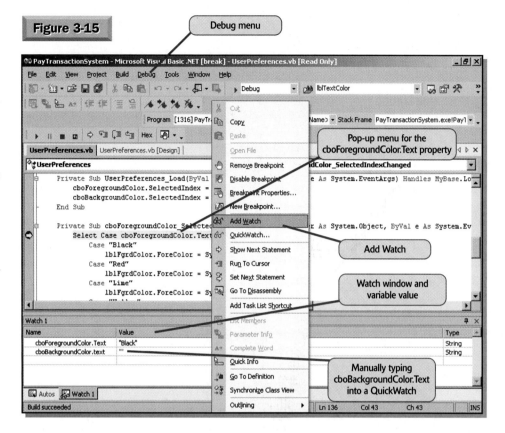

Figure 3-15

Tip In order to add object properties and variables to a Watch window you must be in Break mode.

Tip The best way to identify logical errors is to execute your code one line at a time and examine the values of one or more variables as they change.

Tip Another way to add a watch is to type the name of an object and property, or variable, directly in the name column of the Watch window. Type cboBackgroundColor.text in the name column to add a second property to the Watch window.

Viewing the cboBackgroundColor.Text Breakpoint

We will continue to debug the code in the cboBackgroundColor_
SelectedIndexChanged event to watch the cboBackgroundColor.text value.

Task 6:
To View the cboBackground Color.text Breakpoint

1 Choose **Debug | Start** to continue to the first breakpoint.

> **Tip** When you first start the program, the foreground color is set to "Black" by default and the background is set to blank, which is indicated by double quotes.

Figure 3-16

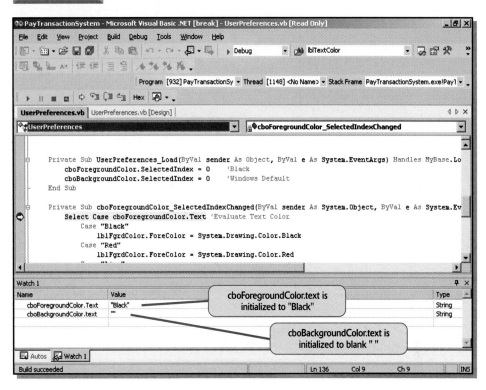

2 Choose **Debug | Start** to continue to the next breakpoint.

3 Verify that **cboBackground Color.text** has been initialized to "Windows Default."

> **Tip** As you reach the second breakpoint, the code has processed logic to set the background color to "Windows Default" and the Watch window keeps you informed of the current values for your watch objects.

Figure 3-17

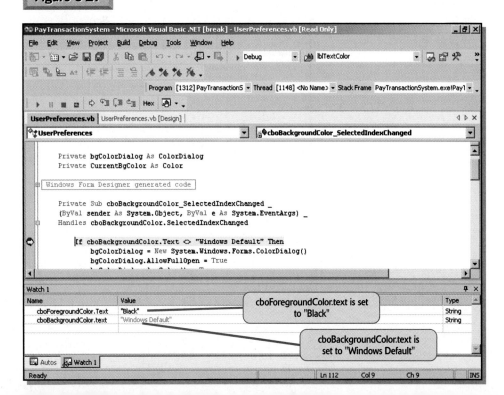

4 Click the Continue [>] button to run and display the User Preferences form.

5 Verify that the default values are Text/Foreground Color = Black and Background Color = Windows Default.

Figure 3-18

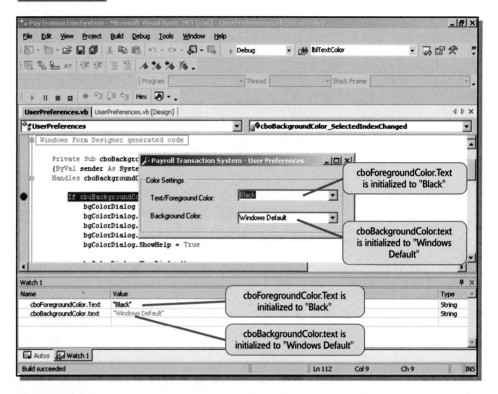

6 Choose **Text/ForegroundColor | Blue**, and verify that the Watch window and screen tip display Blue.

Figure 3-19

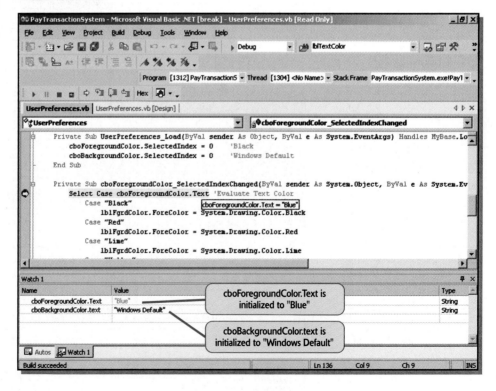

7 Verify that the User Preferences form displays Blue.

Figure 3-20

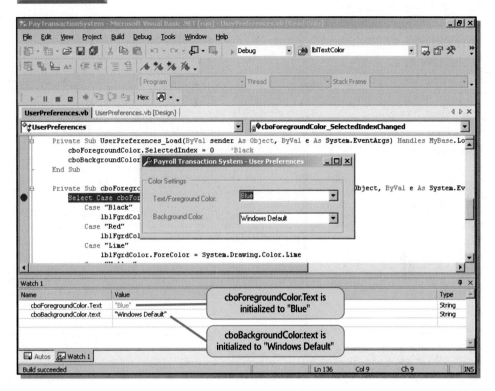

Changing Values at Runtime with the Command Window in Immediate Mode

There will be many scenarios when you want a variable or property to be set to another value during runtime. To do this you need to use the Command window in Immediate mode. Here is how you change a value of a property or variable during runtime using the debugger.

Troubleshooting In order to change the value of a variable in the Command window in Immediate mode, you must set a breakpoint at the cboForegroundColor_SelectedIndexChanged event on the Select Case cboForegroundColor.text line of code. When you run the program, the code will stop at this breakpoint. Now go to the Immediate window and type the code in Task 7, step 2. If you try to change the value without setting a breakpoint, and run until it stops at the breakpoint, you will receive the following message in the Command window: "The expression can not be evaluated while in run mode."

Task 7:
To Change Values at Runtime Using the Command Window in Immediate Mode

1 While in runtime, choose **Debug | Windows | Immediate**.

2 In the Immediate window, type cboForegroundColor.Text= "Red" and press Enter. Notice that the value immediately changes in the Watch window.

3 Choose **Debug | Continue** and verify that the foreground color changes to Red.

4 Choose **File | Save All**.

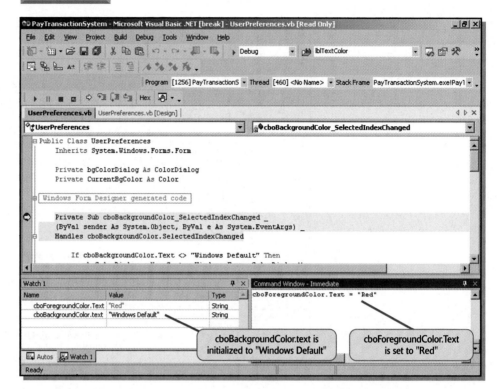

Figure 3-21

Tip

The Command window is used either to issue commands or to debug and evaluate expressions in the integrated development environment (IDE). To view the Command window, press Ctrl + Alt + A, or choose **View | Other Windows | Command Window**. The Command window has two different modes: Command and Immediate. The Command mode is used for executing Visual Studio commands directly in the Visual Studio .NET environment, bypassing the menu system, or executing commands that do not appear in any menu. The Immediate mode is used for debugging, evaluating expressions, executing statements, printing variable values, and so forth. Use Immediate mode to view and change the value of variables when you debug applications, execute functions and statements, and so forth. Typing a question mark character followed by a space and the variable name in the Immediate window and pressing Enter in the immediate window after a breakpoint is reached will also display the current value of the variable.

Identifying Debugging Concepts

As we walked through the code, we learned how to set breakpoints and step through code (Table 3-4).

Table 3-4 Key Debugging Concepts	
Concept	**Procedure**
Set a breakpoint	Click on the indicator bar in the left margin next to the line of code on which you wish to pause execution.
Execute one line of code at a time	Choose **Debug	Step Into** or press F8.
Examine a variable or object property in the code editor	Move the mouse pointer over the variable or object property whose value you want to evaluate.
Display a Watch window	In Break mode, choose **Debug	Watch**. To open the Watch window, the debugger must be running or in break mode.
Stop debugging	Choose **Debug	Stop Debugging**.

SUMMARY AND EXERCISES

SUMMARY

- Debugging terminology was presented to prepare you to debug code and create an executable (*exe*) file.
- When building a project you can select either a debug or release build configuration.
- The Visual Basic .NET debugger enables you to create breakpoints and step through code one line at a time and evaluate current variable values.
- The value of variables can be determined by moving the mouse pointer over the variable, by using watches, or by typing a question mark character followed by a space and the variable name in the Immediate window and pressing Enter after a breakpoint is reached.
- Building a project causes Visual Basic .NET to verify correct syntax for every line of program code.
- It is a good practice to build an executable every day to identify exceptions right away so they can be resolved early in the software development process.
- When Visual Basic .NET identifies an exception, the suspect code is highlighted to draw attention to it to help you quickly get to the root cause of a coding issue.
- When a project is built, a file with an *.exe* extension is created and placed in a bin directory under the project's folder.
- The Configuration Manager enables you to set the build type.
- There are three general types of errors: runtime, logical, and syntax.

KEY TERMS & SKILLS

KEY TERMS

Autos window (p. 3-5)
bin subdirectory (p. 3-5)
breakpoint (p. 3-5)
Build Output box (p. 3-5)
build type (p. 3-5)
Configuration Manager (p. 3-5)

debugging (p. 3-5)
deployment (p. 3-5)
distribution (p. 3-5)
executable file (p. 3-5)
Immediate mode (p. 3-5)
logical errors (p. 3-13)
Run dialog box (p. 3-5)

runtime errors (p. 3-13)
scope (p. 3-5)
syntax errors (p. 3-13)
Watch window (p. 3-5)

SKILLS

Build an executable (p. 3-6)
Change values at runtime using the Command window in Immediate mode (p. 3-22)
Create a variable watch (p. 3-18)

Set a breakpoint (p. 3-14)
Use the Debug menu (p. 3-10)
View the Autos window (p. 3-17)
View the cboBackgroundColor.text breakpoint (p. 3-19)

STUDY QUESTIONS

MULTIPLE CHOICE

1. What function key advances the debugger only one line?
   a. the F1 key
   b. the F5 key
   c. the F8 key
   d. the F9 key

2. When Visual Basic .NET builds a project, it creates a file with a file name extension of
   a. .bas.
   b. .frm.
   c. .vbp.
   d. .exe.

3. In what subdirectory does Visual Basic .NET place the executable file?
   a. object
   b. bin
   c. root
   d. none of the above

4. What line of code ends a Case statement?
   a. End Sub
   b. Case Else
   c. End Case
   d. End Select

5. What ComboBox control event is launched when a value is selected?
   a. Click
   b. Got Focus
   c. SelectedIndexChanged
   d. none of the above

6. X (2 = 1 is an example of what type of error?
   a. logical
   b. syntax
   c. runtime
   d. arithmetic

7. The Software Development Life Cycle consists of which of the following stages?
   a. Design
   b. Code
   c. Testing
   d. all of the above

8. A variable can be changed in Break mode using the
   a. Command window in Immediate mode.
   b. debugger.
   c. Command window in Command mode.
   d. InputBox control.

9. Which of the following cannot be performed using a Watch window?
   a. Read the value of a variable
   b. Change the value of a variable
   c. Delete a watch
   d. Delete a variable

10. What debugging tool displays the return value for a function that is called when debugging?
   a. Autos window
   b. Watch window
   c. Immediate window
   d. Solution Explorer

SHORT ANSWER

1. What is the name of the Visual Basic .NET tool used to walk through code one line at a time?

2. How many types of builds can Visual Basic .NET create and what are they called?

3. What is the best debugging tool to display the value of a variable that changes as the program runs?

4. When a variable is misspelled, Visual Basic .NET considers this what type of error?

5. When a variable used to total multiple other variables computes an incorrect total, Visual Basic .NET considers this what type of error?

6. When a syntax error occurs, how does Visual Basic .NET help identify the exception?

7. When running the program, if the name of a file or the path to its location is incorrect, this is what type of error?

8. If you want to walk one line at a time through code, then avoid entering code you know is correct, which Debug menu option would you select?

9. What is the fastest way to avoid stopping at breakpoints once you know that the code is correct?

10. What function key moves the debugger through the code one line at a time?

FILL IN THE BLANK

1. When you build a project, Visual Basic .NET compiles all code and generates a _____ file that has the three-letter file name extension of _____.

2. When a project is built, the executable file is placed in the _____ directory.

3. A _____ is set to cause the program to pause when running and allow you to review the code and variable values.

4. Visual Basic .NET can create two types of executable files: one as a _____ build and the other as a _____ build.

5. Build status messages are displayed in the _____ _____ box.

6. The _____ Manager allows you to select the build type.

7. The process of verifying that code is correct is called _____.

8. The process of installing files on a target computer is called _____.

9. The primary purpose of _____ is to determine what files are needed in the installation setup.

10. There are three common types of errors: _____, _____, and _____ errors.

FOR DISCUSSION

1. Why should a project be built on a regular basis?

2. Explain how to set a breakpoint.

3. Why are logical errors hard for the debugger to catch?

4. How can you change the value of a variable when the program is in Break mode?

5. Explain where to place a breakpoint if you want to verify the color selected in the cboForegroundColor ComboBox control.

P R O J E C T 4

Expanding Our Application with Windows Form Management

U p to this point, we have written programs that use only one form for input and output. Most commercial and corporate applications include a series of forms that are designed to work together.

We will begin this exercise by creating the Main form that will serve as the "homepage" for our payroll transaction application. This Main form is a special Windows form called a Multiple Document Interface (MDI) that serves as the parent for all of the other forms in the application. There is little difference between a parent (MDI) and a child form, other than that the parent form has an IsMdiContainer property set to True, while the child forms have the IsMdiContainer property set to False and have an additional MdiParent property set to the name of the parent form.

Once we create our parent form, we will integrate the Login form from Project 0 and create a new splash screen that will be displayed upon a successful login. After you have successfully tested the Login to splash to Main form sequence, we will add a module for common code that will be shared by all the forms in the application. The module will centralize the programming features to make it easier to maintain the application, reduce potential redundant coding, and significantly reduce testing and development time.

OBJECTIVES

After completing this project, you will be able to

- Identify terminology related to multiple forms and their events

- Add new forms to a project

- Integrate an existing form into the application

- Add a module

- Control the program startup flow

e-selections) Running Case

Mr. Traylor was asked to give another presentation next week, and he needs to demonstrate what is meant by the term *component-based software design*. The other managers realize that building projects by assembling reusable components can be a very effective and cost-saving approach to providing the high level of IT services that users at e-Selections are expecting. Form objects are considered components of a project. Some forms are created as a standard form or component that will be reused in later projects. The Login form is one example of a reusable component.

Expanding Our Application with Windows Form Management

The Challenge

The next presentation will be in about a week and will demonstrate that Visual Basic .NET can easily create new form components, insert preexisting forms, and integrate all the pieces into a nice flow. This will require resourcefulness, as we have only one week to prepare this project. Mr. Traylor is very pleased with how well you have learned this new tool and is confident that you will be able to build the project.

The Solution

Visual Basic .NET provides a development environment that will work well to provide what Mr. Traylor needs. The human resources staff will be attending the meeting and will be particularly interested in security features that prevent unauthorized users from gaining access to confidential employee information. Since we have already completed a Login form, this will be reused and included in the project.

As new software releases of the Pay Transaction System are rolled out to the user community, and especially to the human resources department, users want to be assured that they are using the latest version. A splash screen will display the version number. The help desk staff will be notified every time a new release is available and instructed to verify the software version with users that call for assistance.

Figure 4-1

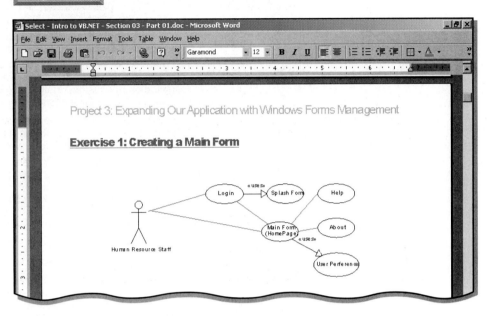

Identifying Terminology Related to Multiple Forms and Their Events

Terminology will now include component-related terms (Table 4-1).

Table 4-1	Multiple Form and Event Terminology
Term	**Description**
Background image	Gets or sets the background image displayed in the control. This option enables you to choose an image to display or tile in the background of the form. You can either type in the image path in the BackgroundImage field, or click the ellipsis (…) button and navigate to the file's location.
Border style	Returns or sets the border style for an object. The following two properties are available: 1 for FixedSingle or 0 for None.
Click event	Occurs when the user presses and then releases a mouse button over an object. It can also occur when the value of a control is changed.
Control alignment	To standardize the layout of the user interface of your Windows application, you can position groups of controls with a single command. Open the form containing the controls you want to position in the Windows Forms Designer. Select the controls you want to align so that the first control you select is the primary control to which the others should be aligned. Choose **Format	Align**, and then choose one of the seven options.
Copyright	Statement of ownership and rules about distribution of files and components and licensing information

(Continued)

Table 4-1   Multiple Form and Event Terminology (*continued*)

Term	Description
Form icon	Designates the picture that represents the form in the taskbar as well as the icon that is displayed next to the application control menu located on the left side of the title bar of the form.
Form Load event	Occurs when a form is loaded. For a startup form, it occurs when an application starts as the result of a Load statement or as the result of a reference to an unloaded form's properties or controls. Typically, you use a Load event procedure to include initialization code for a form—for example, code that specifies default settings for controls, indicates contents to be loaded into ComboBox or ListBox controls, and initializes form-level variables.
Hide	Returns or sets a value that determines whether the object is visible—an object that is visible can be seen by the user in the active application.
IsMDIContainer property	In Visual Basic .NET, any form can be made a MDI parent by setting the IsMdiContainer property to True.
MDI parent form	The foundation of a MDI application is the MDI parent form. This is the form that contains the MDI child windows, which are the "subwindows" wherein the user interacts with the MDI application. Creating an MDI parent form is easy, both in the Windows Forms Designer and programmatically.
PictureBox control	A PictureBox control can display a graphic from a bitmap, icon, or metafile, as well as enhanced metafile, JPEG, or GIF files. It clips the graphic if the control isn't large enough to display the entire image.
Project startup object	By default, the first form in your application is designated as the project startup object. When your application starts running, this form is displayed (so the first code to execute is the code in the Form_Initialize event for that form). If you want to display a different form when your application starts, you must change the startup object.
Splash screen	If you need to execute a lengthy procedure on startup, such as loading a large amount of data from a database or loading several large bitmaps, you might want to display a splash screen on startup. A splash screen usually displays information such as the name of the application, copyright information, and a simple bitmap. The screen that appears when you start Visual Basic is a splash screen.
Unload event	This event is initiated when the form is unloaded. This can occur in several ways; for example, a form can be closed within code using the statement **form.close**, where **form** is the name of the form to be closed. The event can also be initiated by clicking the application Close **X** button.
Visible	Returns or sets a value indicating whether an object is visible or hidden.
Window state	Sets or returns the state of the window. The following are the three window state settings: **vsWindowStateNormal 0** (window is normal), **vsWindowStateMinimize 1** (window is minimized), and **vsWindowStateMaximize 2** (window is maximized).

Adding New Forms to a Project

A form is ultimately a blank slate that you, as a developer, enhance with controls to form a user interface and code to manipulate data. We will add a Main form to the **PayTransactionSystem** project, and then a splash page.

Adding the Homepage (Main) Form

Task 1:

To Add the Homepage Form

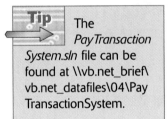

1 In the Visual Basic .NET environment, choose **File | Open | Project** and select the **PayTransactionSystem** project.

> **Tip** The *PayTransaction System.sln* file can be found at \\vb.net_brief\ vb.net_datafiles\04\Pay TransactionSystem.

Figure 4-2

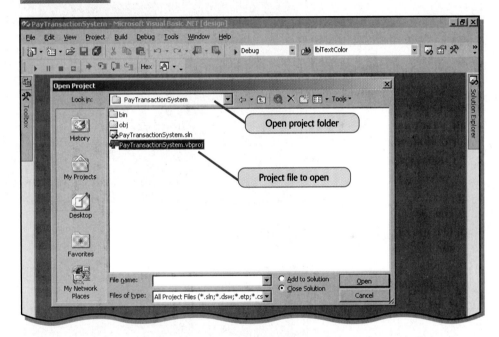

 The PayrollTransactionSystem project may already be on your start page, and you can just double-click the link and avoid having to remember where the project is stored.

2 From the Solution Explorer, right-click the **PayTransactionSystem** project and choose **Add | Add Windows Form**.

Figure 4-3

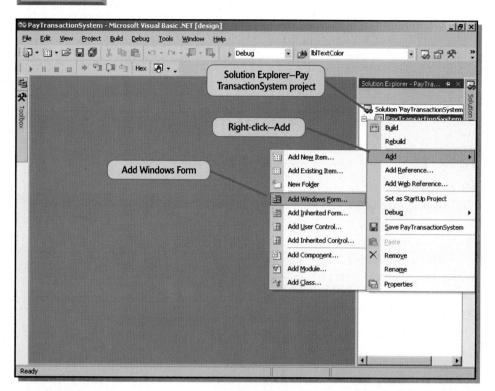

3 Select **Windows Form**, type HomePage.vb for the **Name**, and then click the **Open** button.

Figure 4-4

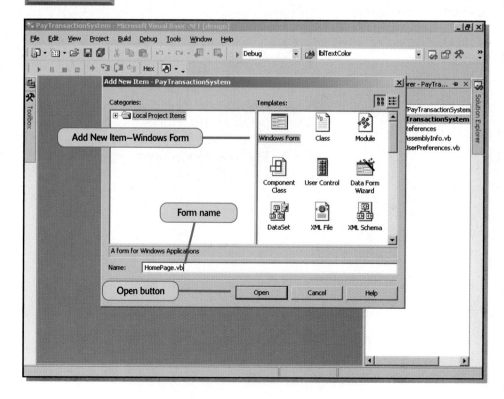

4 Verify that the *HomePage.vb* file appears in the Solution Explorer.

Figure 4-5

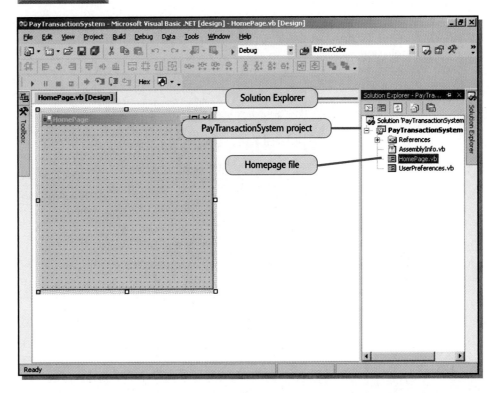

5 Change the form properties according to the values in Table 4-2.

Tip The *Payroll TransLeft BorderBackground.jpg* file and other image files can be found at \\vb.net_brief\vb.net_datafiles\04\images.

Table 4-2	Homepage Form Properties
Property	**Value to Set**
WindowState	Maximized
Text	Payroll Transaction System - Home
Size	800,600
IsMdiContainer	True

6 Select *HomePage.vb* in the Solution Explorer, choose **View | Properties Window**, select the **BackgroundImage** property, and select the *PayrollTransLeftBorder Background.jpg* file.

Figure 4-6

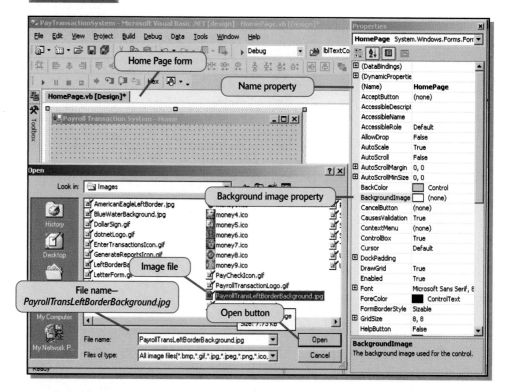

7 Verify that the Home Page form has the correct background image.

8 Choose **File | Save All**.

Figure 4-7

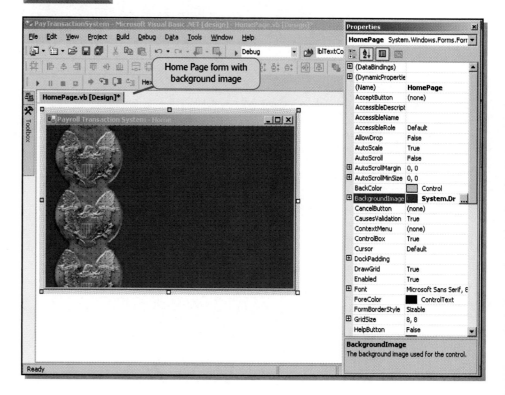

Adding the Splash Screen

Most applications, whether commercial or corporate, incorporate a splash screen to display the current version of the program, copyright notices, and usually a graphical image for a professional touch. The splash screen is typically the first item displayed during the startup of a program.

Figure 4-8 shows an example of the splash screen as it would appear during the program load.

Figure 4-8

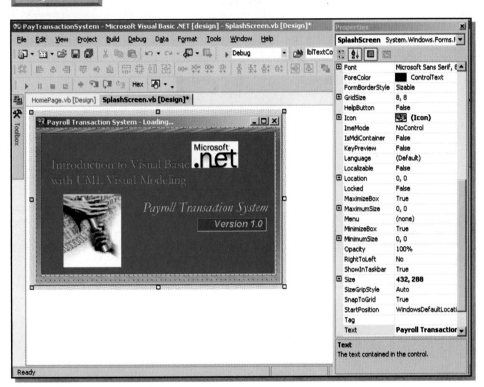

Task 2:
To Add the Splash Screen

1 Right-click the **PayTransactionSystem** project in the Solution Explorer and choose **Add | Add Windows Form**.

2 Type SplashScreen in the **Name** field, then click the **Open** button.

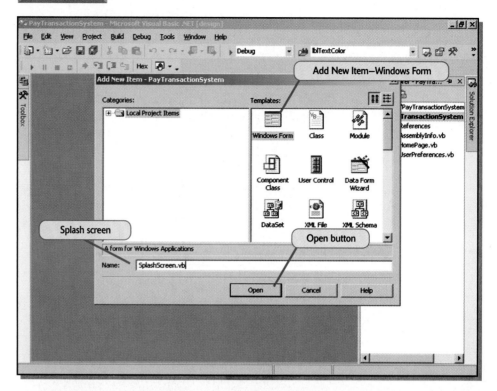

Figure 4-9

3 Change the form properties according to the values in Table 4-3.

Table 4-3   Splash Screen Form Properties

Property	Value to Set
Text	Payroll Transaction System - Loading…
StartPosition	Center Screen
Size	432,288

4 Click the
SplashScreen.vb
file in the Solution Explorer,
choose the Icon property,
click the Ellipsis (…) button,
and choose the *Money3.ico*
icon file.

Figure 4-10

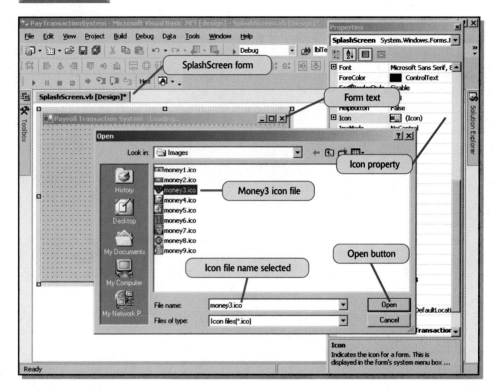

5 Select the
BackgroundImage
property, click the Ellipse
(…) button, and select the
BlueWaterBackground.jpg
image file.

Figure 4-11

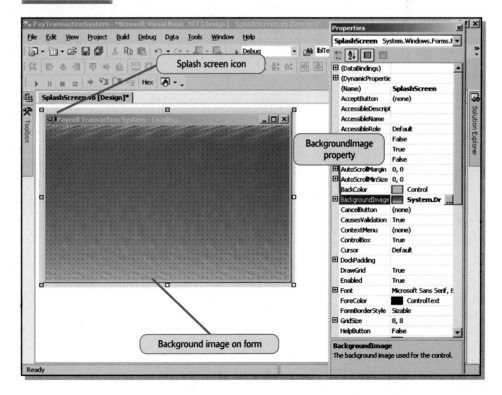

6 Choose **View | Toolbox**, then click the PictureBox control and hold down the left mouse button to drag the PictureBox control onto the form.

Figure 4-12

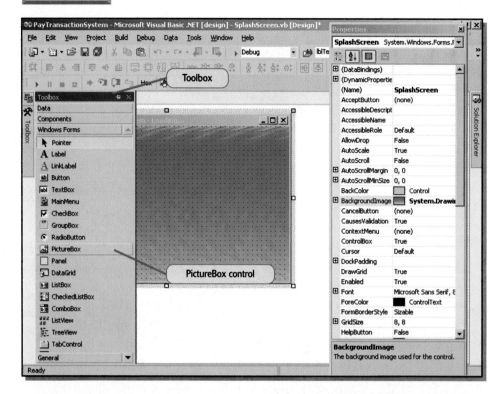

7 Change the PictureBox properties according to the values in Table 4-4.

Table 4-4	Picturebox Property Settings
Property	**Value to Set**
Border Style	Fixed 3D
Location	8,8
Size	408,240

Tip   You can verify that an object is selected when you see active handles that allow you to resize or move the object. You will also see the name of the object in the first field of the Properties window. The PictureBox control above will appear in the center of the splash screen as a background container for other controls once the size and location properties are set.

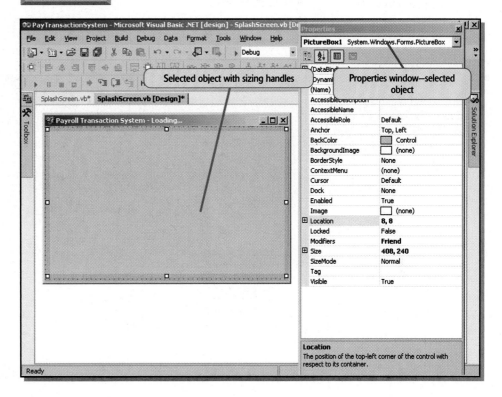

Figure 4-13

Adjusting the Layout and Adding a Few More Controls

Now that the splash screen is almost done, we will adjust the layout of the controls as necessary to complete the form.

Task 3:

To Adjust the Layout and Add a Few More Controls

1 From the Toolbox, click to select a Label control, then click on the Picture Box and draw a rectangle about ¼ inch high and 2 inches wide for the version.

2 Change the Label properties according to the values in Table 4-5.

Table 4-5	Label Properties
Property	**Value to Set**
Name	lblVersion
BackColor	Dark Blue
BorderStyle	Fixed 3D
Font	Arial, 12 pt, style=Bold, Italic
ForeColor	Aqua
Text	Version (we will change this text property dynamically in code later in the project)
TextAlign	Top Right

3 Adjust the layout as necessary to look similar to Figure 4-14.

Tip. The Instructor's solution contains the image as shown in Figure 4-14.

Figure 4-14

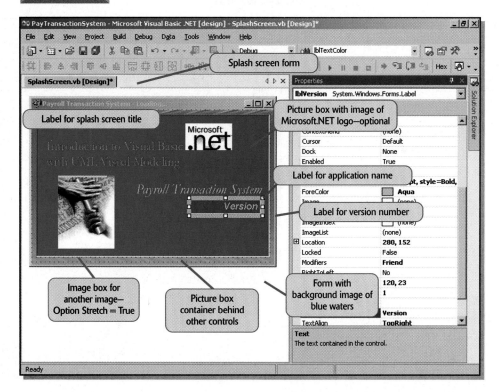

Adding Code to the Form Load Event

When the application starts, developers usually place code in the Form Load event of a form to initialize the values for variables. In addition, control properties and/or data displayed in the controls are also populated. To populate a control you fill it with data statically by setting its property or dynamically through code. We will add code to the Form Load event of the splash screen to initialize the version number displayed in the version label.

Task 4:
To Add Code to the Form Load Event of the Splash Screen

1 Double-click on the outside of the form (in the light blue area) and you will be placed in the Code View for the **SplashScreen_Load** event.

2 Type lblVersion.text = "Version 1.0".

Tip This will change the label text to "Version 1.0" when the application is running.

Figure 4-15

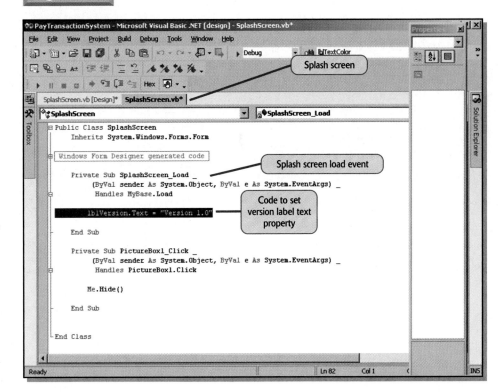

Adding Programming Login to the PictureBox Click Event

The splash screen needs to disappear, or hide itself, at some point—usually after five seconds or after the user clicks on it. We will add code to the Click event of the PictureBox control to hide the form. (This is the PictureBox control used as a background on the splash screen rather than one used as a container for a graphical image).

Task 5:
To Add a Programming Login to the PictureBox Click Event

Figure 4-16

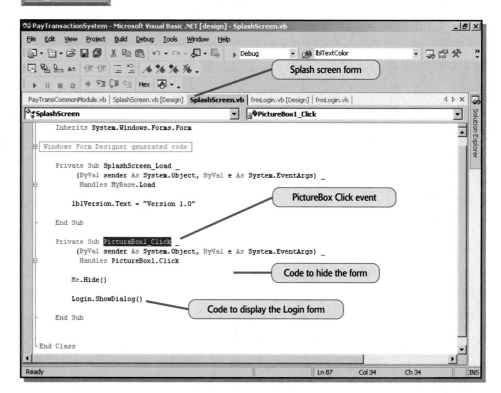

 1 Choose **View | Solution Explorer** and then double-click the *SplashScreen.vb* form.

2 Double-click the PictureBox control to display the Click event in the Code View window.

3 Type **Me.Hide**.

4 Choose **File | Save All**.

> **Tip**
> You can type the subprocedure directly into the Code View windows as shown; however, double-clicking objects such as the form and picture box generates a stub subprocedure and all of the arguments. It is usually more productive to let Visual Basic .NET generate the subprocedures.

Changing the Project Startup Object

When the application starts, the property page of the project is read to determine what code, form object, or other component will begin. The startup object will now be set to the splash screen just created. Once we change this property, we can save and test the application.

Task 6:

To Change the Project Startup Object

1 Right-click the **PayTransactionSystem** project in the Solution Explorer and choose **Properties**.

2 Select **SplashScreen** for the Startup object.

3 Click **OK**.

Figure 4-17

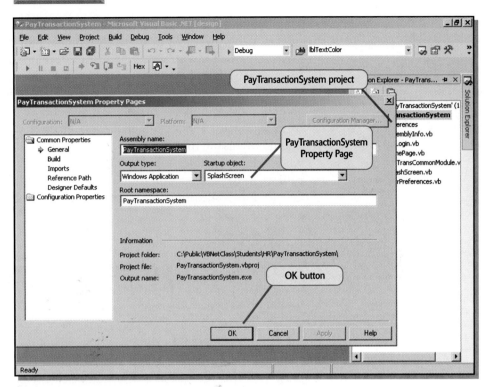

4 Choose **File | Save All**.

5 Choose **Debug | Start**.

6 Verify that the splash screen appears, click the dark blue picture box in the center of the splash screen, and see the splash screen hide (disappear from view).

7 Choose **Debug | Stop Debugging**.

Figure 4-18

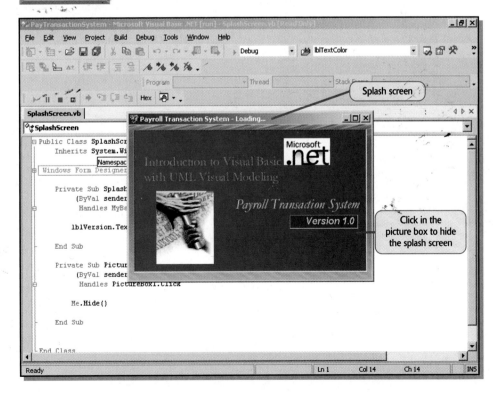

Integrating an Existing Form into the Application

The concept of reusability is an important issue for businesses. Reusability means using the same program for more than one project. This can provide great return on investment, as you can develop new projects faster and reduce the amount of support and maintenance effort necessary to keep programs up and running. The Login form is a good example of a form that should be shared among multiple projects. If we choose to make enhancements to the form (we will in this exercise), every project can benefit from the enhancements. One issue that has to be thought through for projects that share code is where these common objects are to be stored. We suggest that you create a project folder called Common and create subfolders as the application progresses into a file directory structure similar to that shown in Figure 4-19.

Figure 4-19

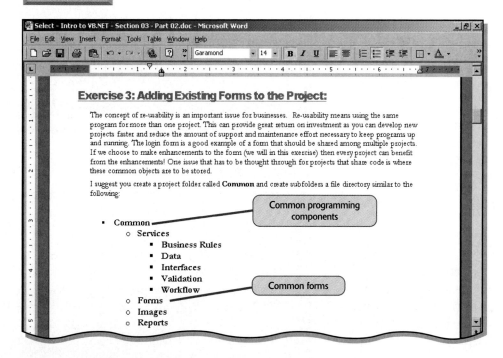

Creating a Common Directory and Forms Subdirectory

Using Windows Explorer, create a directory structure similar to the example described in Task 7. The Common directory should be at a peer level with major systems such as HR. The Pay Transaction System is really a subsystem of HR just like Benefits, Performance Tracking, Compensation, and others.

Task 7:

To Create a Common Directory and a Forms Subdirectory

1 Right-click the **Start** button and choose **Explore**.

2 Click the **Public** folder; then click the **vbNetClass** folder and the **Students** folder.

3 Choose **File | Add | Add Folder** and type **Common** for the new folder name.

4 Click the **Common** folder, choose **File | Add | Add Folder**, and type **Forms** for the new subfolder name.

Figure 4-20

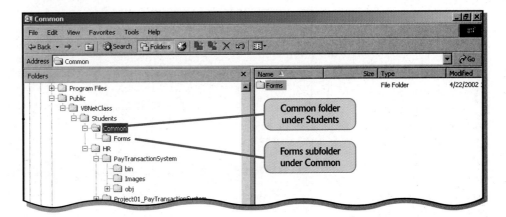

Tip It is important to select the Common folder first and then add the Forms subfolder.

Tip The *login.vb* file can be found at \\vb.net_brief\ vb.net_datafiles\00\ Login.Net.

Adding the Login Form to the PayTransactionSystem Project

We will add the existing *login.vb* form to our project and then save it to the Common\Forms folder.

Opening the Existing Login Project and Saving the *Login.vb* File to the Common\Forms Folder The *login.vb* form was provided in Project 0. We will open that file and save it to a different location. The original file will not be harmed. Before we begin, please minimize the current project to avoid potential confusion.

Task 8:

To Save the *Login.vb* file to the Common\Forms Folder

1 Right-click the **PayTransaction System** project in the Solution Explorer, choose **Add | Add Existing Item**, and then navigate to the existing login project—see tip above—and click the **Add** button.

2 Double-click the *Login.vb* file in the Solution Explorer and click the **View Code** button.

Tip View the code by clicking the View Code button at the top of the Solution Explorer and enter a new blank line somewhere in the code. This will let Visual Basic .NET know that changes have been made and will let you save the form using the **File | Save As** menu option.

3 Click the *Login.vb* file in the Solution Explorer, and then choose **File | Save frmLogin.vb as**—see step 4—to display the Save File As dialog box.

Figure 4-21

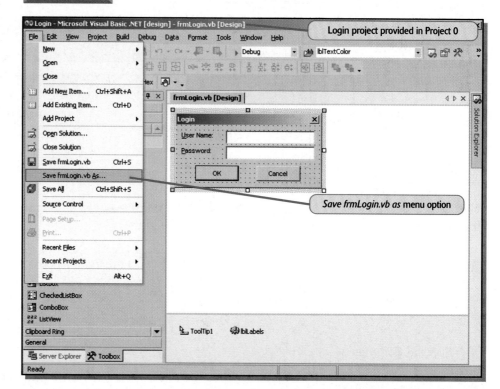

Login project provided in Project 0

Save frmLogin.vb as menu option

Tip A copy of *frmLogin.vb* will be created in your current directory, but we really want this form to be in the Common\Forms directory. This will establish the Login form as a common form that can be used in other projects. This common reusable form may change over time, and other projects that link to this form will dynamically view the latest standard version of the form when they add the *frmLogin.vb* form link from a new project. This is a great design consideration, as only one project will maintain the *frmLogin.vb* form rather than many.

4 Navigate to the C:\Public\vbNetClass\ Students\Common\Forms\ folder and then click the **Save** button and save the file as *Login.vb*.

Figure 4-22

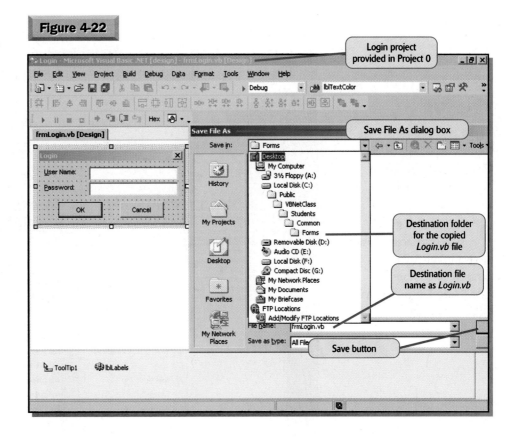

5 Verify that the icon next to *frmLogin.vb* in the Solution Explorer appears with an arrow to indicate that the source code is being stored in a directory outside the immediate project directory.

Tip Click No when prompted to save the original project to avoid changing the original project.

Figure 4-23

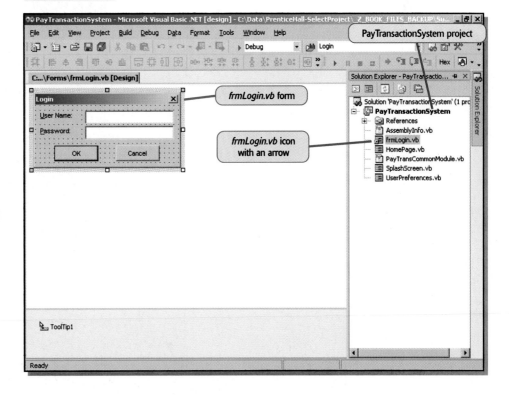

Adding the Login Form to the PayTransactionSystem Project Now that we have copied the existing *Login.vb*-related files to the Common\Forms folder for the PayTransactionSystem project, we need to let Visual Basic .NET know about the file. We will add the *Login.vb* file to our project.

Task 9:
To Add the Login Form to the PayTransaction System Project

1 Right-click the **PayTransactionSystem** project in the Solution Explorer and choose **Add | Add Existing Item**.

Figure 4-24

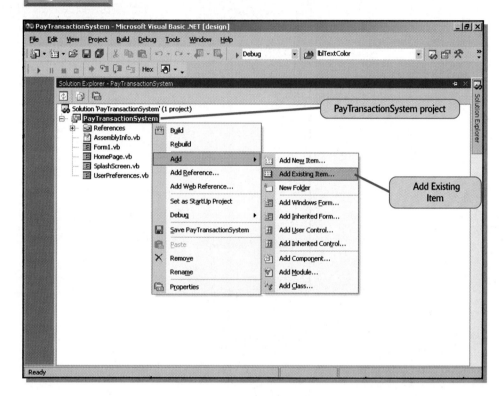

2 Navigate to the C:\Public\vbNetClass\ Students\Common\Forms folder and add the *Login.vb* file.

Figure 4-25

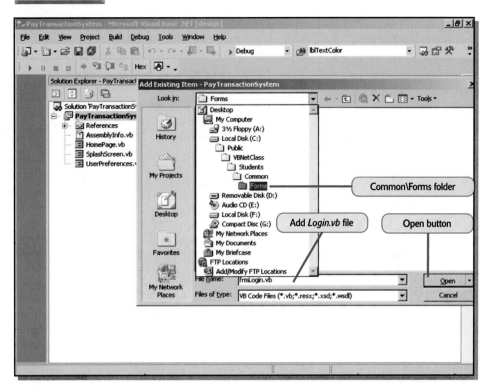

3 Verify that *Login.vb* appears in the Solution Explorer.

4 Double-click the *Login.vb* form to view code.

Figure 4-26

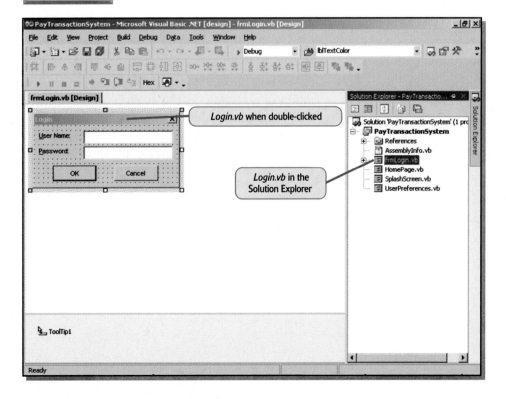

5 Type **Home.Show()** after Me.Show statement.

6 Choose **File | Save All**.

Figure 4-27

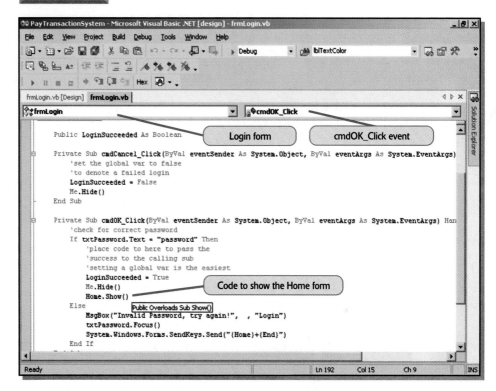

Adding a Module

A module is a special program that incorporates all variables, procedures, and functions that are common across all the forms and classes (more on classes later) in a project. Most professional programmers also use the subprocedure Main of a module as the startup object of the project. We will add a module called PayTransCommonModule for code and will create a Main procedure to control the flow of navigation from the splash screen to the login and finally to the homepage upon a successful login.

Task 10:
To Add a Module

1 Right-click the
PayTransactionSystem
project in the Solution
Explorer and choose
Add | Add Module.

Figure 4-28

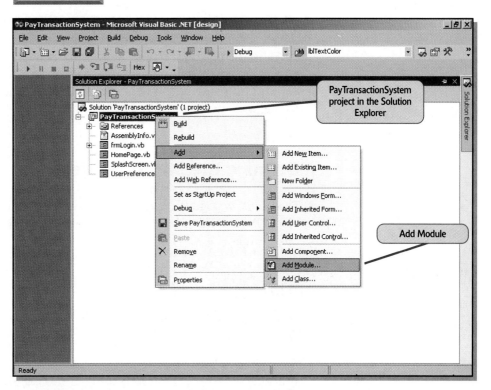

2 Type **PayTrans
CommonModule.vb**
in the **Name** field and then
click the **Open** button.

Figure 4-29

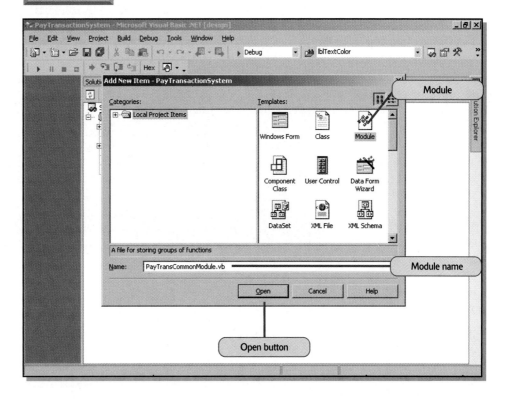

Controlling the Program Startup Flow

When the application is started, the Sub Main procedure determines that the splash screen will appear. Once the splash screen is presented and the user clicks it, the program will hide the splash screen and display the Login form. After a successful login the homepage appears. The following steps are needed: defining the startup object, adding code to the Sub Main procedure, and adding code to show the Login form.

Defining the Startup Object

The property page of the project contains a startup object setting that instructs Visual Basic .NET what to do first when the application starts. We will update this setting.

Task 11:
To Define the Startup Object

1 Right-click the **PayTransactionSystem** project in the Solution Explorer.

2 Choose **Properties**, click the **Startup object** list box and select **Sub Main**, and then click **OK**.

Figure 4-30

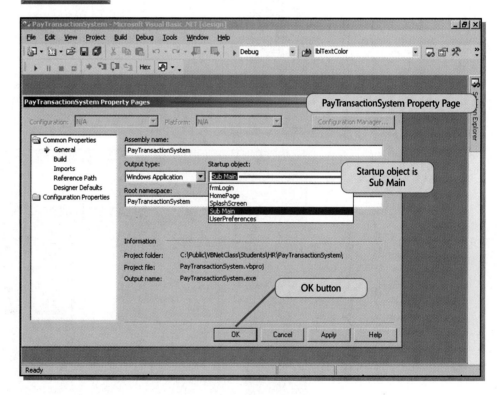

Adding Code to the Sub Main Procedure of the Module

Code needs to be added in the Sub Main procedure of the PayTrans-CommonModule that declares object names and shows the splash screen. We will add this code now.

Task 12:
To Add Code to the Sub Main Procedure of the Module

1 Double-click the **PayTransCommon-Module** file in the Solution Explorer to display a Code View window.

2 Type the code as shown in Figure 4-31.

Figure 4-31

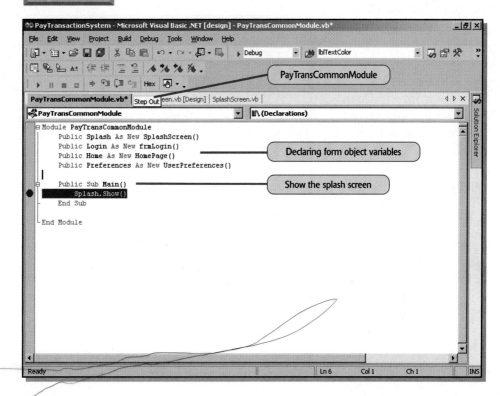

Adding Code to Show the Login Form

When the splash screen appears, it will remain visible until the user clicks it, or another event such as a five-second timer initiates the next step in the program flow. We will enter code into the Click event of the splash screen to show the Login form and then show the homepage form if the login is successful.

Task 13:
To Add Code to Show the Login Form

1 Double-click the *SplashScreen.vb* form in the Solution Explorer and then click the **View Code** button.

2 Double-click the picture box to see the Click event code.

3 Type **Me.Hide()** and press Enter.

4 Type **Login.Show Dialog()** and press Enter.

5 Verify the code as it appears in Figure 4-32.

6 Right-click the **PayTransactionSystem** project in the Solution Explorer, choose **Properties**, and then choose **Startup Object | Splash Screen**.

7 Choose **File | Save All**.

8 Choose **Debug | Start** to test the program and then choose **Debug | Stop Debugging**.

Figure 4-32

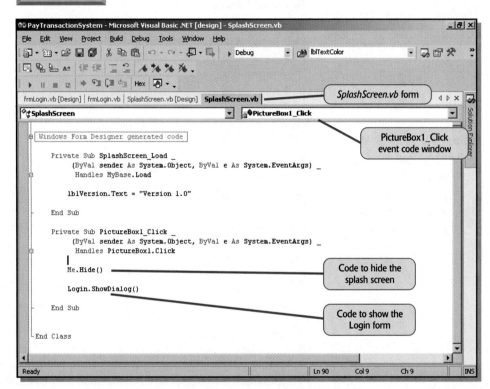

Tip

The Login.ShowDialog() code displays the login form modally. This requires the user to complete the login form or click **Cancel** before the code resumes. The Home.Show() code displays the homepage form only if the login was successful.

SUMMARY AND EXERCISES

SUMMARY

- Window state sets or returns the state of the window. The following are the three window state settings: vsWindowStateNormal 0 (window is normal), vsWindowStateMinimize 1 (window is minimized), and vsWindowStateMaximize 2 (window is maximized).

- A parent form (MDI) serves as a parent for all other forms in the application.

- Child forms have the IsMDIContainer property set to False.

- Splash screens always appear when the application starts to identify version and other basic program information.

- Modules are used to centralize code.

- A background image appears behind other controls for decoration.

- The Form Load event is used to set variables and populate controls.

- The Sub Main procedure of a module is often used to control program flow.

KEY TERMS & SKILLS

KEY TERMS

background image (p. 4-3)
border style (p. 4-3)
Click event (p. 4-3)
control alignment (p. 4-3)
copyright (p. 4-3)
form icon (p. 4-4)
Form Load event (p. 4-4)
hide (p. 4-4)

IsMDIContainer property (p. 4-4)
MDI parent form (p. 4-4)
PictureBox control (p. 4-4)
project startup object (p. 4-4)
splash screen (p. 4-4)
Unload event (p. 4-4)
visible (p. 4-4)
window state (p. 4-4)

SKILLS

Add a module (p. 4-25)
Add a programming login to the PictureBox Click event (p. 4-16)
Add code to show the Login form (p. 4-28)
Add code to the Form Load event of the splash screen (p. 4-15)
Add code to the Sub Main procedure of the module (p. 4-27)
Add the Homepage form (p. 4-5)
Add the Login form to the Pay TransactionSystem project (p. 4-22)

Add the splash screen (p. 4-10)
Adjust the layout and add a few more controls (p. 4-13)
Change the project startup object (p. 4-17)
Create a Common directory and a Forms subdirectory (p. 4-19)
Define the startup object (p. 4-26)
Save the *Login.vb* file to the Common\Forms folder (p. 4-20)

STUDY QUESTIONS

MULTIPLE CHOICE

1. Why are reusable components important in software development?
   a. Reduces development time and support effort
   b. Reduces the scope of code to be tested
   c. Code developed can be used in other projects
   d. all of the above

2. Code that is going to be used for one or more projects is best stored
   a. in a folder named Common.
   b. within the project folder.
   c. in a folder on a separate computer.
   d. none of the above

3. Which of the following is used to create folders?
   a. the Solution Explorer
   b. Windows Explorer
   c. Internet Explorer
   d. the Toolbox

4. Once a form has been copied from its original location to the destination directory of a project, how does Visual Basic .NET become aware of it?
   a. after debugging the application the first time
   b. when the application is compiled
   c. when it is found in the project folder and recognized by the project
   d. when the Solution Explorer adds the existing form to the project

5. A module contains which of the following?
   a. procedures
   b. functions
   c. variables
   d. all of the above

6. To display a form and require the user to close the form before doing anything else in the application, we use which of the following methods?
   a. Startup form object
   b. Startup position
   c. ShowDialog
   d. Show

7. Which code event of the picture box is used to hide the form?
   a. Activate
   b. Double-Click
   c. Click
   d. Form Load

8. Which of the following forms commonly provides a menu?
   a. Splash
   b. About
   c. Login
   d. Home or Main

9. When you want to see a picture on the title bar, you set which of the following form properties?
   a. Picture
   b. Icon
   c. Text
   d. none of the above

10. Which menu option is commonly used to position multiple controls in a standard way?
    a. Format
    b. Align
    c. Edit
    d. Lock Controls

SHORT ANSWER

1. What common security feature is used to prevent unauthorized individuals from using an application?
2. What is the name of the property that can maximize a form to make it fill the entire screen?
3. What happens when you hide a form?
4. How can you easily restart an application you recently worked on?
5. What property would you set to display a picture behind other controls on a form?
6. What component of the Interactive Development Environment would you use to add a PictureBox control to the form?
7. How can you tell visually what object has been selected?
8. What property is used to set a form's height and width values?
9. What property is used to position the form centered on the screen?
10. How are new Windows forms added to a project?

FILL IN THE BLANK

1. The _____ form is usually the first form that appears when an application starts and displays the version number.
2. A _____ form acts as a container for other forms (child forms) and usually contains a menu.
3. The _____ property is used to identify a form that contains other forms.
4. A _____ is used to centralize programming code that is common to the application and used by one or more forms.
5. The _____ _____ procedure is used in the project properties to indicate that the program should process code rather than just display a form when the application starts.
6. The _____ _____ property is used to select a form that you want to see when the application starts.
7. The _____ is often used to identify ownership and warn individuals that it is illegal to use unlicensed software.
8. A FixedSingle property setting is usually associated with the _____ _____ property of an object.
9. The _____ _____ event is where code is usually placed within a form to populate controls with data.
10. When you do not want to see a form but want to keep it loaded in memory, you call the form's _____ method.

FOR DISCUSSION

1. In this project, if you click the label or the light blue section of the splash screen, it does not hide. What other events could you program that would make sure the splash screen goes away regardless of where the user clicks it?

2. Forms that have graphics or a significant amount of variables and programming logic take up memory. A form such as a splash screen will not usually be needed again during a user session once it has been displayed once. What other methods besides "Me.Hide" could you use to have the splash screen disappear and not continue to use up available memory?

P R O J E C T 5

Expanding Our Application with Menus and Help Screens

Now that we have successfully tested the Login to splash screen to Main form sequence, we will create a Help form and add an About form (from an existing template) to integrate with our User Preferences form into the application. Finally, we will build a menu structure into our Main form and use the menu items to invoke User Preferences, the About form, and the Windows Help facility.

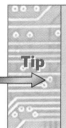

Tip

The *PayTransactionSystem.sln* file can be found at
\\vb.net_brief\vb.net_datafiles\05\PayTransactionSystem.
The *Question.ico* file can be found at
\\vb.net_brief\vb.net_datafiles\05\PayTransactionSystem\Images.
The *HelpInfo.txt* file can be found at
\\vb.net_brief\vb.net_datafiles\05\PayTransactionSystem\bin.
The *About.vb* file can be found at
\\vb.net_brief\vb.net_datafiles\05\PayTransactionSystem\Templates.

e-selections   Running Case

Great news—the demonstration went very well and everyone seems to feel that Visual Basic .NET is a tool that will be used for other exciting projects. Having created a few small components and integrated them into the payroll transaction system so easily proves that we can learn to design and develop systems faster and have fun too. Mr. Traylor wants to add a Help Information form that displays messages, a menu to reach forms without a mouse, and the ability to use access keys.

OBJECTIVES

After completing this project, you will be able to:

● Identify menu terminology

● Add a new Help Information form

● Add the About form from a template

● Add a menu using the MainMenu control

● Add access keys for menu commands

● Name menu items and add separators

● Add event procedures to your menu items

● Add event procedures with an "Under Construction" message from a module

● Test the program

Expanding Our Application with Menus and Help Screens

The Challenge

Mr. Traylor is pleased with the work done so far and now we will enhance the application to be more production oriented. We need to provide a menu, a Help About screen, and a Help Information screen.

The Solution

The help desk staff requested a way to ensure that payroll transaction system users know how to obtain help if they have a question. A Help Information screen will be added to display instructions on how to operate the application, and an About screen will be added that displays a version number. A MainMenu control will be added that provides an alternative method for launching forms without the mouse by using access keys. Finally, code will be added behind each menu item's event procedure to carry out an action.

Figure 5-1

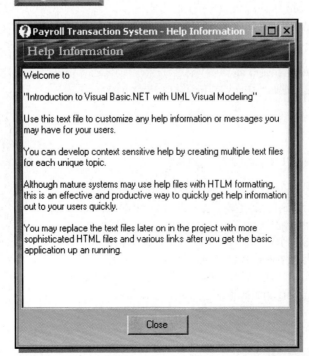

Identifying Menu Terminology

As we continue to enhance our project we begin to learn about new properties relating to the menu and other system components. Each project will add to our knowledge of Visual Basic .NET terminology (see Table 5-1).

Table 5-1

Term	Description
About form	A form that contains copyright information, the application name and version, and other information needed for support.
Access keys	Many users prefer to execute commands using the keyboard rather than mouse clicks. This is especially important in data entry activities and in situations where the keyboard is more efficient for end users (depending on their touch-typing skills). Access keys are identified by an underline. When you press the [Alt] key in conjunction with the access key, it invokes the option the same as if you had clicked it using the mouse.
Ampersand (&)	An access key is an underlined character in the text of a menu, in a menu item, or on the label of a control such as a button. It enables the user to "click" a button by pressing the [Alt] key in combination with the access key. For example, if a button runs a procedure to print a form, and therefore its Text property is set to "Print," adding an ampersand before the letter P causes the letter P to be underlined in the button text at runtime. The user can run the command associated with the button by pressing [Alt] + [P].
BackColor—Transparent	Setting the BackColor property of the UserControl object to Transparent allows whatever is behind your control to be seen between the constituent controls on your UserControl surface. When the BackStyle property is set to Transparent, the BackColor and Picture properties of the UserControl are ignored.
Font	Lists the available fonts, such as Times New Roman or Arial.
Font dialog box	Use the Text Tool Font dialog box to change the font, style, or size of the cursor font. Changes are applied to the text displayed in the Text area.
Font Size	Lists the available point sizes for the specified font, such as 8, 9, 10, 11, 12, 14, 16, 18, and more.
Font Style	Lists the available styles for the specified font, such as Regular, Bold, Italic, and Bold Italic.
Form—AcceptButton	Optional property that sets AcceptButton=True. Press [Enter] to launch this button click event. Choose **Form | View Properties**, select **AcceptButton**, and select **btnOK**.
Form—CancelButton	Optional property that sets CancelButton=True. Press [Esc] to launch this button click event. Choose **Form | View Properties**, select **CancelButton**, and select **btnOK**.
Form—MaximizeBox	False value removes the Maximize button from the form at runtime.
Form—MinimizeBox	False value removes the Minimize button from the form at runtime.
Form—ShowDialog()	Forms and dialog boxes are either modal or modaless. A modal form or dialog box must be closed or hidden before you can continue working with the rest of the application. Dialog boxes that display important messages should always be modal. The About dialog box in Visual Studio is an example of a modal dialog box. A message box is a modal form you can use. Modaless forms let you shift the focus between the form and another form without having to close the initial form. The user can continue to work elsewhere in any application while the form is displayed. Modaless forms are harder to program, because users can access them in an unpredictable order. You have to keep the state of the application consistent no matter what the user does. Often, tool windows are shown in a modaless fashion. The Find dialog box, accessible from the Edit menu in Visual Studio, is an example of a modaless dialog box. Use modaless forms to display frequently used commands or information.

(Continued)

Table 5-1 *(continued)*

Term	Description
Location	Sets the location of the label in pixels.
MainMenu control	The Windows Forms MainMenu control displays a menu at runtime. If you add this component in the Windows Forms Designer, the Menu Designer enables you to visually set up the structure of the main menu. The MainMenu control enables you to create and maintain menus in your forms. With the tool you can add, change, and delete menu items; reorder them; and set up access keys. There are properties to help customize menus, and you can use event procedures to invoke the menu commands when they are selected at runtime.
Menu—Separator	Visual Basic .NET enables you to insert a gray line called a separator above the currently selected menu item. To add a separator, select a menu subitem, then right-click and choose **Insert Separator**. In Windows, most of the menus include separators to group similar processes. For instance, under the File menu, **New**, **Open**, and **Close** are all file commands and should be grouped together. Grouping menu items is not a perfect science and can vary by individual and organizational preferences.
Menu Designer	A Visual Basic .NET tool that enables you to create structured menus and context menus.
	To add menus using the Menu Designer, you need to have either a MainMenu or ContextMenu control added to your form. With either of these controls added (and selected within the control tray at the bottom of the Windows Forms Designer), you will see the text "Type Here" or "Context Menu" just below the caption bar of the form. Clicking this text and typing will create a menu item whose Text property is specified by the name you type.
	Additionally, by right-clicking the Menu Designer, you can insert new menu items, add a separator to the menu you are designing, or open the Name Editor (which enables you to modify the Name property of the menu items you are creating).
Multiline property	A multi-line text box enables you to display more than one line of text in the control. If the WordWrap property is set to True, text entered into the multi-line text box is wrapped to the next line in the control. If the WordWrap property is set to False, text entered into the multi-line text box control will be displayed on the same line until a new-line character is entered.
	You can add scroll bars to a text box using the ScrollBars property to display horizontal and/or vertical scroll bars. This enables the user to scroll through text that extends beyond the dimensions of the control.
	Note: This property is set to False by default for all derived classes, with the exception of the RichTextBox control.
Size Mode	Auto Size—Allows the image to be stretched if the form is resized.
StartPosition	Start the form centered on the parent form.
TextAlign-TopLeft	Aligns the text to the top left of the label.

Adding a Help Information Form

We will add a new Help Information form to the project to describe key concepts or steps that users will need when using the payroll transaction system. The form you develop will look similar to Figure 5-1. This form uses an icon to identify the form more easily, a title bar that describes the form, a yellow label, a text box to display variable information, and a Close button to close the form.

Adding the Help Information Form

Task 1:
To Add a Help Information Form

1 Right-click the **PayTransactionSystem** project in the Solution Explorer and choose **Add | Add New Item**.

Figure 5-2

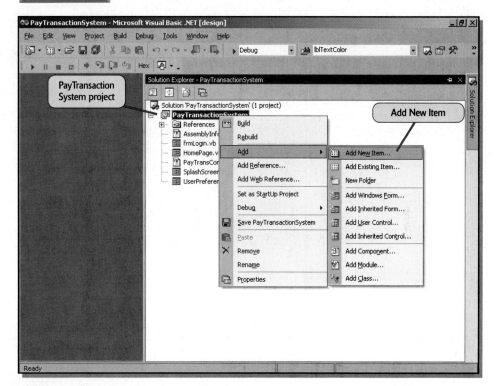

2 Select **Windows Form**, type HelpInformation.vb as the form name, and click the Open button. Using Table 5-2, update the form properties.

Figure 5-3

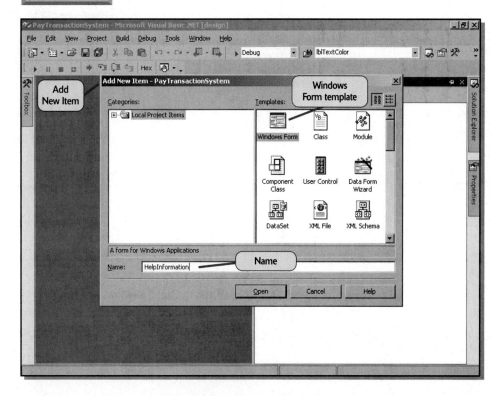

Tip Notice that an additional form named *HelpInformation. vb* is added to the PayTransactionSystem project as shown in the Solution Explorer (Figure 5-4).

Figure 5-4

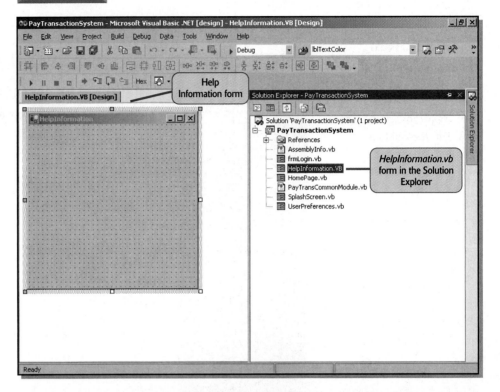

Table 5-2	Form Properties
Property	**Value to Set**
Text	Pay Transaction System - Help Information
Size	350,390
BackgroundImage	Blue Water Background.jpg

3 Select the Icon property, click the Ellipse (…) button, select *Question.ico*, and then choose **Center Form** for the StartPosition property.

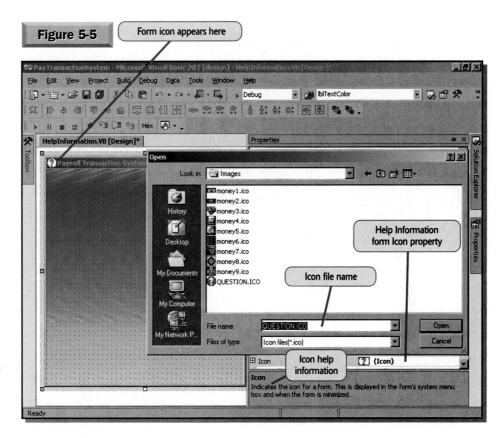

Figure 5-5

Form icon appears here

Help Information form Icon property

Icon file name

Icon help information

4 Add a TextBox control to the form. From the toolbox, drag a TextBox control onto the form and stretch the width to be the width of the form.

5 In the Properties window, type txtHelpInfo for the Name property, select **True** for the Multiline property, and delete **TextBox1** from the Text property.

6 Type **4, 32** for the Location property.

7 Type **332, 288** for the Size property.

8 Add a Label control above the text box, type lblHelpInfo for the name (changing it from Label1), and then delete **Label1** from the Text property.

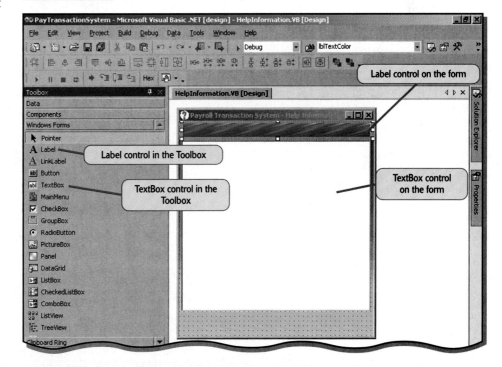

Figure 5-6

Label control on the form

Label control in the Toolbox

TextBox control in the Toolbox

TextBox control on the form

Tip Click and hold down the left mouse button on the TextBox control and then drag the TextBox down until it appears vertically centered on the form.

Other Ways You can also click the bottom right size handle of the text box, hold down the left mouse button, and drag until you have reached the desired size. Release the mouse button to set the size of the text box.

9 Select the BackColor property, click the **Web** tab, and select **Transparent**.

Other Ways To set a BackColor property to Transparent, you could just type in the value Transparent.

Figure 5-7

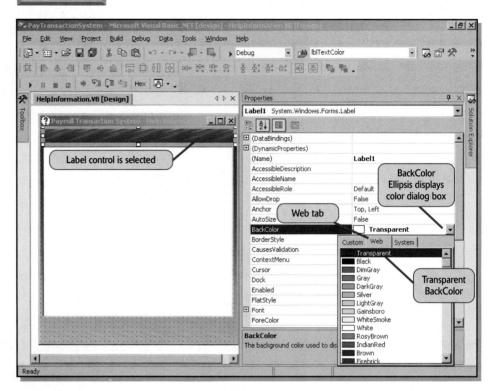

10 Set additional Label control properties as shown in Table 5-3.

Tip The Font property is similar in that it may be easier to click the Plus sign ⊞ button and set the font name, size, and style in the dialog box as shown.

Figure 5-8

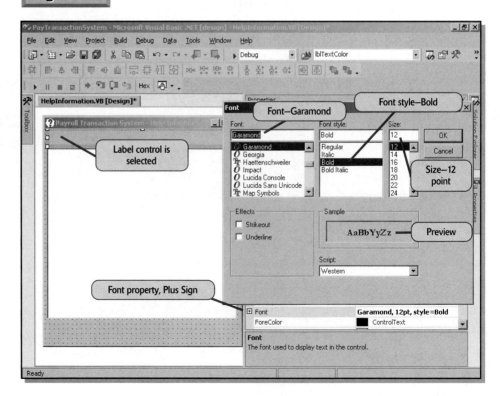

Figure 5-9

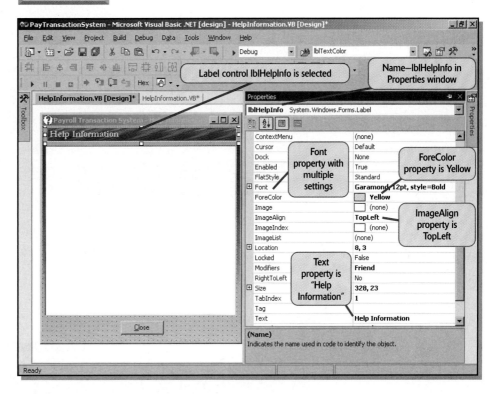

Property	Value to Set	Purpose
BorderStyle	Fixed3D	Makes the label look as if it is beveled into the form for a nice visual effect
ForeColor	Yellow	Sets the color of the characters to yellow
ImageAlign	TopLeft	Aligns the text to the top left of the label
Text	Help Information	Sets the contents of the label

Table 5-3   Form Properties

Adding Code to Read Help Text from a File

Task 2:
To Add Code That Reads Help Information from a File

1 Add a Button control to the form. From the Toolbox, drag a Button control onto the form and place it centered just below the **txtHelpInformation** text box. Change the name from **Button1** to btnClose and set the Text property to &Close.

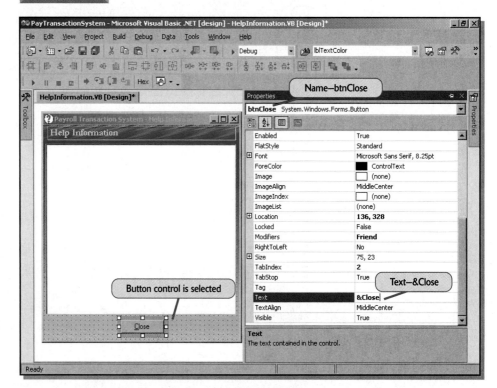

Figure 5-10

Tip

The & character for the Text property (&Close) will display an access key for the letter that follows. In this example, the letter C in **Close** will appear underlined. This enables the user to hold down the [Alt] key then press C to launch the click event of the Close button rather than having to click with the mouse.

2 Add programming logic for the Close button. Double-click the Close button control, and you will be placed in the Code View window for the btnClose_Click event.

3 Type Me.Close() in the btnClose_Click event. This will cause the Help Information form to close. This will also remove the form from memory.

4 Import the *System.IO foundation class*. Go to the very top line of the Code View window and type Imports System.IO.

5 Add programming logic to load data into the text box. Double-click the form background to enter the Code View window inside the HelpInformation_ Load event and type the code in Figure 5-11 into the Load event.

Figure 5-11

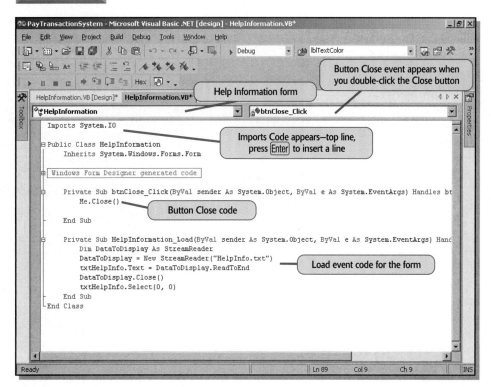

This Imports System.IO statement enables you to use the StreamReader object that we will be using to populate the text box with data in the next step. The System.IO Namespace class enables you to read and write characters to and from streams or files, using specific encoding to convert characters to and from bytes. It includes a pair of classes, StreamReader and StreamWriter, which enable you to read or write a sequential stream of characters to or from a file.

Troubleshooting You need to place a file called *HelpInfo.txt* into the \Bin subdirectory directly under the \PayTransactionSystem directory for this code to work. Visual Basic .NET by default creates the *PayTransactionSystem.exe* file in the bin directory when you start the debugger. Since we have not specified a directory path in the StreamReader("HelpInfo.txt") statement, it assumes the application will be run from the current directory. You may think you are running from the \PayTransactionSystem directory but you are really running from the \PayTransactionSystem\Bin directory when you are testing your applications. The HelpInfo.txt file was provided in the data files for Project 5.

6 Change the project's startup object. Right-click the **PayTransactionSystem** project in the Solution Explorer and choose **Properties**. Select **HelpInformation** for the Startup object and then click the OK button.

Figure 5-12

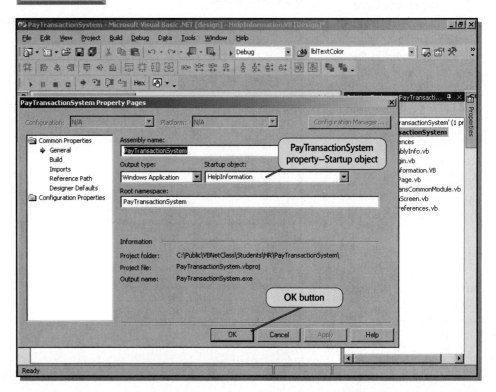

7 Choose **File | Save All**.

8 Test the Program. Click the Start button or choose **Debug | Start**.

9 Click the Close button and verify that the Help Information form disappears.

Figure 5-13

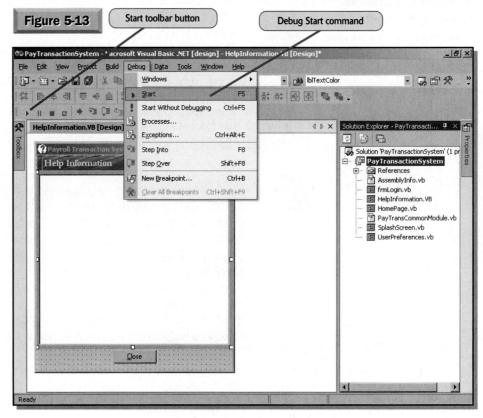

Adding the About Form from a Template and Verifying Property Settings and Code

We will add an existing form to the project to display information on the authors, a copyright notice, and the version of the program. Once you have added this form from the Templates directory, you can personalize it by changing the background image, label text properties, and label background colors. The form should look similar to Figure 5-14 when you are finished.

Figure 5-14

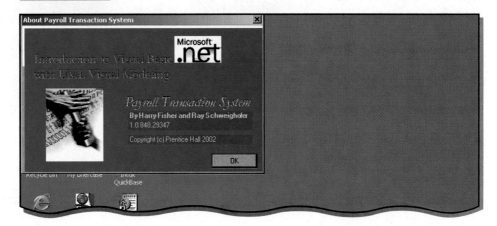

Adding the About Form from a Template

We will add an existing form. This is a common procedure when working in a development environment. Usually a form that will be reused is created just once, and then it is added to a new project and modified. We will add this Template-type form to this project and then review the code.

Task 3:

To Add the About Form from a Template

1 Add an existing form to the project. Right-click the **PayTransactionSystem** project in the Solution Explorer; choose **Add | Add Existing Item**, select *About.vb* from the Templates directory, and then click the Open button.

Figure 5-15

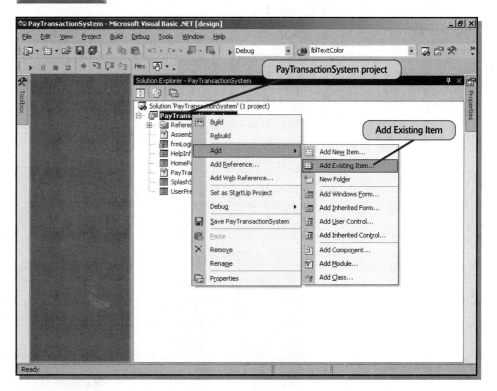

2 Identify the form you wish to add. From the Add Existing Item dialog box, browse to the Templates directory and double-click *About.vb*.

Figure 5-16

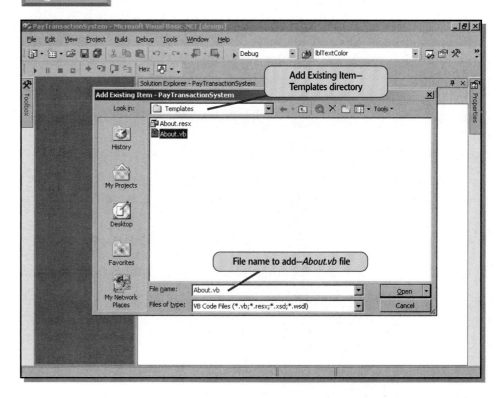

Tip Notice that an additional form named *About.vb* is added to the PayTransactionSystem project as shown in the Solution Explorer.

Figure 5-17

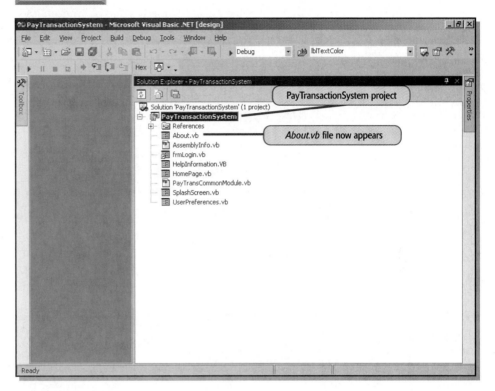

3 Change the project's startup object. Right-click the **PayTransaction System** project in the Solution Explorer and choose **Properties**. Change the Startup object to **About** and then click the OK button.

4 Test the program. Click the **Save All** icon to save all the files in your solution. Next click the debug start button to run the debugger and test your program.

Tip After you click the Start button, the program will compile and the About form will be displayed as shown in Figure 5-18.

Figure 5-18

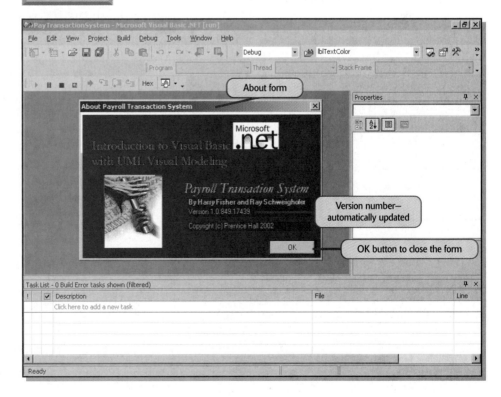

Tip Notice how the version number is automatically assigned and replaces the default property value of "Version Info." You have now completed all of the forms indicated in our Use Case diagram for this phase of the project.

Verifying Property Settings and Reviewing Code

Now that the form has been added, it might be helpful to review the property settings and the code. The following is a quick review of the object property changes used to create this form.

Verify Property Settings Property settings are made in the Properties window. There are several different objects on the form; Table 5-4 lists the object name, property, value to set, and purpose. You can also click the About form and view the property settings in the Properties window.

Table 5-4   Object Property Settings for the About Form

Object Name (Object Type)	Property	Value to Set	Purpose
About (WinForm)	Name	About	Defines the name of the form.
	AcceptButton	btnOK	Optional property that sets AcceptButton=True. Press Enter to launch this button click event. Select the form, choose **View | Properties**, select **AcceptButton**, and select **btnOK**.
	CancelButton	btnOK	Optional property that sets CancelButton=True. Press Esc to launch this button click event. Select the form, choose **View | Properties**, select **CancelButton**, and select **btnOK**.
	Form Border Style	FixedDialog	Defines the form style.
	MaximizeBox	False	Removes the Maximize button from the form at runtime.
	MinimizeBox	False	Removes the Minimize button from the form at runtime.
	Size	424,272	Defines the exact size of the form in pixels.
	StartPosition	CenterParent	Starts the form centered on the parent form that called the About form.
	Text	About Payroll Transaction System	Sets the title bar to "About Payroll Transaction System".

(Continued)

Table 5-4   Object Property Settings for the About Form *(continued)*

Object Name (Object Type)	Property	Value to Set	Purpose
PctBxLogo (Picture Box)	Name	PctbxLogo	Defines the name of the PictureBox object.
	Image	SplashScreenLogo2	Sets the image to be displayed in the picture box.
	Size	414, 241	Sets the size of the picture box.
	Size Mode	Auto size	Allows the image to be stretched if the form is resized.
lblAuthors (Label)	Name	lblAuthors	Defines the name of the label object.
	BackColor	Midnight Blue	Sets the background color of the label to Midnight Blue.
	Font	Microsoft Sans Serif, Bold, 8	Sets the font, appearance, and size.
	ForeColor	Cyan	Sets the color of the text for the label.
	Location	184, 144	Sets the location of the label in pixels.
	Size	216, 16	Sets the size of the label.
	Text	By Harry Fisher and Ray Schweighofer	Defines the contents of the label.

Tip The lblVersion and lblCopyRight settings are very similar to lblAuthors.

Reviewing Code Although a Template form is assumed to be fully tested once completed, it may become necessary to modify the code in the future. Let us review the code for the About form.

Task 4:
To Review the Code

1 Choose the *About.vb* object in the Solution Explorer window and then click the View Code button. Verify the code as it appears in Figure 5-19.

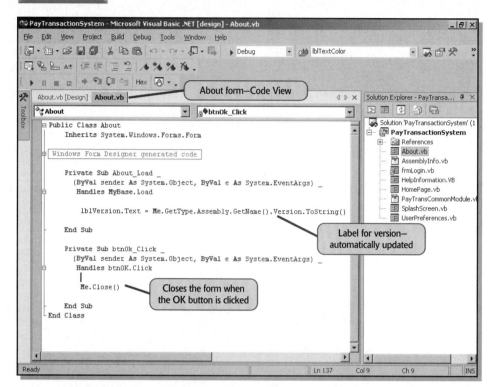

Figure 5-19

About form—Code View

```
Public Class About
    Inherits System.Windows.Forms.Form

Windows Form Designer generated code

    Private Sub About_Load _
        (ByVal sender As System.Object, ByVal e As System.EventArgs) _
        Handles MyBase.Load

            lblVersion.Text = Me.GetType.Assembly.GetName().Version.ToString()

    End Sub

    Private Sub btnOk_Click _
        (ByVal sender As System.Object, ByVal e As System.EventArgs) _
        Handles btnOK.Click

            Me.Close()

    End Sub
End Class
```

Label for version—automatically updated

Closes the form when the OK button is clicked

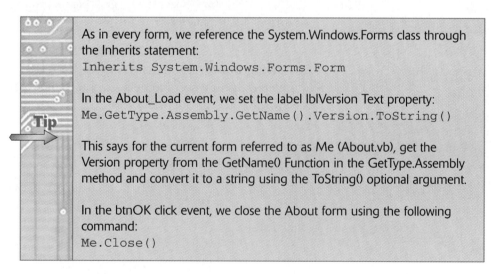

Tip

As in every form, we reference the System.Windows.Forms class through the Inherits statement:

```
Inherits System.Windows.Forms.Form
```

In the About_Load event, we set the label lblVersion Text property:

```
Me.GetType.Assembly.GetName().Version.ToString()
```

This says for the current form referred to as Me (About.vb), get the Version property from the GetName() Function in the GetType.Assembly method and convert it to a string using the ToString() optional argument.

In the btnOK click event, we close the About form using the following command:

```
Me.Close()
```

Adding a Menu Using the MainMenu Control

The MainMenu control enables you to create and maintain menus in your forms. With this tool you can add, change, and delete menu items; reorder them; and set up access keys. There are properties to help customize menus, and you can use event procedures to invoke the menu commands when they are selected at runtime. We will now create a menu for the PayTransaction System project homepage.

Create the Top-Level Menu

The top-level menu appears by default. Once an item is selected, the subitem menu appears. We will now create the top-level menu and then create the subitem menu in the next section.

Task 5:
To Add a Menu Using the MainMenu Control

1 Double-click the *HomePage.vb* in the Solution Explorer window.

2 Select the **MainMenu** object from the Toolbox and drag it onto the homepage form.

3 Click the Menu Designer and then type **File**.

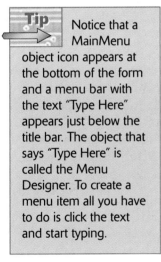

Tip Notice that a MainMenu object icon appears at the bottom of the form and a menu bar with the text "Type Here" appears just below the title bar. The object that says "Type Here" is called the Menu Designer. To create a menu item all you have to do is click the text and start typing.

Figure 5-20   Toolbox

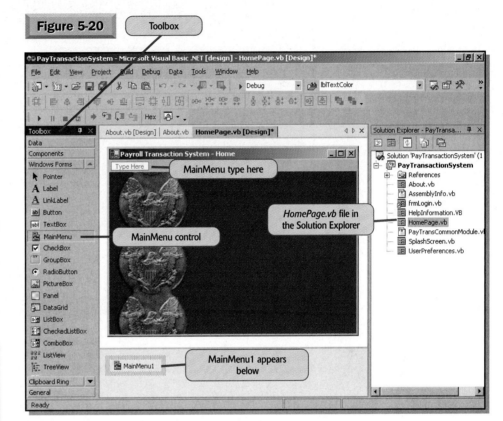

MainMenu type here

MainMenu control

HomePage.vb file in the Solution Explorer

MainMenu1 appears below

4 Click the Menu Designer to the right of **File** and type **Edit**. Repeat this for **View, Insert, Tools, Window,** and **Help** so that your form looks similar to Figure 5-21.

Tip If you are unsure of what the main items in your application should be, use a similar program as an example, such as Microsoft Word or Microsoft Access.

Figure 5-21

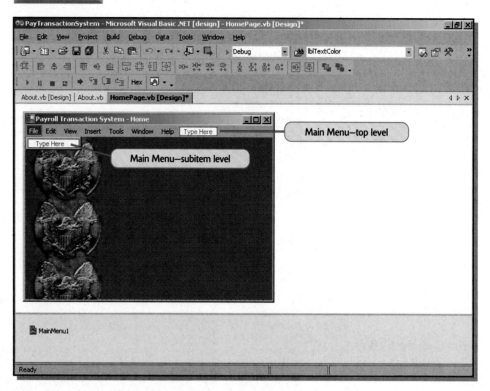

Create the Subitem-Level Menu

Now that the top-level menu is completed, we will click to select an item and type the subitem name in the Menu Designer on the MainMenu control. We will now create the subitem level, and then add code to each subitem later. Figure 5-22 shows an example of the File menu from Microsoft Word 2002. Using this as a guideline, we will create a File menu for our application that has **New, Open, Close, Save, Search, Page Setup, Print, Preferences,** and **Exit** as our menu items.

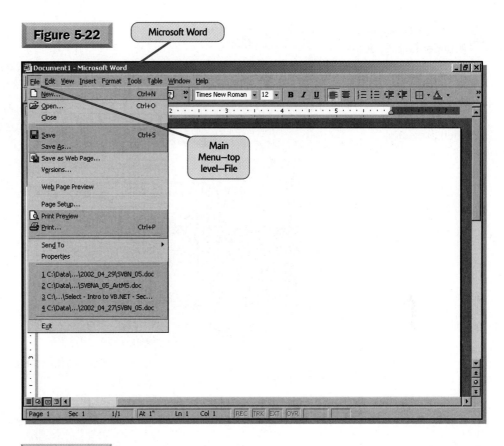

Figure 5-22

Microsoft Word

Main Menu—top level—File

Task 6:

To Create the Subitem-Level Menu

1 Create the subitems under **File**. Click the Menu Designer below **File** and type **New…** and then press Enter; type **Open…** and then press Enter; repeat the process until the menu looks like Figure 5-23.

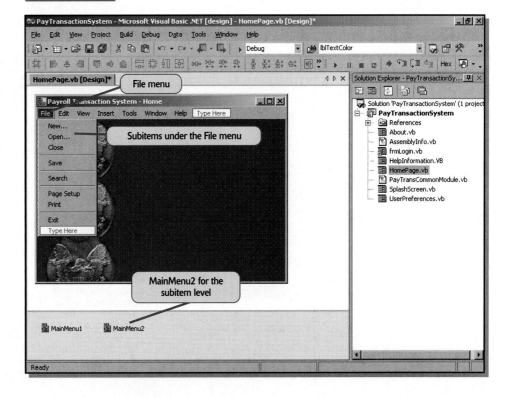

Figure 5-23

File menu

Subitems under the File menu

MainMenu2 for the subitem level

2 Create the subitems under **Edit**. Click the Menu Designer below **Edit** and type Copy and then press [Enter]; type Paste and then press [Enter]; type Find and then press [Enter].

Figure 5-24

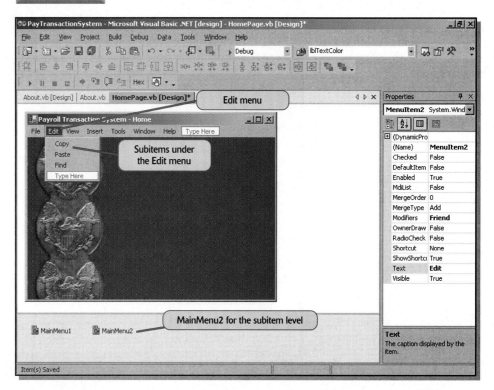

3 Create the subitems under **Tools**. Click the Menu Designer below **Tools** and type Spell Check and then press [Enter]; type User Preferences and then press [Enter].

Figure 5-25

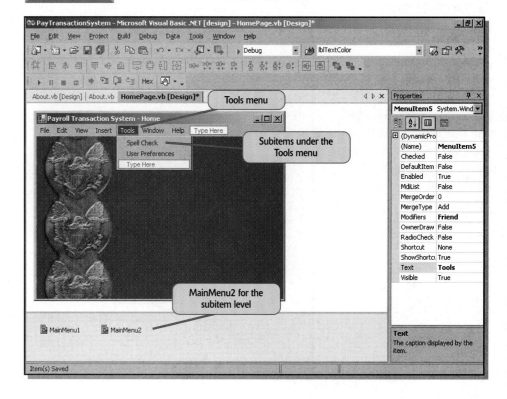

4 Create the subitems under **Help**. Click the Menu Designer below **Help** and type Index... and then press Enter; type Payroll Transaction System Help and then press Enter; type About and then press Enter.

Figure 5-26

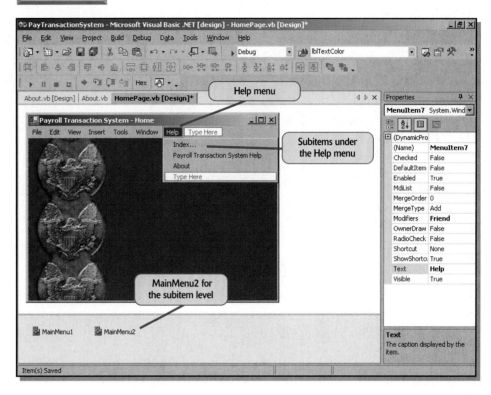

Adding Access Keys for Menu Commands

Many users prefer to execute commands using the keyboard rather than mouse clicks. This is especially important in data entry activities and in situations where the keyboard is more efficient for end users (depending on their touch-typing skills). Access keys are identified by an underline. When you press the Alt key in conjunction with the access key, it invokes the option the same as if you had clicked it using the mouse.

Tip
Windows 2000 and Windows XP do not display the access key underlines until you press and hold the Alt key. To add an access key to a menu item, click the desired menu item in the Menu Designer and type & (ampersand) before the letter you want to designate as an access key.

Task 7:
To Add Access Keys for Menu Commands

1 Add access key designations to the File menu. Choose **File** and type **&File** for **File**; choose **New...** and type **&New...** for **New...**; choose **Open...** and type **&Open...** for **Open...**; choose **Close** and type **&Close** for **Close**; choose **Save** and type **&Save** for **Save**; choose **Search** and type **Searc&h** for **Search**; choose **Page Setup** and type **Page Set&up** for **Page Setup**; choose **Print** and type **&Print** for **Print**; choose **Exit** and type **E&xit** for **Exit**.

> **Tip** To add access keys to the existing menus, choose **View | Properties** (or press `F4`) to display the Properties window, select the menu (or submenu) item for which you want to add the access key, and insert the & character in the Text property. This should take only a few minutes; there is no need to retype the entire menu text.

2 Add access key designations to the Edit menu. Choose **Edit** and type **&Edit** for **Edit**; choose **Copy** and type **&Copy** for **Copy**; choose **Paste** and type **&Paste** for **Paste**; choose **Find** and type **&Find** for **Find**.

Figure 5-27

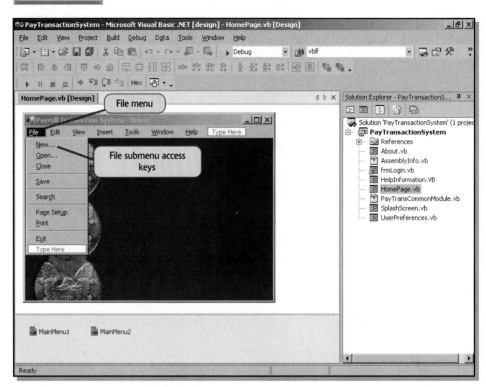

Figure 5-28

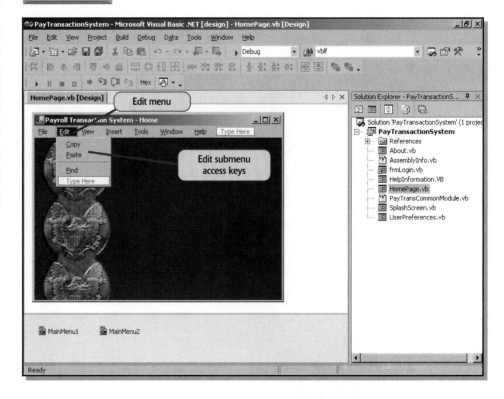

3 Add access key designations to the Tools menu. Choose **Tools** and type &Tools for **Tools**; choose **Spell Check** and type &Spell Check for **Spell Check**; choose **User Preferences** and type &User Preferences for **User Preferences**.

Figure 5-29

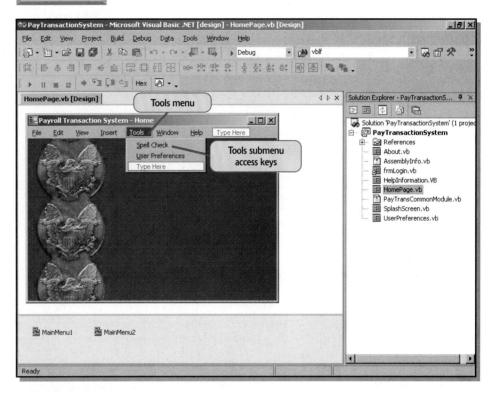

4 Add access key designations to the Help menu. Choose **Help** and type &Help for **Help**; choose **Index...** and type &Index... for **Index...**; choose **Payroll Transaction System Help** and type Payroll Transaction System &Help for **Payroll Transaction System Help**; choose **About** and type &About for **About**.

Figure 5-30

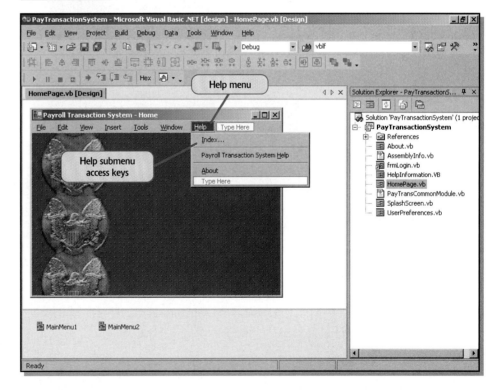

Tip

If you wish to change the order of your menu items, just click the item to be moved and then drag it to the desired place in the menu. To delete a menu item, click the item and then press Delete (the Delete key).

Naming Menu Items and Adding Separators

Once menu items are configured they become new objects with events in the program. When a user clicks a menu item or invokes its access key sequence, an event procedure is be executed. Just like a command button click event, you can place the programming code inside the event procedure to display forms and execute processes.

> **Tip**
>
> Visual Basic .NET creates event procedures based on the names of the menu items. By default the items will be named MenuItem(1) through MenuItem(n). Using these default names will make your code difficult to read and maintain. It is suggested that you take the time to rename all of the menu items to something meaningful, such as MenuItem_File, MenuItem_FileNew, MenuItem_FileOpen and so on.

Task 8:

To Name Menu Items and Add Separators

1 Rename menu items to meaningful names. Right-click the File menu and choose **Properties**.

Figure 5-31

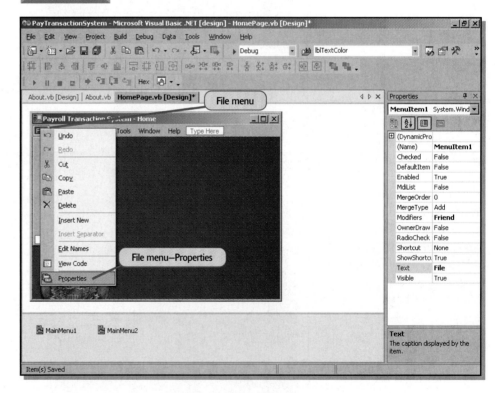

2 Change **MenuItem1** to **MenuItem_File** by clicking in the Name property and typing **MenuItem_File**.

3 Rename each menu item on your form according to Table 5-5.

Figure 5-32

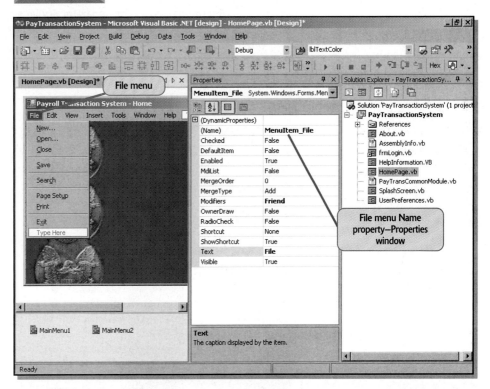

Table 5-5	Sample Menu Item Names					
File	**Edit**	**View**	**Insert**	**Tools**	**Window**	**Help**
MenuItem_File	MenuItem_Edit	MenuItem_View	MenuItem_Insert	MenuItem_Tools	MenuItem_Window	MenuItem_Help
MenuItem_New	MenuItem_Copy			MenuItem_Spell		MenuItem_HelpIndex
MenuItem_Open	MenuItem_Paste			MenuItem_UserPref		MenuItem_HelpPayTrans
MenuItem_Close	MenuItem_Find					MenuItem_HelpAbout
MenuItem_Save						
MenuItem_Search						
MenuItem_PgSetup						
MenuItem_Print						
MenuItem_Exit						

 Tip Once you have renamed all of your menu items to correspond with Table 5-5, you are ready to program the logic that goes behind each menu item.

To help organize submenu items into groups, a gray line called a separator is often used. To insert a separator above an existing menu item, right-click the submenu item above which you want the line to appear and choose **Insert Separator**. See Figure 5-33 for an example of a separator.

4 Insert a separator in the File menu. Choose **File | Save,** then right-click and choose **Insert Separator**.

Figure 5-33

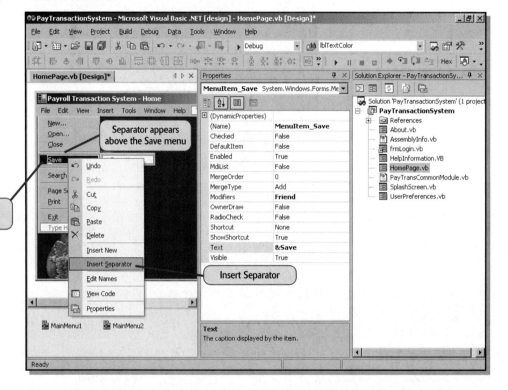

In Windows, most of the menus include separators to group similar processes. For instance, under the File menu **New, Open,** and **Close** are all file commands and should be grouped together. Grouping menu items is not a perfect science and can vary by individual and organizational preferences. The following is a suggestion on how to define separators for your menus.

5 Insert additional separators in the File menu. Choose **File | Search**, then right-click and choose **Insert Separator**; choose **File | Exit**, then right-click and choose **Insert Separator**.

Figure 5-34

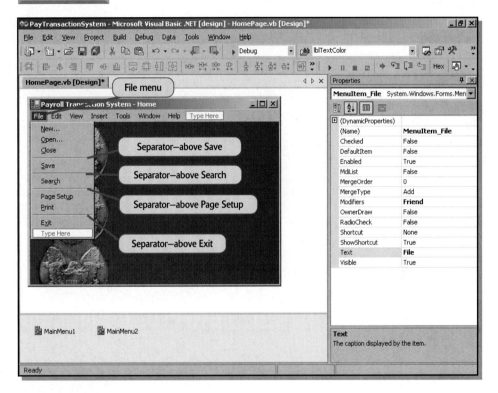

6 Insert separators in the Edit menu. Choose **Edit | Find**, then right-click and choose **Insert Separator**.

Figure 5-35

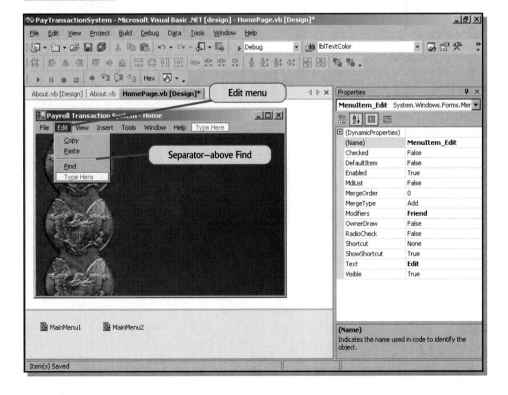

7 Insert separators in the Help menu. Choose **Help | Payroll Transaction System Help**, then right-click and choose **Insert Separator**; choose **Help | About**, then right-click and choose **Insert Separator**.

Figure 5-36

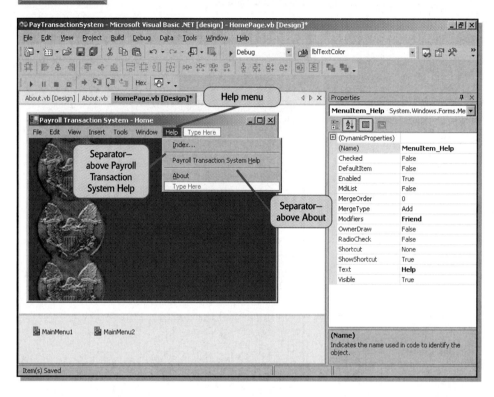

Adding Event Procedures to Menu Items

Now that the menu structure is complete, we will add code to the click event behind each menu subitem. We want the User Preferences form to be displayed when the **Tools | User Preferences** submenu item is clicked.

Task 9:
To Add Event Procedures to Menu Items

1 Create event proce-
dures for **Tools | User
Preferences**. Double-click
the **User Preferences** submenu item to display the
Code View window.

2 Enter programming
commands to show the
User Preferences form and
hide it after it is closed. Type
Preferences.ShowDialog()
and then type
Preferences.Hide().

Figure 5-37

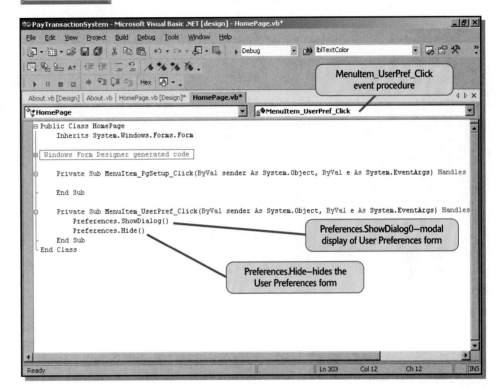

The Preferences.ShowDialog() statement displays the User Preferences
form modally when the User Preferences submenu item is clicked, and
then hides the form when the form is closed.

Adding Event Procedures with an "Under Construction" Message from a Module

There are times when you need to display a message to the user that indicates
that a particular feature may not be complete in the current version of the
application. We will construct a simple procedure in the existing code module,
and then call this UnderConstruction procedure when a menu item is selected
that is not fully implemented.

To finish the coding we will create a common procedure in the module called
UnderConstruction. This will be placed in the *PayTransCommon.vb* module.
We will also have to declare the HelpInformation form and the About form in
the module so we can use them in our project.

Task 10:

To Add Event Procedures with an "Under Construction" Message from a Module

Tip To add a procedure to a module, just click above the last line (the End Module statement), type Public Sub UnderConstruction0, and press Enter.

1 Create the common UnderConstruction message box. Double-click the *PayTransCommon.vb* file in the Solution Explorer. Enter a new subprocedure called UnderConstruction.

2 Add the declarations for the HelpInformation and About forms. Double-click the *PayTransCommon.vb* file from the Solution Explorer. Declare the forms Public, as shown in Figure 5-39.

Figure 5-38

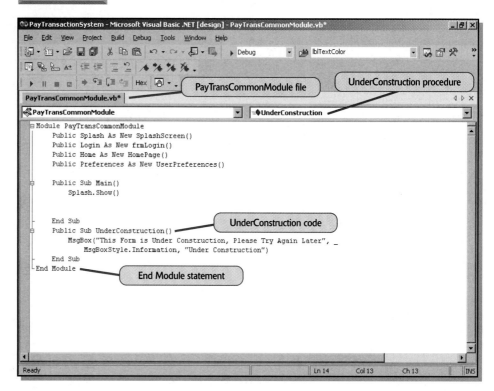

Figure 5-39

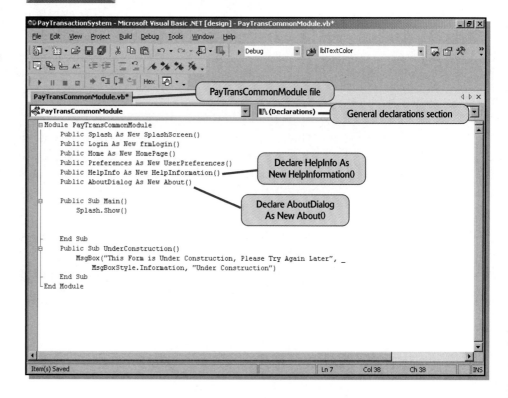

3 Call the UnderConstruction procedure for each menu item. As an example, for each menu item that will be under construction, follow the pattern of the Print menu item. Double-click the Print menu to view code.

Figure 5-40

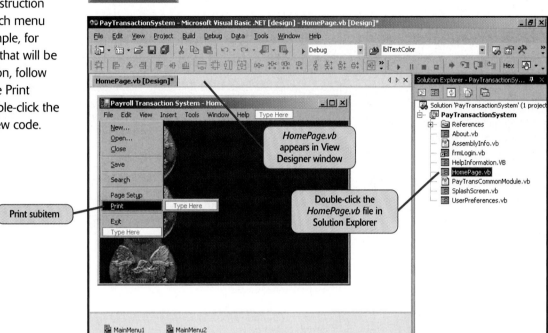

4 Code the procedure. Type **Call UnderConstruction** in the click event procedure and press [Enter].

Tip When you press [Enter], Visual Basic .NET will append brackets( ) at the end of the statement. The brackets indicate it is a separate procedure. You can send or receive arguments to/from the procedure inside of these brackets (more on arguments later).

Figure 5-41

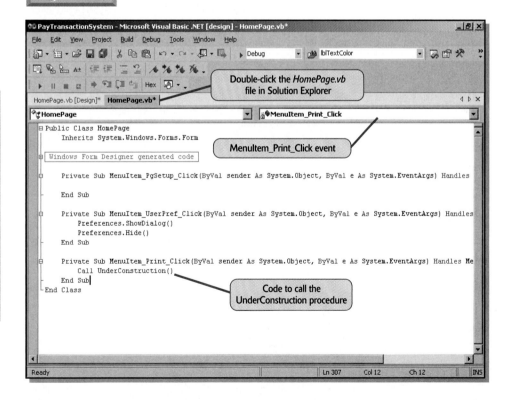

Other Ways In addition to choosing a menu, then double-clicking the submenu item to view and add code, from the Code View window you can also choose **MenuItem_Print** from the object selector, select the click event from the event selector, and just type in the code.

Figure 5-42

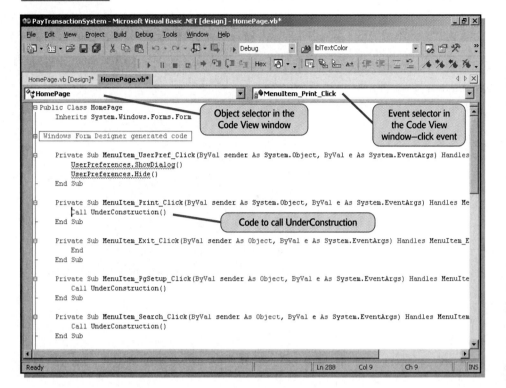

Tip After you have placed a Call UnderConstruction command in all of the menu item click events, you can go back and change the items for the forms that you have already completed in your project. For instance, you will add User Preferences to the Tools menu, and About to the Help menu. When you are done, your programs should look similar to Figures 5-43, 5-44, and 5-45.

5 Verify code in the Menultem_UserPref_ Click, Menultem_Print_Click, Menultem_Exit_Click, Menultem_PgSetup_Click, and Menultem_Search_Click events as shown in Figure 5-43.

Figure 5-43

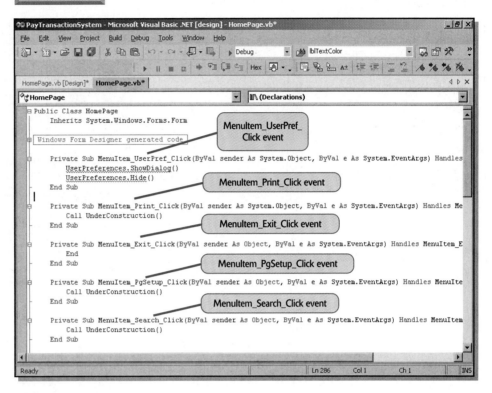

6 Verify code in the Menultem_Save_Click, Menultem_Close_Click, Menultem_Open_Click, Menultem_New_Click, Menultem_Copy_Click, and Menultem_Paste_Click events as shown in Figure 5-44.

Figure 5-44

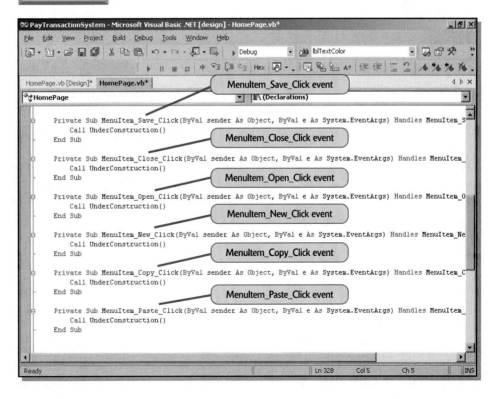

7 Verify code in the MenuItem_UserPref_ Click, MenuItem_Print_Click, MenuItem_Exit_Click, MenuItem_PgSetup_Click, and MenuItem_Search_Click events as shown in Figure 5-45.

Figure 5-45

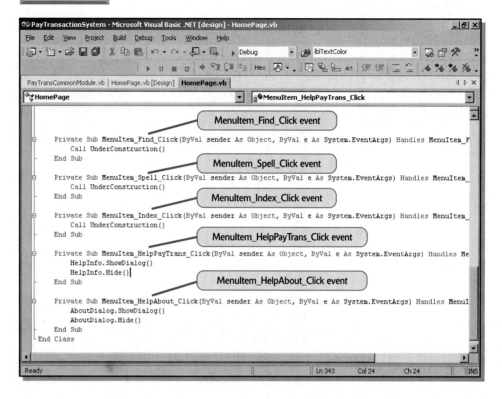

Testing the Program

Now you should be able to run the program and invoke the User Preferences screen from the File menu, and the Help and About screens from the Help menu. After each screen is closed, you are returned to your homepage.

Tip
Splash screens usually appear first when an application is started. Now that we have a splash screen, the startup object needs to be changed from About to SplashScreen. Right-click the **PayTransactionSystem** project within the Solution Explorer and choose **Properties**. Click the Startup Object Dropdown List control and choose **SplashScreen**. Click **OK** to save the change.

Task 11:
To Test the Program

1 Choose **File | Save All**.

2 Choose **Debug | Start** and verify that the splash screen appears.

Figure 5-46

3 Click the image of the baton in the lower-left corner and verify that the splash screen disappears and the login screen appears.

Figure 5-47

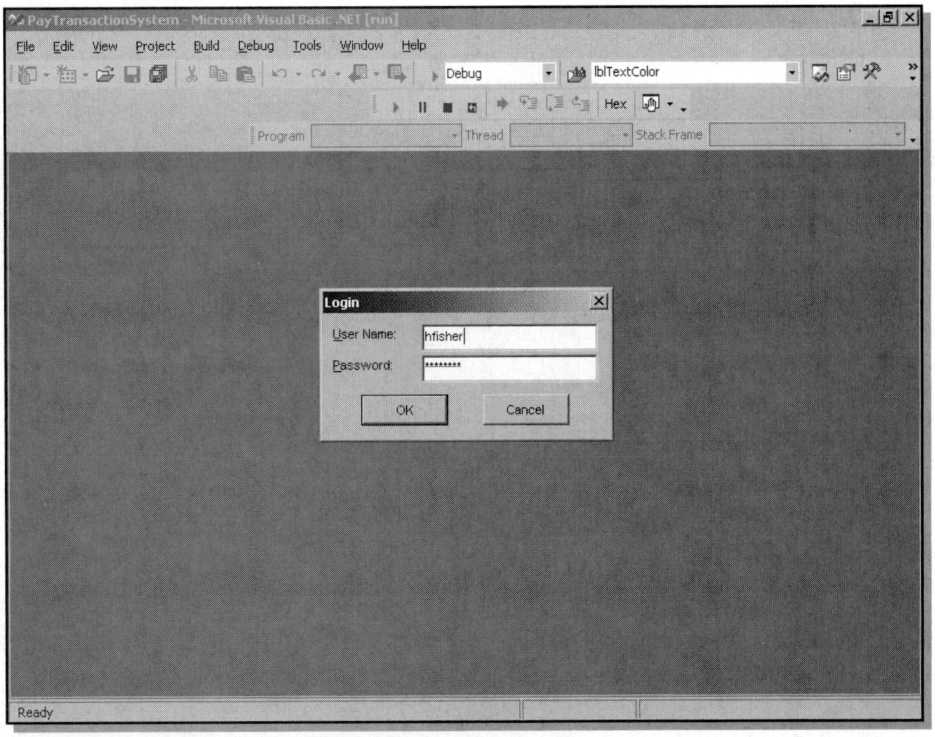

4 Type **your name** for the User Name, type **password** for the Password, click the OK button, and verify that the login screen disappears and the home-page appears.

> **Tip** The Login screen only validates the password value so you can type any name for the user name to successfully login. In the real world you would have to enter a valid username/password combination to successfully login to the application.

Figure 5-48

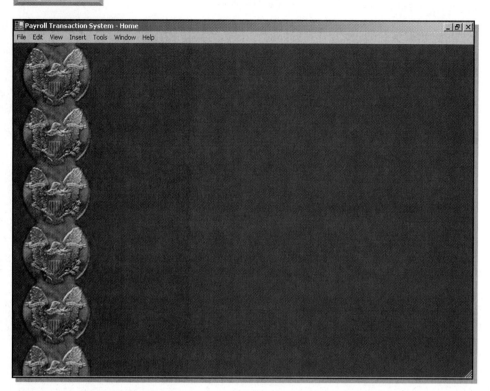

5 Choose **Tools | User Preferences** and verify that the User Preferences form appears.

Figure 5-49

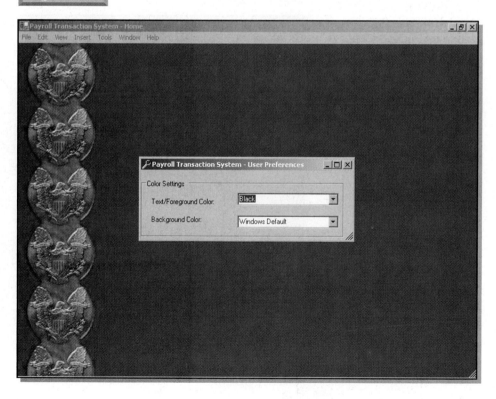

6 Click the Close button to close the User Preferences form, then choose **Help | About** and verify that the Help About form appears. Click the OK button and verify that the About form disappears.

Figure 5-50

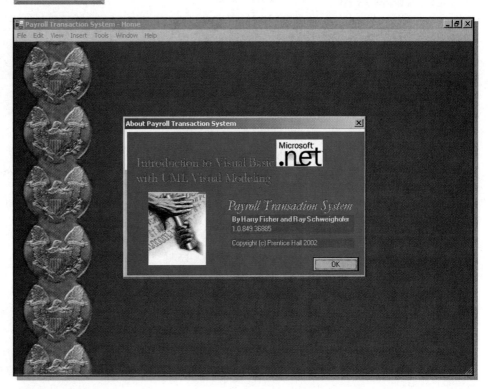

7 Choose **File | Print** and verify that the "Under Construction" message appears.

Figure 5-51

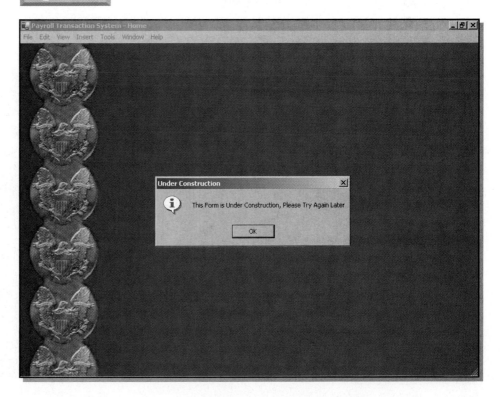

8 Choose **Help | Payroll Transaction System Help** and verify that the Help Information form appears.

Figure 5-52

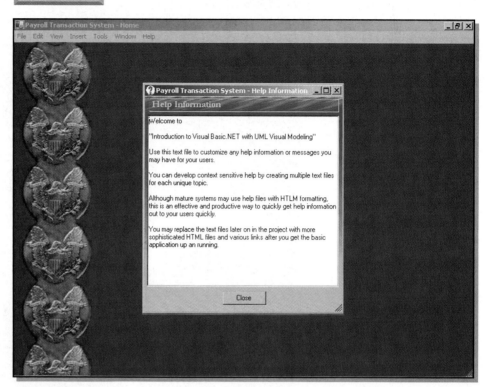

9 Choose **Help | About** and verify that the About form appears.

10 Choose **File | Exit** and verify that the application ends without errors.

Figure 5-53

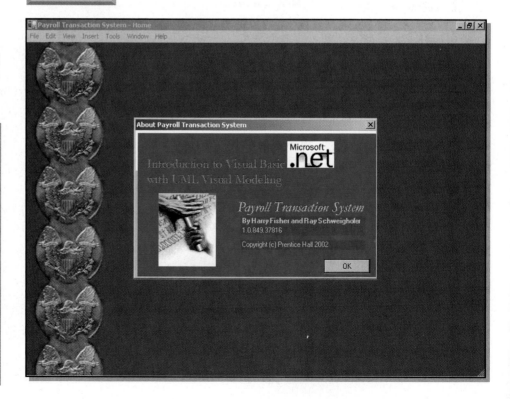

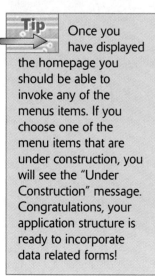

Tip Once you have displayed the homepage you should be able to invoke any of the menus items. If you choose one of the menu items that are under construction, you will see the "Under Construction" message. Congratulations, your application structure is ready to incorporate data related forms!

SUMMARY AND EXERCISES

SUMMARY

- Menu and Menu Event coding examples were utilized to enable the menu on the form.
- A MainMenu control enables the programmer to create menus and access keys.
- A Template form, such as the About form, is provided, copied, and then modified to meet the needs of the project being developed based on a standard pattern.
- Visual Basic .NET supports module-based procedure code, such as the UnderConstruction command used to display a message. Using modules centralizes code and thus reduces the total coding effort by eliminating redundancy.
- The most common event for menu programming is the click event.

KEY TERMS & SKILLS

KEY TERMS

About form (p. 5-3)
access keys (p. 5-3)
ampersand (&) (p. 5-3)
BackColor—Transparent
  (p. 5-3)
font (p. 5-3)
Font dialog box (p. 5-3)
Font Size (p. 5-3)
Font Style (p. 5-3)
Form—AcceptButton
  (p. 5-3)

Form—CancelButton
  (p. 5-3)
Form—MaximizeBox
  (p. 5-3)
Form—MinimizeBox
  (p. 5-3)
Form—ShowDialog()
  (p. 5-3)
ImageAlign—Left
  (p. 5-9)
Location (p. 5-4)

MainMenu control
  (p. 5-4)
Menu—Separator
  (p. 5-4)
Menu Designer (p. 5-4)
Multiline property
  (p. 5-4)
Size Mode (p. 5-4)
StartPosition (p. 5-4)
System.IO foundation
  class (stream reader)
  (p. 5-11)

SKILLS

Add a Help Information form (p. 5-5)
Add a menu using the MainMenu
  control (p. 5-19)
Add access keys for menu commands
  (p. 5-24)
Add code that reads help information
  from a file (p. 5-10)
Add event procedures to menu items
  (p. 5-31)

Add event procedures with an "Under
  Construction" message from a
  module (p. 5-32)
Add the About form from a template
  (p. 5-14)
Create the subitem-level menu (p. 5-21)
Name menu items and add separators
  (p. 5-26)
Review the code (p. 5-18)
Test the program (p. 5-37)

STUDY QUESTIONS

MULTIPLE CHOICE

1. What form property would you set to center a form on the screen?
a. Align
b. StartPosition
c. WindowState
d. Size

2. What form property is used to define the picture that appears on the left side of the form title bar?
a. Picture
b. Image
c. Icon
d. BackgroundImage

3. What character is used when creating a menu to provide an access key that displays an underlined letter on a menu or button?
a. +
b. ^
c. @
d. &

4. A value of 12 is an example of what Font property?
a. Width
b. Font Identifier
c. Style
d. Point Size

5. The Label control's Location property is measured in what units?
a. twips
b. pixels
c. inches
d. millimeters

6. What form property is used to set the caption that appears in the form title bar?
a. Text
b. Caption
c. Title
d. Name

7. What form property is used to affect the graphic that appears behind everything else?
a. Image
b. Icon
c. Picture
d. BackgroundImage

8. What action is required to insert a menu separator?
a. menu click
b. right-click
c. double-click
d. Insert button click

9. The Size Mode Auto Size value of the PictureBox control
a. allows the image to be stretched when the form is resized.
b. causes the image to be centered in the client area.
c. shrinks the image to fit the PictureBox control.
d. places the image in the upper left corner of the PictureBox control.

10. Which PictureBox property is used to create a beveled look?
a. Format
b. BorderStyle Fixed3D
c. BackColor
d. Style

SHORT ANSWER

1. What statement enables you to use the StreamReader object?
2. What is the name of the common procedure that displays a message when a menu option is not available in the payroll transaction system?
3. What happens when a form is shown with the ShowDialog method?
4. In what event would you type code to handle a menu selection?
5. How do you create a menu?
6. What form property would you set if you wanted the [Esc] key to launch the click event of a button?
7. Name the BackColor value of a label that permits the background to appear around the label control?
8. What is the name of the control used to create a menu?
9. What would you use to create a horizontal line between menu items?
10. What property of the TextBox control would you set to see more than one line of text?

FILL IN THE BLANK

1. The _____ form contains copyright information, the application name and version, and other information needed for support and additional help.
2. The _____ Designer enables you to create structured menus and context menus.
3. The _____ _____ box is used to change the font style or size of the cursor font.
4. The _____ button property of the form is used to launch a button click event when the [Enter] key is clicked.
5. The _____ button is used to make the currently active form fill the screen completely.
6. The _____ method is used to display a form modally and require the user to click a button or close the form.
7. _____ _____ are used to provide a means to launch a menu or click a button by pressing the [Alt] key followed by an underlined letter.
8. The _____ Position property is used to center a form on the screen.
9. Using the _____ property enables a TextBox control to display more than one line of text.
10. The _____ property allows an image to be stretched if the form is resized.

FOR DISCUSSION

1. Why would you use access keys?

2. When might you set the MaximizeBox property to False?

3. Why would you set the BackColor property of a label to Transparent?

4. When might a user visit the About form?

5. Why are menu separators used?

FROM THE FILES

You Will Need

✔ BlueWaterBackground.jpg

✔ Money9.ico

PROJECT 6

Introducing Common Controls Provided with Visual Basic .NET

T his project will focus on many *common controls* provided with Visual Basic .NET that are used in just about every application. When you understand the capabilities of controls, you can reduce or eliminate the need for programming code in many situations.

Tip

The *BlueWaterBackground.jpg* file can be found at \\vb.net_brief\vb.net_datafiles\06\Student\HR\PayTransaction System\Images.

The *Money9.ico* file can be found at \\vb.net_brief\vb.net_ datafiles\06\Student\HR\PayTransactionSystem\Images.

e-selections) Running Case

Other developers in the e-Selections Division of Selections, Inc. have been reviewing the prototype application used in the recent demo; they want to know more about common controls and how they are used to reduce development time.

OBJECTIVES

After completing this project, you will be able to:

- Create the Fundamentals project
- Use the TextBox control
- Use the Button control
- Build the Help Desk Tracker
- Understand standard naming conventions
- Use the CheckBox control
- Use the Label control
- Use the DateTimePicker control
- Use the MonthCalendar control
- Use the ComboBox control
- Use the CheckedListBox control
- Use the Multi-line TextBox control
- Use the RadioButton controls within a GroupBox control
- Use the ListBox control
- Test the Help Desk Tracker

Standard Naming Conventions

Learn How Using Standard Naming Conventions Can Help Make Code More Readable

Understanding complex code can be difficult, especially if someone else wrote it. Using a three-letter prefix for controls can clarify code. This can be especially helpful when debugging code. For example, a checkbox that will indicate a closed state might be named chkClosed. The first three letters are lowercase, and the first initial of the name is capitalized. If applied consistently, **standard naming conventions** (see the following table) greatly increase the readability of your code.

Standard Naming Convention Prefixes

User Interface Controls	Sample Name	User Interface Controls	Sample Name
AnimatedButton	aniControl	Image	imgControl
Button	btnControl	Item	itmMyitem
CheckBox	chkControl	Label	lblControl
Class	clsClassName	Line	linControl
ComboBox	cboControl	ListBox	lstControl
CommandButton	cmdControl (common in VB6 but referred to as a button in VB.NET)	ListView	lsvControl
		Menu	mnuFile
		OLEControl	oleControl
		OptionButton	optControl
DataControl	datControl	PictureBox	pbxControl
DirListBox	dlbControl	RemoteDataControl	rdcControl
DriveListBox	drbControl	Shape	shpControl
FileListBox	flbControl	TextBox	txtControl
Form	frmForm	Timer	tmrControl
Frame	fraControl (Group Box)	TreeView	trvControl
HScrollBar	hsbControl	VScrollBar	vsbControl

Introducing Common Controls Provided with Visual Basic .NET

The Challenge

Mr. Traylor would like to present a demonstration to the development group rather than managers next week. He would like to respond to many questions he has received focusing on how Visual Basic .NET can provide powerful applications using controls that are included in the software and simple coding techniques. This will require development of a few small demonstration-oriented projects apart from the PayTransactionSystem project.

The Solution

Visual Basic .NET has powerful built-in features that include a variety of controls; we will learn about many common controls in this project.

To demonstrate all the important fundamentals we will create the Visual Basic .NET Fundamentals project. It will include a *Switchboard* form that contains a button for each of the three major parts of this project. It also reinforces that it is useful to consider designing applications that provide users with just a few choices at startup, thus simplifying the application. Finally, you will create a HelpDeskTracker form that uses all the controls on a single form. Mr. Traylor would like you to accompany him to the next meeting to present a demonstration of the Fundamentals project.

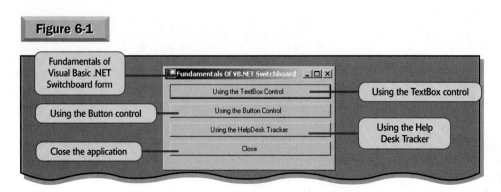

Figure 6-1

Creating the Fundamentals Project

Common controls form the building blocks of our applications. By selecting the most appropriate controls and adding relevant properties and code, we can quickly develop prototype and production grade applications. We will begin this project by creating a new Windows Forms–type project, and then enhance it piece by piece until we learn all the fundamentals we will need for the PayTransactionSystem application.

Task 1:
To Create the Fundamentals Project

1 Launch Visual Basic .NET and select **New Project**.

2 Select **Visual Basic Project** as the project type.

3 Choose **Windows Application** as the template.

4 Type **Fundamentals OfVBNET** as the name of the new project.

5 Choose **Browse | Navigate** and go to the *c:\Public\VBNetClass\ Students* folder. While in the Project Location window, right-click in the white center area and select **New Folder**. A folder will appear highlighted in the project location window. Rename the folder named NewFolder to **FundamentalsOfVBNET** and then double-click the FundamentalsOfVBNET folder just created to make it appear selected in the top of the Project Location window. Click the Open button to close the Project Location Window.

6 Verify that the information matches Figure 6-2 and then click the OK button.

Figure 6-2

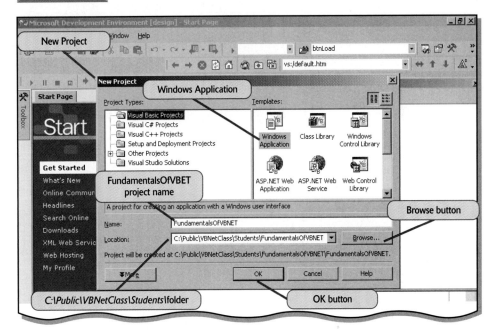

7 Click on the Switchboard form until the sizing handles are visible. Using the Properties window, type **Switchboard** for the name property, and then type **Fundamentals OfVB.NET Switchboard** for the Text property. Change the StartPosition property to **CenterScreen**.

Figure 6-3

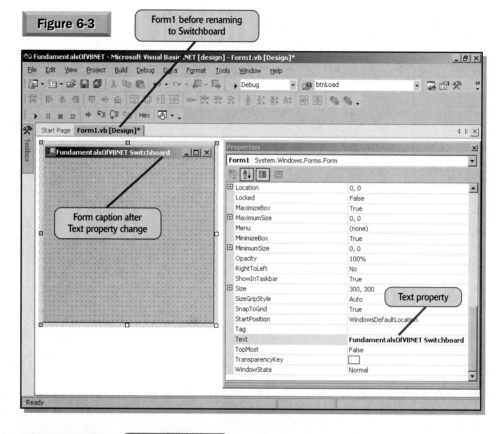

Form1 before renaming to Switchboard

Form caption after Text property change

Text property

8 Choose **File | Save Switchboard** and then click the OK button.

You can right-click on Switchboard.vb in the Solutions Explorer and select save.

Figure 6-4

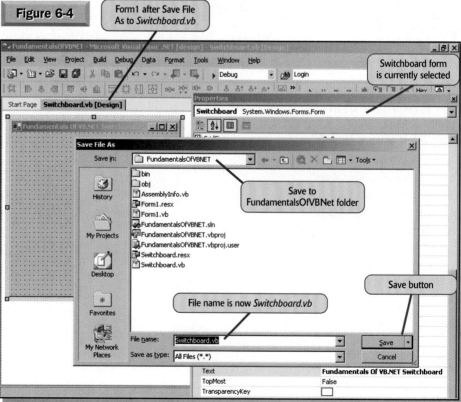

Form1 after Save File As to *Switchboard.vb*

Switchboard form is currently selected

Save to FundamentalsOfVBNet folder

Save button

File name is now *Switchboard.vb*

9 Set the Size property to 300, 176.

10 Choose **View | Toolbox**.

11 Click the *Button control* and draw a button on the Switchboard form.

12 Once you size the first button, right-click the Button1 control, choose **Copy**, click the Switchboard form, then right-click and choose **Paste**. Repeat two more times for a total of four buttons. Align each button vertically with one blank row between buttons. Complete the control properties as shown in Table 6-1.

13 Review Figure 6-5 and verify that the buttons appear correctly.

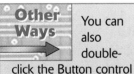
Other Ways You can also double-click the Button control on the Toolbox to add a control to the currently active form. Once added, the buttons can be arranged.

Figure 6-5

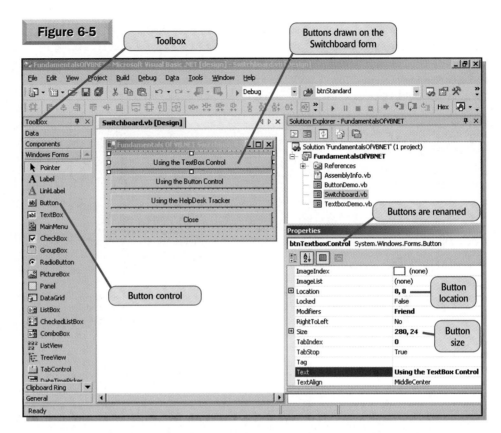

Table 6-1   Button Properties

Control Name	Location	Size	Text
btnTextboxControl	8,8	280,24	Using the Textbox Control
btnButtonControl	8,40	280,24	Using the Button Control
btnHelpDeskTracker	8,72	280,24	Using the Help Desk Tracker
btnClose	8,104	280,24	Close

Tip You can use the Align Tool to make each button the same size, align them to the left or right, and make them equidistant in the spacing between them.

14 Right-click the **Fundamentals OfVBNET** project within the Solution Explorer, choose **Properties**, and then click the selection under **Startup object**. Change the startup object from **Form1** to **Switchboard** and then click the OK button.

15 Choose **File | Save All**.

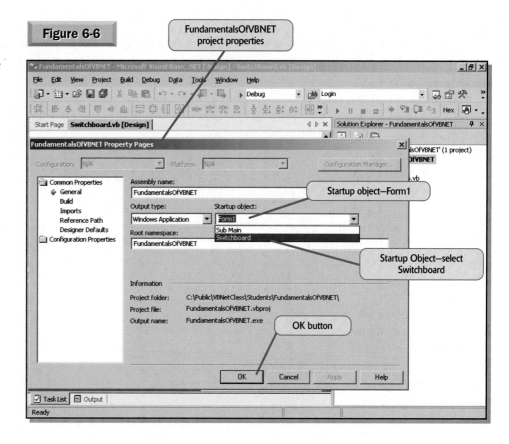

Figure 6-6

FundamentalsOfVBNET project properties

Startup object—Form1

Startup Object—select Switchboard

OK button

Using the TextBox Control

The *TextBox control* holds text or possibly multiple lines of text. It can also be configured as read-only and may support scroll bars. This control is commonly used to enable a user to enter information on a data entry form. When the ReadOnly property is set to True, the TextBox control will display information but not permit changes. This is helpful when users with different levels of access are using the system. If you set the read-only property to false, only authorized individuals who also have update privileges will be able to change values.

Several commonly used TextBox properties are listed in Table 6-2.

Table 6-2 TextBoxProperties

Property	Description
AcceptsTab	Indicates whether pressing the Tab key in a multi-line TextBox control inserts tabs in the control itself, rather than moving the focus to the next control in the tab order
AcceptsReturn	Indicates whether pressing [Enter] in a multiline TextBox control creates a new line of text in the control or activates the default button for the form
Autosize	Determines whether the size of the control automatically adjusts when the assigned font is changed
BackColor/ForeColor	Indicates the background or foreground color of the control
MaxLength	Sets the maximum number of characters that can be entered in the TextBox control
Multi-line	Specifies whether the text box can contain multiple lines of text
PasswordChar	Indicates the character used to mask characters in a single-line TextBox control usually used to enter passwords
ReadOnly	Marks the text box as read-only when true or read-write when false
SelectedText	Contains the currently selected text in the control
SelectionLength	Indicates the length of the selected text
SelectionStart	Indicates the starting point of text selected in the text box
TextAlign	Indicates how text is aligned in the TextBox control, using a HorizontalAlignment value of Center, Left, or Right
WordWrap	Indicates whether a multi-line TextBox control automatically wraps words to the beginning of the next line when necessary

To help us better understand the TextBox control, we will create a new form that contains several key points about the TextBox control. Then we will add controls and create a link from the Switchboard form to the TextboxDemo form using the TextBox control button (btnTextboxControl). Finally, we will test the TextboxDemo form. We will explore the AcceptsReturn, AcceptsTab, Multi-line, ScrollBars, TabIndex, PasswordChar, and ReadOnly properties.

Adding the TextboxDemo Form

Let's begin by adding the TextboxDemo form to the FundamentalsOfVBNET project.

Task 2:
To Add the TextboxDemo Form

1 Choose **Project | Add Windows Form**. Type **TextboxDemo.vb** for the name property and then click the Open button.

2 Type **Textbox Demo** for the Text property. Change the Size property to **504,300** and the Location property to **0,0**, and then choose **StartPosition | CenterScreen**.

Figure 6-7

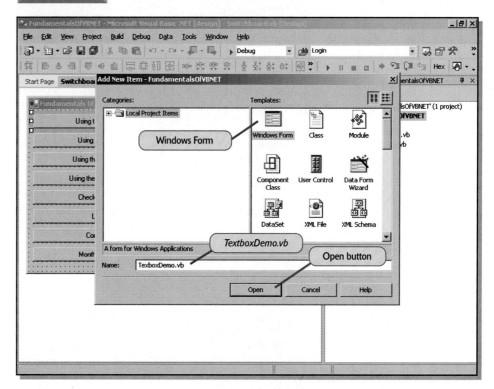

Adding the Controls to the Form

3 From the Toolbox, double-click the Label control four times, double-click the TextBox control four times, and then double-click the Button control once to add the controls to the form.

To complete the setup, we will add four Label controls, four TextBox controls, and one Button control to the form. In the next section we will add code.

Tip   The tab order is the order in which a user moves focus from one control to another by pressing the Tab key. Each form has its own tab order. By default, the tab order is the same as the order in which you created the controls. Tab-order numbering begins with zero. The TabIndex property is used to determine the tab sequence.

Arrange the layout of the Label, TextBox, and button controls similar to Figure 6-8. Complete the control properties as shown in Table 6-3.

Figure 6-8

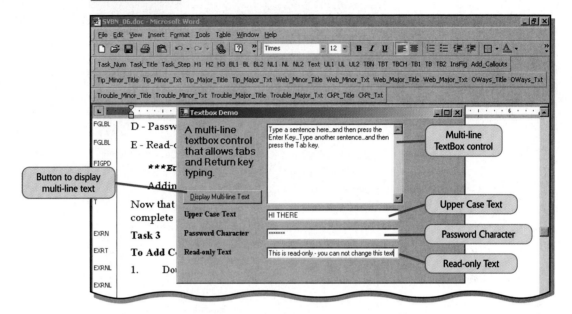

Table 6-3   Control Properties

Control Name	Properties
lblMulti-lineCaption	Font = Microsoft Sans Serif
	Font Style = Bold
	Font Size = 12
	Location = 8,8
	Size = 136, 104
	Text = A multi-line text box control that allows Tab and Enter key typing.
txtMulti-lineTextbox	AcceptsReturn = True
	AcceptsTab = True
	Location - 152,8
	Multi-line = True
	ScrollBars = Vertical
	Size = 240, 136
	TabIndex = 0
	Text = Type a sentence here…and then press the Enter key…Type another sentence…and then press the Tab key.
btnDisplayMulti-LineText	Location = 8, 120
	Size = 136, 23
	Text = &Display Multi-line Text
	TabIndex = 1

(Continued)

Table 6-3 Control Properties *(continued)*	
Control Name	**Properties**
lblUpperCaseCaption	Font = Times New Roman
	Font Style = Bold
	Font Size = 10
	Location = 8, 152
	Size = 136, 23
	Text = Upper Case Text
txtUpperCase	CharacterCasing = Upper
	Location = 152, 152
	Size = 232, 20
	TabIndex = 2
	Text = (Delete contents to leave the text empty)
lblPasswordCaption	Font = Times New Roman
	Font Style = Bold
	Font Size = 10
	Location = 8, 184
	Size = 136, 23
	Text = Password Character
TxtPassword	Location = 152, 184
	Size = 232, 20
	TabIndex = 3
	Text = (Delete contents to leave the text empty)
	PasswordChar = * (Shift 8 Asterisk)
lblReadonlyCaption	Font = Times New Roman
	Font Style = Bold
	Font Size = 10
	Location = 8, 216
	Size = 136, 23
	Text = Read-only Text
TxtReadonly	Location = 152, 216
	Readonly = True
	Size = 232, 20
	TabIndex = 4
	Text = This text is read-only. You cannot change it.

Adding Code to the Controls

Now that the Graphical User Interface (GUI) is finished, we must add code to complete the programming for the controls.

Task 3:
To Add Code to the Controls

1 Within the TextboxDemo form, double-click the btnDisplayMulti-LineText button to view code. Type the following code: MessageBox.Show (txtMulti-lineTextbox.text, "You typed this text:").

Figure 6-9

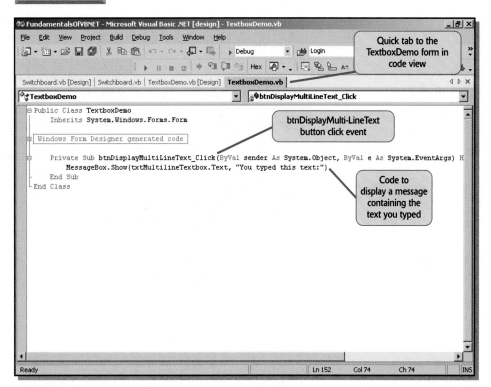

2 Double-click the Switchboard form in the Solution Explorer and then double-click on the Using the Textbox Control button to view code.

3 Type the code as provided in Figure 6-10.

4 Choose **File | Save All**.

Figure 6-10

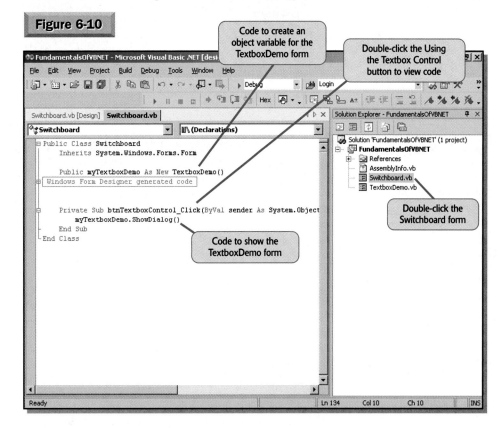

Testing the Textbox Demo Form

Since the Switchboard form appears when the application starts, and we have added code to link the top button to the TextboxDemo form and display the multi-line text box message, we are ready to test the form.

Task 4:

To Test the TextboxDemo Form

1 Choose **Debug | Start**, and then click the Using the Textbox Control button to display the TextboxDemo form.

2 Type some text in the multi-line text box, and then click the Display Multi-line Text button and verify that a message appears. Click the OK button to close the message window.

3 Press Tab to move the cursor to the Upper Case Text field and type **hello**.

4 Press Tab to move the cursor to the Password Character field and type **secret**.

5 Press Tab to move the cursor to the Read-only Text field, type **Try**, and verify that you cannot change the text.

6 Choose **Debug | Stop Debugging**.

Figure 6-11

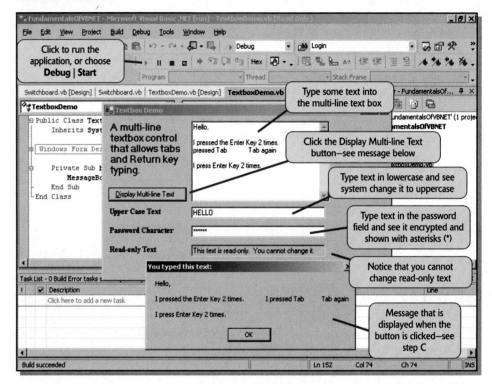

Tip   When using a multi-line TextBox control that has the AcceptsTab property set to True, Tab moves within the control. Press Ctrl + Tab to move to the next control in the tab index sequence.

Using the Button Control

The button is the simplest control, but is an import component in our screen design toolbox. It typically responds to a mouse click or key press. Table 6-4 presents the key properties of the Button control.

Table 6-4	Button Control Properties
Property	**Description**
ContentAlignment	Determines where on the button to display text. The following are alignment options: BottomCenter, BottomLeft, BottomRight, MiddleCenter, MiddleLeft, MiddleRight, TopCenter, TopLeft, TopRight.
FlatStyle	Indicates the appearance of the Button control. It can have the following values:
	Flat—The control appears flat. When the cursor is over the button, the text color changes to indicate that the button has the focus.
	Popup—The button control appears flat until the cursor moves over it, and then it becomes three-dimensional.
	Standard—The button appears three-dimensional, like a standard push button.
	System—The operating system determines the appearance.
Image	Determines which image is displayed somewhere on the button. This is an optional property setting. This control also has a background image that displays an image over the entire surface area of the button.
ImageAlign	Determines the alignment of the image on the button.
ImageIndex	Along with the ImageList control, determines which image to display.
IsDefault	Determines whether the button is the default button that responds when the Enter key is pressed.
TextAlign	Determines the alignment of the text on the button.

We will now add a new form with four buttons and then add code. Each button will demonstrate a different property or style. Images will also appear in one button. Afterward, a link from the Switchboard form will launch the new ButtonDemo form. This application uses the FlatStyle, ImageAlign, and TextAlign properties. The Standard Style button will display a message.

Adding the ButtonDemo Form

Let's begin by adding the ButtonDemo form to the FundamentalsOfVBNET project.

Task 5:
To Add the ButtonDemo Form

1 Choose **Project | Add Windows Form**. Type **ButtonDemo.vb** for the name and then click the Open button.

2 Type **Button Demo** for the Text property. Choose **StartPosition | CenterScreen**.

3 Choose **File | Save All**.

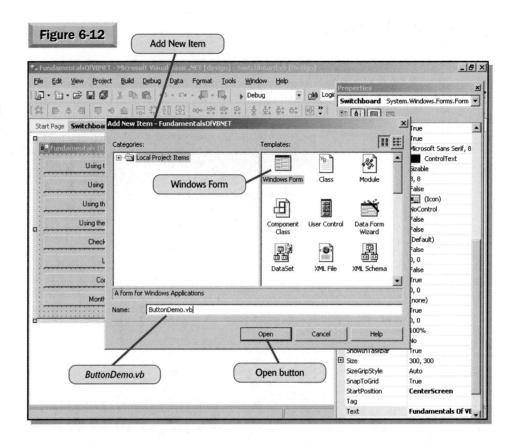

Figure 6-12

Adding Button Controls to the Form

Several buttons will be added to the form.

Task 6:
To Add Button Controls to the Form

1 From the Toolbox, double-click the Button control four times to add four Button controls to the ButtonDemo form.

2 Complete the control properties as shown in Table 6-5.

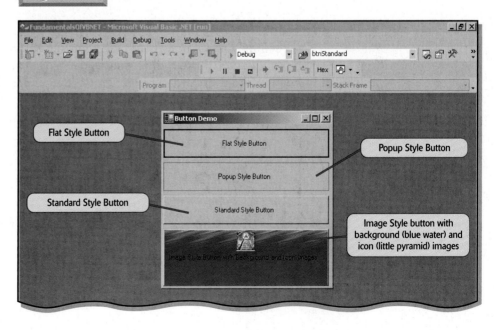

Figure 6-13

Tip See the From the Files section at the beginning of this project for the location of the image files you will need.

Table 6-5 Button Properties	
Control Name	**Properties**
btnFlatStyleButton **(top button)**	FlatStyle = Flat Location = 0, 8 Size = 288, 48 Text = Flat Style Button
btnPopupStyleButton **(second button from the top)**	FlatStyle = Popup Location = 0,64 Size = 288, 48 Text = Popup Style Button
btnStandardStyleButton **(third button from the top)**	FlatStyle = Standard Location = 0,120 Size = 288, 48 Text = Standard Style Button
btnImageStyleButton **(bottom button)**	Background Image = *BlueWaterBackground.jpg* FlatStyle = Standard Icon = *Money9.ico* ImageAlign = TopCenter (Cclick top center button within the Image Align property dialog box). Location = 0, 176 Size = 288, 48 StartPosition = Center Screen Text = Image Style Button with Background and Icon Images

Adding Code to the Standard Style Button

To help demonstrate the ContentAlignment property, we will add code to the Standard Style button click event. When the Standard Style button is clicked, it will display a message using a message box.

Task 7:

To Add Code to the Standard Style Button

1 Double-click the Standard Style Button to view code.

2 Type the code as shown in Figure 6-14.

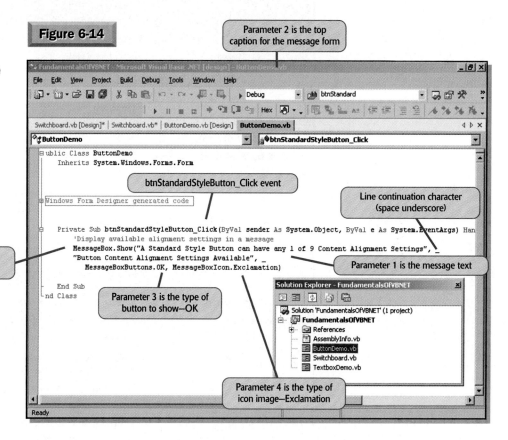

Figure 6-14

Parameter 2 is the top caption for the message form

btnStandardStyleButton_Click event

Line continuation character (space underscore)

MessageBox.Show method displays a form with a message

Parameter 1 is the message text

Parameter 3 is the type of button to show—OK

Parameter 4 is the type of icon image—Exclamation

Linking and Testing the ButtonDemo form

We will again create a link from the Switchboard form to the ButtonDemo form.

Task 8:
To Link and Test the ButtonDemo Form

1 Choose **View | Solution Explorer**, double-click the Switchboard form, and then double-click the btnButtonControl button to view code for the button click event.

2 Type the code as shown in Figure 6-15.

3 Choose **File | Save All**.

4 Choose **Debug | Start** and then click the Using the Button Control button to display the ButtonDemo form.

5 Position the mouse pointer over the Flat Style Button and verify that the button changes color.

6 Position the mouse pointer over the Popup Style Button and verify that it appears to pop up with a white outline on the left and top sides of the button.

7 Click the Standard Style Button and verify that a message appears.

8 Verify that the Image Style button has a background image and icon.

Figure 6-15

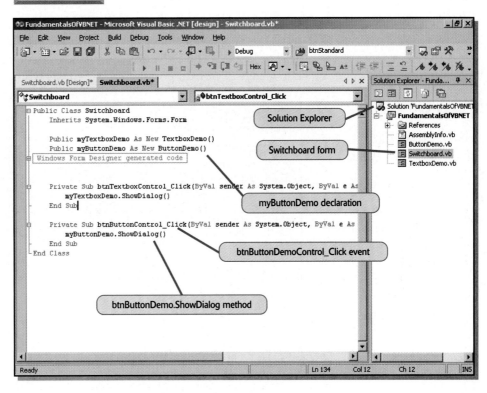

Creating the HelpDeskTracker Form

In this section you will add a new form and link to it from the Switchboard form. In the tasks that follow, you will gradually develop the Help Desk Tracker application by adding controls. In the next project, we will extend our knowledge of how to populate the controls by reading values from them.

Task 9:

To Create the HelpDeskTracker Form

1 Choose **Project | Add Windows Form** and select a Windows Form template. Type HelpDeskTracker.vb for the name and then click the Open button.

2 Complete the form properties as shown in Table 6-6.

Figure 6-16   Add New Item

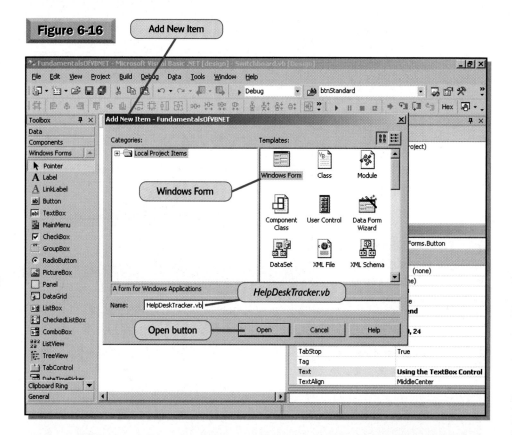

Table 6-6	Form Properties
Control Name	**Properties**
HelpDeskTracker (Form)	Location = 0, 0
	Size = 416, 456
	StartPosition = CenterScreen
	Text = Help Desk Tracker - Common Controls Demo

> **Tip** The completed HelpDeskTracker form appears in Figure 6-17. The remaining tasks in this project will gradually add controls until the form is complete.

3 Choose **File | Save All**.

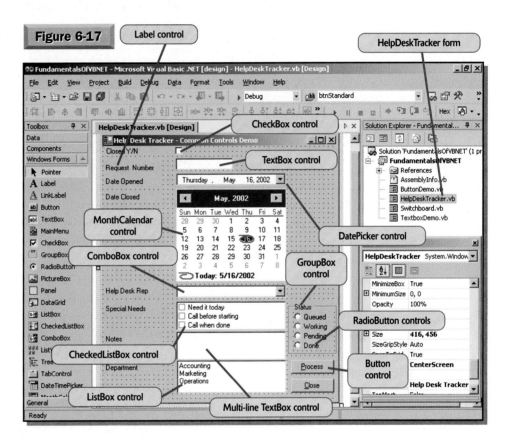

Figure 6-17

Using the CheckBox Control

The *CheckBox control* is used when the application needs to provide the user with one or more choices. The CheckBox control supports three possible states: Checked when the control is clicked, Unchecked when the control is empty, and Indeterminate when the control displays a shaded appearance of a checkmark symbol. Table 6-7 presents the properties of the CheckBox control.

Table 6-7	CheckBox Control Properties
Property	**Description**
Appearance	Configures the appearance of a check box.
Autocheck	Determines whether the Checked or CheckState value and the check box's appearance are automatically changed when it is clicked.
CheckAlign	Determines the horizontal and vertical alignment of a check box using the ContentAlignment options: topleft, topmiddle, topright, middleleft, middle, middleright, bottomleft, bottommiddle, and bottomright.
Checked	Determines whether the check box is checked using the CheckState enumeration rather than a boolean (True/False) value. This is important since the CheckBox control has three possible state values.
TextAlign	Indicates the alignment of the text on the button controls.
	BottomCenter—Content is vertically aligned at the bottom and horizontally aligned at the center.
	BottomLeft—Content is vertically aligned at the bottom and horizontally aligned on the left.
	BottomRight—Content is vertically aligned at the bottom and horizontally aligned on the right.
	MiddleCenter—Content is vertically aligned in the middle and horizontally aligned at the center.
	MiddleLeft—Content is vertically aligned in the middle and horizontally aligned on the left.
	MiddleRight—Content is vertically aligned in the middle and horizontally aligned on the right.
	TopCenter—Content is vertically aligned at the top and horizontally aligned at the center.
	TopLeft—Content is vertically aligned at the top and horizontally aligned on the left.
	TopRight—Content is vertically aligned at the top and horizontally aligned on the right.
ThreeState	Determines whether the check box supports three states of selection rather than just two.

Task 10:
To Use the CheckBox Control

1 In the Toolbox, double-click the CheckBox control to add it to the form.

2 Complete the control properties as shown in Table 6-8.

Table 6-8	CheckBox Control Properties
Control Name	**Properties**
chkClosed	Location = 3,0
(CheckBox)	Size = 136,16
	Text = Closed Y/N
	TextAlign = MiddleRight

Tip

The CheckBox control appears to have a label next to the box. This is a part of the CheckBox control and does not require a secondary Label control. In this example, the label portion of the CheckBox control was left-justified by setting the TextAlign property to MiddleRight. By default, the label portion appears to the right of the box.

Using the Label Control

 The *Label control* is a container for static text. It is often used to provide a caption that appears next to a text box or other type of control. It is also used to provide a read-only view of data.

Task 11:
To Use the Label Control

1 In the Toolbox, double-click the Label control six times to add six Label controls to the form.

2 Complete the control properties as shown in Table 6-9.

Table 6-9	Label Control Properties
Control Name	**Properties**
lblRequestNumber (Label)	Location = 3, 24 Size = 100, 23 Text = Request Number
lblDateOpened (Label)	Location = 3, 47 Size = 100, 23 Text = Date Opened
lblDateClosed (Label)	Location = 3, 73 Size = 100, 23 Text = Date Closed
lblHelpDeskRep (Label)	Location = 3, 231 Size = 100, 23 Text = Help Desk Rep
lblSpecialNeeds (Label)	Location = 3, 261 Size = 100, 23 Text = Special Needs
lblDepartment (Label)	Location = 3, 360 Size = 100, 23 Text = Department

Adding a TextBox Control for the Request Number

Now that we have a label caption, let's add a text box to enable the user to type in a request number. In a production application, we would eventually link the information collected in the HelpDeskTracker form to a database. The system could record each request, generate reports, and help track requests over time. In addition, the system would be able to assign the request number by taking the largest request number taken so far, and adding 1 to increment the number. This is usually done by using a sequence object in a relational database such as Oracle or SQL Server.

Task 12:

To Add the TextBox Control for the Request Number

Table 6-10 TextBox Control Properties	
Control Name	**Properties**
TxtRequestNumber (TextBox)	Location = 126, 20
	Size = 100, 20
	Text = (Delete contents to leave the text empty)

1 In the Toolbox, double-click the TextBox control to add it to the form.

2 Complete the control properties as shown in Table 6-10.

Using the DateTimePicker Control

DateTimePicker

The *DateTimePicker control* enables the user to select a date and time, and to display that date and time in the specified format. It returns a single date and time selected by the user. The default value is today's date unless the MaxDate value has passed. This control is similar to the ComboBox control (the ComboBox control will be discussed later in this project) because it is initially small, and when it is clicked it appears larger. The DateTimePicker control when clicked displays a full-sized calendar; once a date is selected, the calendar disappears to maximize available screen space. In the next section, we will explore the MonthCalendar control, which looks similar to the DateTimePicker control but can return multiple dates rather than just one, and appears as a calendar all the time rather than just after the control has been clicked. Table 6-11 presents the properties of the DateTimePicker control.

Table 6-11 DateTimePicker Control Properties	
Property	**Description**
MinDate	The minimum date and time that can be selected in the control. The default is 1/1/1753 00:00:00.
MaxDate	The maximum date and time that can be selected in the control. The default is 12/31/9998 23:59:59.

Task 13:
To Use the DateTimePicker Control

1 In the Toolbox, double-click the DateTimePicker control to add it to the form.

2 Complete the control properties as shown in Table 6-12.

Figure 6-18

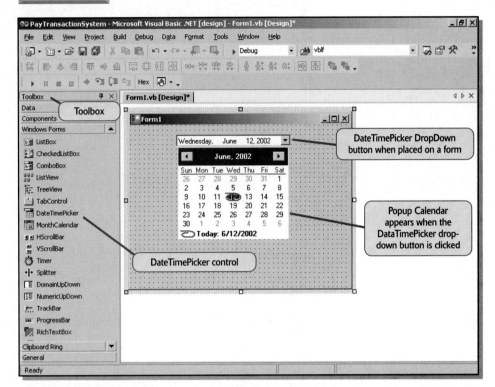

Table 6-12	DateTimePicker Control Properties
Control Name	**Properties**
dtpDateOpened	Location = 127, 46
(DateTimePicker)	Size = 192, 20

Using the MonthCalendar Control

 MonthCalendar

Visual Basic .NET provides an extremely useful *MonthCalendar control* that enables the user to select a date (or range of dates) using a friendly user interface. You can limit the dates and times that can be selected by setting the MinDate and MaxDate properties. Table 6-13 presents the properties of the MonthCalendar control.

Table 6-13   MonthCalendar Control Properties

Property	Description
BoldedDates	Indicates whether dates are shown in bold
CalendarDimensions	Indicates the number of columns and rows of months displayed in the MonthCalendar control
FirstDayOfWeek	Indicates the first day of the week for the MonthCalendar control
MaxDate	Indicates the maximum date and time that can be selected in the control. The default is 12/31/9998 23:59:59.
MonthlyBoldedDates	Indicates which monthly dates are shown in bold
SelectionEnd	Indicates the end date of the selected range of dates
SelectionRange	Retrieves the selection range for the MonthCalendar control
SelectionStart	Indicates the start date of the selected range of dates
SelectionRange	Retrieves the selection range for a MonthCalendar control
ShowToday/ShowTodayCircle	Indicates whether the MonthCalendar control displays today's date at the bottom of the control, as well as whether it circles the current date
ShowWeekNumbers	Indicates whether the MonthCalendar control displays the week numbers (1–52) to the left of each row of days
TodayDate	Indicates the date shown as Today in the MonthCalendar control. By default, Today is the current date at the time the MonthCalendar control is created.
TodayDateSet	Indicates whether the user has explicitly set the TodayDate property. If TodayDateSet is True, TodayDate returns whatever the user has set it to.

Task 14:

To Use the MonthCalendar Control

1 In the Toolbox, double-click the MonthCalendar control to add it to the form.

2 Complete the control properties as shown in Table 6-14.

Figure 6-19

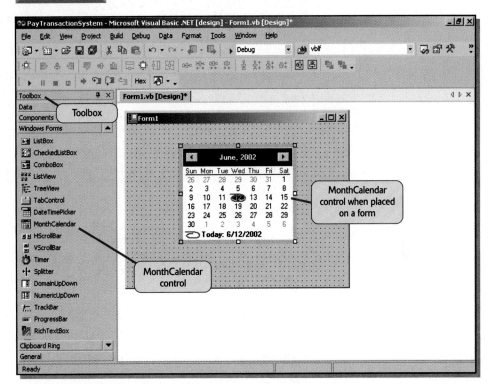

Table 6-14   MonthCalendar Control Properties

Control Name	Properties
calDateClosed	Location = 127, 72
(MonthCalendar)	Size = 192, 55

Using the ComboBox Control

 ComboBox

Like a ListBox control (which will be reviewed later in this project), a *ComboBox control* enables the user to make a selection from a set of choices. It provides a down arrow that reduces the space required to provide users with valid items. Once an item is selected, the drop-down list contracts. You can also type a few letters of the valid item name and the combo box will seek the value; this reduces the need to type all the letters, or even to use the mouse. Table 6-15 presents the properties of the ComboBox control.

Table 6-15   ComboBox Control Properties

Property	Description
DropDown	The text portion is editable. The user must click the arrow button to display the list.
DroppedDown	Indicates whether the drop-down portion of the combo box is dropped down.
MaxDropDownItems	Indicates the maximum number of items to be shown in the drop-down portion of the combo box. This number can range from 1 to 100.
DropDownList	The user cannot directly edit the text portion. The user must click the arrow button to display the list.
DropDownStyle	Indicates the type of combo box. The following styles are provided: DropDown—The text portion is editable. The user must click the arrow button to display the list. DropDownList—The user cannot directly edit the text portion. The user must click the arrow button to display the list. Simple—The text is editable. The list is always visible.
MaxLength	Indicates the maximum length of the text the user can type into a combo box.
SelectedIndex	Indicates the zero-based index of the selected item in the combo box list. It the value is -1, there is no selected item.
SelectedItem	Indicates the handle to the object selected in the combo box list. A handle is a unique integer value defined by the operating environment and used by a program to identify and switch to an object, such as a form or control.
SelectedText	Indicates the selected text in the combo box.
SelectionLength	Indicates the length, in characters, of the selection in the combo box.
Simple	The text is editable. The list is always visible.
Text	The text displayed in the combo box that represents the default or chosen item. Provides the text within the edit box. This is generally the most useful property of the control.

Tip

The terms *ComboBox* and *ListBox* are sometimes used interchangeably. The primary difference between a ComboBox and a ListBox is that the ListBox permits the user to select multiple items. The ListBox is also generally larger in size when placed on the form. A ComboBox differs in that the user can type a different value to quickly find a match in a list of available items. The ComboBox is generally very small in size, opens when clicked, and closes to a small size after a selection has been made. Only a single item can be selected with this control.

Task 15:
To Use the ComboBox Control

1 In the Toolbox, double-click the ComboBox control to add it to the form.

2 Complete the control properties as shown in Table 6-16.

| Table 6-16 | ComboBox Control Properties |
Control Name	Properties
cboHelpDeskRep (ComboBox)	Items—Click the Items property to make the ellipse (...) button appear, and then click it to view the String Collection Editor. Type the following values and press Enter after each line to move down. Harry Fisher Enter Ray Schweighofer (and then click the OK button) Location = 127, 234 Size = 192, 21 Text = (Delete contents to leave the text empty)

Tip If you click to select a control from the Toolbox, the mouse pointer will change to a plus sign (+). This is intended to prepare you to draw the control. If you change your mind and need the mouse pointer reset to normal, select the *Pointer control* in the Toolbox.

Using the CheckedListBox Control

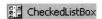 CheckedListBox

The *CheckedListBox control* enables you to group related check box options in a scrollable list control. The user can place a check mark next to one or more items. The CheckedListBox object supports three states through the CheckState enumeration: Checked, Indeterminate, and Unchecked. You must set the state of Indeterminate in the code because the user interface for a CheckedListBox does not provide a mechanism to do so.

Task 16:
To Use the CheckedListBox Control

1 In the Toolbox, double-click the CheckedListBox to add it to the form.

2 Complete the control properties as shown in Table 6-17.

| Table 6-17 | CheckedListBox Control Properties |
Control Name	Properties
clbSpecialNeeds (CheckedListBox)	Items—Click the Items property to make the ellipse (...) button appear, and then click it to view the String Collection Editor. Type the following values and press Enter after each line to move down. Need it today Enter Call before starting Enter Call when done (and then click the OK button) Location = 127,261 Size = 192,49

Using the Multi-line TextBox Control

The multi-line TextBox control is useful for taking notes or for fields that require several paragraphs of text. In many applications, there are "comments" that need to be entered. Multi-line TextBoxes are also useful for capturing the contents of letters, e-mails, and so forth.

Task 17:

To Use the Multi-line TextBox Control

1 In the Toolbox, double-click the TextBox control to add it to the form.

2 Complete the control properties as shown in Table 6-18.

Table 6-18 TextBox Control Properties	
Control Name	**Properties**
txtNotes	Location = 127, 312
(Multi-line TextBox)	Multi-line = True
	Size = 192, 48
	Text = (Delete contents to leave the text empty).

Using the GroupBox and RadioButton Controls

The *RadioButton control* can be either selected or not selected. This is very similar to the check box except for the CheckChanged event, which is fired when the Checked value changes. Typically, multiple RadioButton controls are logically and physically grouped together to function as a whole. For example, if you have a set of seven RadioButton controls representing the days of the week, you may wish to ensure that only one is selected. In Visual Basic .NET you would always use the *GroupBox control*. By placing all seven of the RadioButton controls inside the GroupBox control, you can limit only one RadioButton control to be selected. Radio buttons are also known as option buttons.

Tip The terms Radio button and option button are synonomous.

Task 18:
To Use the GroupBox and RadioButton Controls

1 In the Toolbox, double-click the GroupBox control to add it to the form.

2 Complete the control properties as shown in Table 6-19.

Table 6-19   GroupBox Control Properties

Control Name	Properties
grpStatus (GroupBox)	Location = 323, 264 Size = 85, 87 Text = Status
optQueued (Option or RadioButton)	Location = 10, 16 Size = 70, 16 Text = Queued
optWorking (Option or RadioButton)	Location = 10, 32 Size = 70, 16 Text = Working
optPending (Option or RadioButton)	Location = 10,48 Size = 70,16 Text = Status
optDone (Option or RadioButton)	Location = 10,64 Size = 70,16 Text = Done

Using the ListBox Control

 ListBox   Having predefined valid choices ensures that users make a selection easily. The *ListBox control* enables you to display a list of items that the user can select by clicking. A ListBox control can provide single or multiple selections using the SelectionMode property. The ListBox also provides the MultiColumn property to display items in columns instead of in a straight vertical list. This allows the control to display more visible items and prevents the need for the user to scroll to an item. Table 6-20 presents the properties of the ListBox control.

Table 6-20 ListBox Control Properties	
Property	**Description**
ScrollAlwaysAvailable	Determines whether the associated scroll bar is shown at all times.
SelectedIndex	Indicates the index of the currently selected item in the list (if any). A value of -1 indicates "no selection." If the value is 0 or greater, the value is the index of the currently selected item.
SelectedIndices	Returns a collection of the indices of the selected items in the list box. If no selected items are in the list box, the result is an empty collection.
SelectedItem	Indicates the value of the currently selected item in the list. If the value is null, there is currently no selection.
SelectedItems	Returns a collection of all selected items (for a multiselection list box).
SelectionMode	Controls how many items at a time can be selected in the list box.
Sorted	Indicates whether the list box is sorted (alphabetically).
Text	The text of the currently selected item in the control.
TopIndex	Returns the top index of the first visible item in a list box.

Task 19:

To Use the ListBox Control

1 In the Toolbox, double-click the ListBox control to add it to the form.

2 Complete the control properties as shown in Table 6-21.

Table 6-21 ListBox Control Properties	
Control Name	**Properties**
lstDepartments (ListBox)	Items—Click the Items property to make the ellipse (...) button appear, and then click it to view the String Collection Editor. Type the following values and press Enter after each line to move down.
	Accounting Enter
	Marketing Enter
	Operations (and then click the OK button)
	Location = 128,360
	Size = 192,56

Since we have already reviewed the Button control we will simply add two additional buttons for Process and Close. The Process button will receive code in the next project; when clicked, it will display a MessageBox that contains a summary of the help desk request. The Close button will close the form and display the Switchboard form again.

Task 20:

To Add the Process and Close Buttons

1 In the Toolbox, double-click the Button control twice to add two Button controls to the form.

2 Complete the control properties as shown in Table 6-22.

Table 6-22	Button Control Properties
Control Name	**Properties**
btnProcess (Button)	Location = 328, 360
	Size = 75, 23
	Text - &Process
btnClose (Button)	Location = 128, 392
	Size = 75, 23
	Text = &Close

Tip Remember the ampersand (&) character is used to identify the shortcut keys so that Alt + P will invoke the process button and Alt + C will invoke the close button.

Testing the HelpDeskTracker Form

To this point, we have focused on adding controls to the HelpDeskTracker application. Although we manually added items to several controls, such as the CheckListBox and ListBox controls, we would usually populate them in code and often fill the ComboBox and ListBox with items retrieved from a database. This example should help you better understand how the controls work in runtime.

Creating a Link from the Switchboard Form to the HelpDeskTracker Form

Now that the forms are complete, let us create the final link from the Switchboard form to the HelpDeskTracker form. This will be similar to the first two buttons on the Switchboard form.

Task 21:
To Create a Link from the Switchboard Form to the HelpDeskTracker Form

1 Double-click the Switchboard form in the Solution Explorer.

2 Double-click the Using the HelpDeskTracker button to view the code.

3 Type **Public myHelp DeskTracker as New HelpDeskTracker** in the Declarations section.

4 Type **myHelpDesk Tracker.ShowDialog** in the btnHelpDesk Tracker_Click event.

5 Choose **File | Save All**.

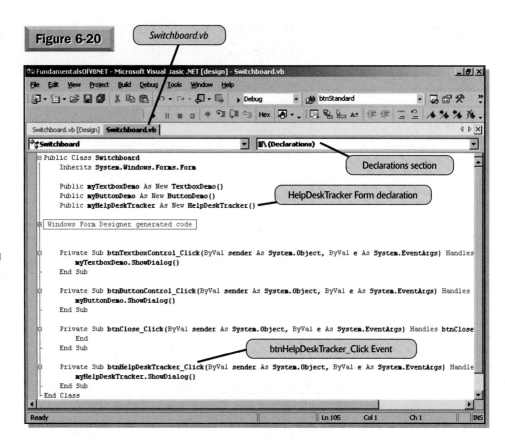

Figure 6-20

Task 22:
To Test the HelpDeskTracker Form

1 Choose **Debug | Start**.

2 Click the HelpDesk Tracker button (third from the top).

3 Complete the control properties as shown in Table 6-23, verify that the form is working properly, and then choose **Debug | Stop Debugging**.

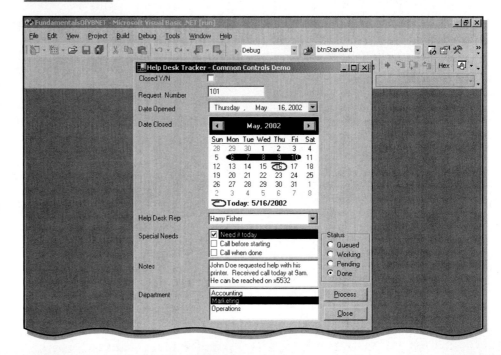

Figure 6-21

Table 6-23   Sample HelpDeskTracker Test Scenarios

Control	Action	Expected Result
ClosedYN	Check it	See the checkmark
(CheckBox)	Uncheck it	No checkmark
RequestNumber (TextBox)	Type 101	Value is displayed
DateOpened (DateTimePicker)	Click, select a date	Calendar appears and date is filled in afterward
DateClosed (MonthCalendar)	Select five days from Monday thru Friday	Click and drag to highlight multiple dates
HelpDeskRep (ComboBox)	Click, select **Harry**	Click shows two names, and the comboBox control displays **Harry** and then contracts to small size when clicked
Notes (Multi-line TextBox)	Type John Doe requested help with his printer. Received call today at 9am. He can be reached on x5532	As you enter text, the text wraps and continues on the line below. If the text exceeds the space available, you can reach additional text using the up and down arrows
Department (ListBox)	Select **Marketing**	The selected item appears highlighted
Process (Button)	Click the button	Nothing happens, since code will be added in the next project
Close (Button)	Click the button	Nothing happens, since code will be added in the next project

SUMMARY AND EXERCISES

SUMMARY

- A TextBox control displays multiple lines of text, and also provides a scroll bar if desired, when the Multi-line property is set to True.

- A Button control supports background and icon images in Visual Basic .NET.

- The HelpDeskTracker form demonstrated that by utilizing common controls we can reduce coding and streamline the data entry process for users of an application.

- The CheckBox control has three possible states: Checked, Unchecked, and Indeterminate.

- The Label control can be used to display read-only information and usually correlates to a TextBox.

- The DateTimePicker control expands to display a large calendar when clicked; it contracts after a date has been selected to maximize screen space.

- The MonthCalendar control enables users to select a range of dates rather than just a single date and does not contract like the DateTimePicker control.

- The ComboBox control, when clicked, expands to display valid choices; after a choice has been made, it contracts again.

- The CheckedListBox control is useful when more than one selection is permitted.

- The ListBox control is typically used to make a single selection and is limited to available choices. It doesnot include the ability to add items outside the list.

- The RadioButton and GroupBox controls are complementary. Users can select only one radio button when multiple radio buttons are contained in a group box.

KEY TERMS & SKILLS

KEY TERMS

AcceptsTab (p. 6-9)

Background Image
(p. 6-15)

Button control
(p. 6-7)

CharacterCasing
(p. 6-11)

CheckBox control
(p. 6-21)

CheckedListBox control
(p. 6-29)

ComboBox control
(p. 6-27)

common controls
(p. 6-1)

DateTimePicker control
(p. 6-24)

GroupBox control
(p. 6-30)

Icon Image (p. 6-16)

Label control (p. 6-23)

ListBox control
(p. 6-31)

MaxLength (p. 6-28)

MonthCalendar control
(p. 6-25)

Multi-line (p. 6-9)

PasswordChar (p. 6-9)

Pointer control
(p. 6-29)

RadioButton control
(p. 6-30)

ReadOnly (p. 6-9)

standard naming
conventions (p. 6-2)

Switchboard (p. 6-4)

TextAlign (p. 6-9)

TextBox control
(p. 6-8)

SKILLS

Add Button controls to the form
(p. 6-16)

Add code to the controls (p. 6-13)

Add code to the Standard Style button
(p. 6-18)

Add the ButtonDemo form
(p. 6-16)

Add the Process and Close buttons
(p. 6-33)

Add the TextBox control for the
request number (p. 6-24)

Add the TextboxDemo form (p. 6-10)

Create a link from the Switchboard
form to the HelpDeskTracker form
(p. 6-34)

Create the Fundamentals project
(p. 6-5)

Create the HelpDeskTracker form
(p. 6-20)

Link and test the ButtonDemo form
(p. 6-19)

Test the HelpDeskTracker form
(p. 6-34)

Test the TextboxDemo form (p. 6-14)

Use the CheckBox control (p. 6-22)

Use the CheckedListBox control
(p. 6-29)

Use the ComboBox control (p. 6-29)

Use the DateTimePicker control
(p. 6-25)

Use the GroupBox and RadioButton
controls (p. 6-31)

Use the Label control (p. 6-23)

Use the ListBox control (p. 6-32)

Use the MonthCalendar control
(p. 6-27)

Use the Multi-line TextBox control
(p. 6-30)

STUDY QUESTIONS

MULTIPLE CHOICE

1. Which control is used to select a single date?
   a. TextBox
   b. MonthCalendar
   c. DateTimePicker
   d. Label

2. Which control permits only a single selection from a group of similar controls?
   a. RadioButton
   b. RadioButton within a GroupBox
   c. CheckBox
   d. CheckedListBox

3. Which control enables a user to select only one choice from a list of many valid choices within a single control?
   a. both b and c
   b. ComboBox
   c. ListBox
   d. CheckedListBox

4. The Multi-line property is generally associated with which type of control?
   a. ListBox
   b. TextBox
   c. ComboBox
   d. CheckedListBox

5. What three-letter standard naming convention prefix would you use to name a checkbox named Control?
   a. cmd
   b. cls
   c. cbo
   d. chk

6. Which of the following is NOT a valid state for the Checkbox control?
   a. Checked
   b. Indeterminate
   c. Cleared
   d. Unchecked

7. What control must you select to reset to be able to click and select another control rather than draw a control on a form?
   a. MousePointer
   b. Pointer
   c. GroupBox
   d. Button

8. When using the Button control, what property would you set to place characters or words on the button?
   a. Name
   b. Text
   c. Caption
   d. Enabled

9. The ListBox is unique in that it has a property that enables the user to see many choices without scrolling. What property displays choices horizontally as well as vertically?
   a. Items
   b. Multi-Line
   c. ListIndex
   d. MultiColumn

10. If you need to display a message that contains the word value rather than a numeric value for the item selected by the user in a ListBox control, which property would you set?
   a. Text
   b. SelectedItem
   c. SelectedIndex
   d. SelectedItems

SHORT ANSWER

1. Which control is most commonly used for data entry when the user needs to be able to type freely?
2. Why might you need a MonthCalendar control rather than a DateTimePicker control?
3. What TextBox control property would you set to True if the user did not have sufficient privileges to change information?
4. The State field on a contact address data entry form should not accept more than two characters. What property would you change to limit the user to type only two characters?
5. When an application is started, the focus where the cursor appears is determined by what property, and what value would be found in the first field that has the focus?
6. What three-letter word is used behind a Close button or Exit menu item that stops an application?
7. If we do not want to display the characters typed into a TextBox control for security reasons, what property would we change?
8. What property would help ensure that information collected in a text box is consistently formatted in upper case?
9. In a multi-line TextBox control, what property must we change from the default setting if we want to press [Tab] and see the cursor move within the control rather than from one control to the next control in the tab order sequence?
10. If we want to display a small image within an button but not fill the entire button, which property would the image be loaded into?

FILL IN THE BLANK

1. One of the most important benefits of using common controls provided with Visual Basic .NET is to _____ _____ time.
2. A _____ screen sometimes contains only a few buttons that each launch another form. This is done to simplify the user interface.
3. Common controls are the _____ blocks of our applications.
4. To add a control to a form, you may click to draw a control, or you can simply _____ on the control within the Toolbox. This will add it to the currently active form. Once the control is added, its properties can be changed and the control can be aligned and resized.
5. The _____ property of a TextBox control is changed to True when more than one line of text needs to be collected and displayed.
6. The _____ property of a TextBox control ensures that the number of characters that can be typed into the control does not exceed a predefined limit.
7. _____ _____ _____ is a naming convention commonly used for naming controls and variables; it provides a three-character prefix to identify the type of control or data type for a variable.

8. The _____ property of the CheckBox control positions the box and text. There are many possible values, such as MiddleRight and MiddleLeft.

9. The Label control is often used for captions and also when it is necessary to provide a _____ view of the data.

10. The _____ control enables the user to select only a single date rather than a range of dates.

FOR DISCUSSION

1. How can standard naming conventions clarify code for a maintenance programmer?

2. Why would you use a DateTimePicker control rather than a TextBox control?

3. When would you use a GroupBox control?

4. How can the GroupBox control be used to organize controls, and why is this a benefit?

5. Why were the various controls provided on the HelpDeskTracker form used rather than just providing several TextBox controls?

PROJECT 7

Introducing Programming Fundamentals with Visual Basic .NET

This project will focus on the fundamentals of programming by creating several small projects that evolve as new controls are discovered. During this process, we will explore variables to define what they are, learn how variables are commonly used, and discover where they can be seen. Sometimes programs must repeat or perform actions more than once. We will build simple Do loops and For Next loops that check the value and either loop again or move on to another block of code. We will also create functions and procedures from scratch.

Tip

The *Fundamentals.sln* file can be found at
\\vb.net_brief\vb.net_datafiles\07\Students\FundamentalsOfVBNET\.

The *PayTransactionSystem.sln* file can be found at
\\vb.net_brief\vb.net_datafiles\07\Students\HR\PayTransactionSystem.

e-selections) **Running Case**

It seems that your recent demonstration using common controls provided with Visual Basic .NET made it appear that it was too easy to create simple applications. Although common controls such as the MonthCalendar provide a lot with little or no programming, there are times when programming is necessary. Developers who are accustomed to writing a lot of code in the e-Selections division of Selections, Inc. want to know more about basic programming techniques. It's time to learn some of the tricks Visual Basic .NET provides for creating applications that include writing code.

OBJECTIVES

After completing this project, you will be able to:

- Use ToolTips with controls
- Integrate variables into the program
- Create procedures and functions
- Write control statements
- Add finishing touches
- Link code to the PayTransactionSystem Toolbox

Introducing Programming Fundamentals with Visual Basic .NET

The Challenge

Mr. Traylor would like to present a demonstration to the lead programmers during their meeting next week. To prepare for the meeting you will have to learn how to declare variables, assign values to them, and loop through code. Although these are very important fundamentals to programming and they are needed for the Payroll Transaction System project, we will initially continue to use the Fundamentals project. Once we have a good grasp of the programming terminology and have actually written code that populates the common controls used in the last project, we will be ready to start up the Payroll Transaction System and add code.

The Solution

Visual Basic .NET has an interesting and unique capability to attach highlighted code to the Toolbox. This is a very convenient way to grab and reuse code that you have written and tested. In addition to enhancing the Fundamentals project, we will collect some of the code we learn and place it on a new tab of the Toolbox called CodeSnippets. This project will focus on populating the controls used in the last project, working with variables, and looping within code. Once you have completed this project, you will be familiar with the fundamentals of writing code. In the next project, we will explore error handling in preparation for connecting our forms to a database.

Figure 7-1

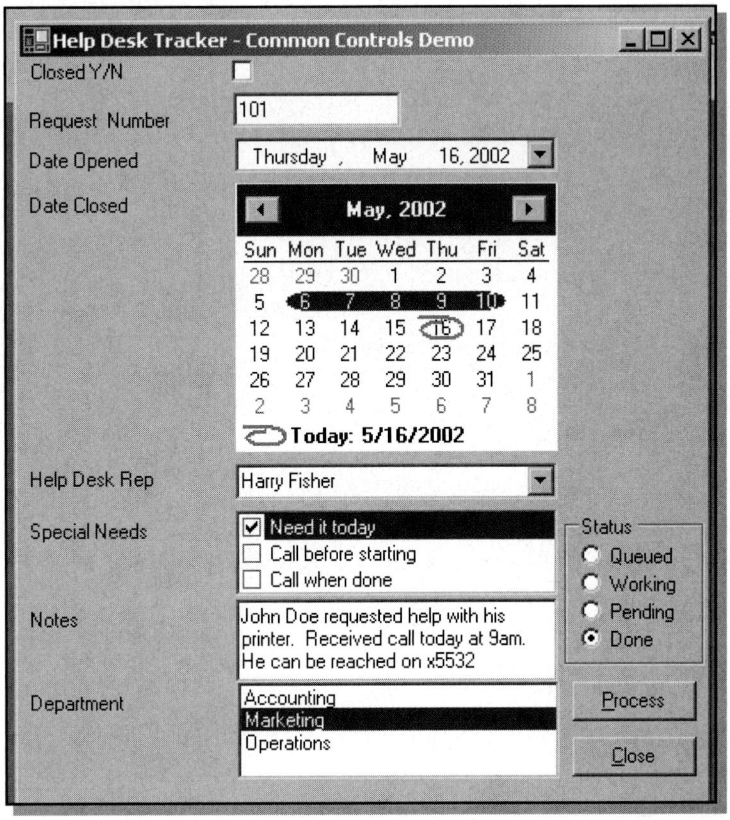

Using ToolTips with Controls

The *ToolTip* feature provides a small floating window that displays a helpful message when the mouse pointer *hovers* over a control. We will open the Fundamentals project and then assign ToolTips to each control. The commonly used ToolTip properties are given in Table 7-1.

Table 7-1	ToolTip Properties
Property	**Description**
Active	Indicates whether the ToolTip is active. You may have a menu item that disables all ToolTips; this property enables advanced users to turn ToolTips off.
AutomaticDelay	Indicates the time (in milliseconds) that passes before the ToolTip appears.
AutoPopDelay	Indicates the time (in milliseconds) that the ToolTip remains visible when the cursor is stationary in the ToolTip region. The default value is 10 times the AutomaticDelay property value.
GetToolTip()	Returns the ToolTip text assigned to a specific control.
InitialDelay	Indicates the time (in milliseconds) that the cursor must remain stationary in the ToolTip region before the ToolTip text is displayed. The default value is equal to that of the AutomaticDelay property.
SetToolTip()	Associates a ToolTip with a specific control.

Task 1:

To Use ToolTips with Controls

1 Navigate to the *Fundamentals.sln* file, open the project, and then double-click *HelpDesk Tracker.vb* within the Solution Explorer to display the form.

2 Choose **View** | **Toolbox** and double-click the ToolTip control to add it to the form; then type tipHelpDeskTracker for the ToolTip's Name property.

3 Click to select the CheckBox control chkClosed and then type Please check this box when the Help Desk Request has been closed. This will remove this particular request item from the Open Requests Report. in the ToolTips On tipHelpDeskTracker property.

4 Choose **File** | **Save All**.

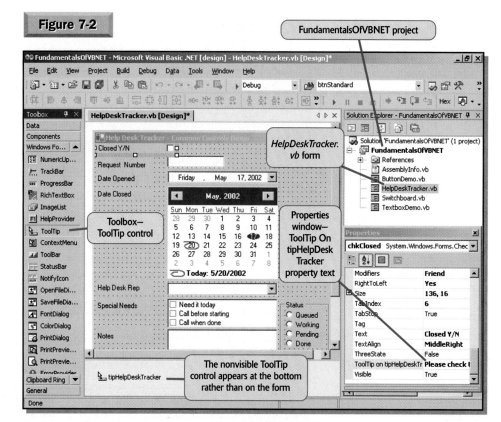

Figure 7-2

Tip
Only one ToolTip control will be needed for each form. To associate the new tip with a control, select the control that should activate the ToolTip and set the ToolTip On property. Once the control is added, it will appear at the bottom of the IDE below the form. This indicates that it is a nonvisible type of control. Nonvisible components added to the Windows Forms Designer are placed on the tray below it in the development environment so that they are easily accessible without cluttering the visual design space.

5 Choose **Debug | Start** and then click the Help Desk Tracker button on the Switchboard form.

6 Hover the mouse over the Closed Y/N (chkClosed) check box entry field and verify that the ToolTip appears.

7 Choose **Debug | Stop Debugging**.

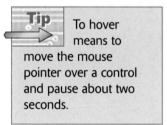

Tip To hover means to move the mouse pointer over a control and pause about two seconds.

Figure 7-3

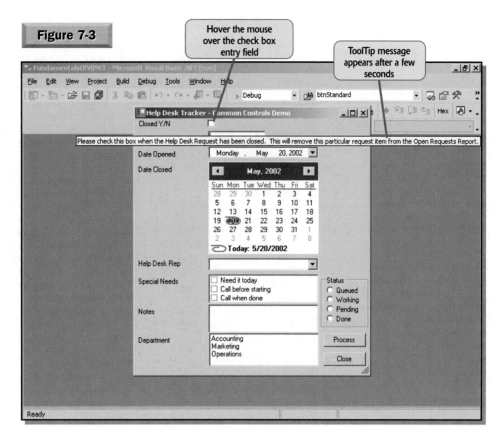

Integrating Variables into the Program

Programming in Visual Basic .NET can be very easy as long as you do not overprogram. Beginners always want to begin coding. It is important to understand what your project is capable of with no additional code from you. You might want to consider the expression "less is best." In this section we will review the standard naming conventions for variables, how to declare variables and constants while understanding variable scope.

Standard Naming Conventions

Establishing *standard naming conventions* for controls helps identify the type of control being used and the associated properties available. As variables are created in code, we use standard naming convention prefixes (Table 7-2) to establish meaningful variable names.

Table 7-2 Standard Naming Prefixes for Variables and Code Structures		
Variables and Code Structures	**Sample Name**	**Prefix**
Byte	bNumber	b
Character string	strString	str
Constant	cName	c
Currency	curCurrency	cur
Date/time	dtDate	dt
Decimal	decDecimal	dec
Double	dNumber	d
Flag long	flFlag	fl
Flag short	fsFlag	fs
Integer	iNumber	i
Return code	rcReturnvalue	rc
Single	sNumber	s

Declaring Variables

Variables and *assignments* are at the core of every programming language. Variables enable you to store information for later use, and assignment is how you put information into variables.

A variable is a bucket or container. It is a place to hold information until you need it. You will use variables throughout your programs to hold temporary values during calculations, to store user input, and to prepare information that will be displayed to users.

Variable names in Visual Basic .NET can be up to 255 characters long and usually begin with a letter. After the initial letter, any combination of letters, numbers, and underscores is allowed. All characters in a variable name are significant, but as with most things in Visual Basic .NET, case is irrelevant. FirstName is the same as Firstname. Assignments are done with an equal (=) sign. For example, ZipCode = "19709."

In addition, you cannot use words reserved by VB.NET for variable names unless you surround them with brackets. For example, Friend is not acceptable as a variable name, but [Friend] would be fine, although you probably would choose a more unique name. Visual Basic .NET underlines the keyword and presents an error message with a ToolTip if you try to use a *reserved word* as a variable name. Table 7-3 presents a partial listing of the Visual Basic .NET language keywords.

Table 7-3   Visual Basic .NET Language Keywords

Alias	DirectCast	Friend	MustOverride	On	Protected	To
Ansi	Each	Handles	MyBase	Option	Public	True
As	Else	In	MyClass	Optional	ReadOnly	TypeOf
Assembly	Elself	Is	New	Overloads	Resume	Unicode
Auto	End	Lib	Next	Overridable	Shadows	Until
ByRef	Error	Loop	Nothing	Overrides	Shared	When
ByVal	Explicit	Me	NotInheritable	ParamArray	Static	While
Case	False	Module	NotOverridable	Preserve	Step	WithEvents
Default	For	MustInherit	Off		Private	Then	WriteOnly

Task 2:

To Declare a Variable

1 Double-click the *HelpDeskTracker.vb* form in the Solution Explorer and then double-click the Process button to view code for the btnProcess Button control.

2 Type Dim requestInfo As String in the click event to declare a local-level, string-type variable. Table 7-4 lists variable conversion functions, intrinsic data types, and data verification functions.

3 Type the code provided in Figure 7-4.

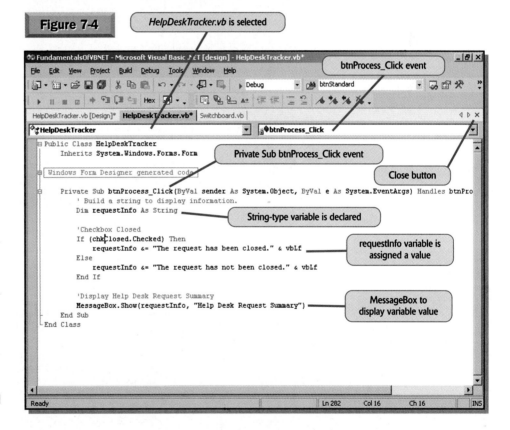

Figure 7-4

HelpDeskTracker.vb is selected

Tip   The entry process begins by starting the application, clicking the Help Desk Tracker button on the Switchboard, and then filling in the blanks. The last step is to click the Process button and view the message that appears. When the Process button is clicked, a local string-type variable named requestInfo is declared and a test is performed that determines whether the chkClosed check box is checked. Based on the condition of either checked or not checked, the variable is assigned a value. The command "& vblf" adds a line feed to the message ("vbcrlf" is also a valid command to add a line feed). The last step displays a message using the requestInfo variable and a MessageBox object with a title of Help Desk Request Summary.

Function or Data Type	Examples
Table 7-4	**Variable Conversion Functions, Intrinsic Data Types, and Verifying Data Type Functions**
Variable conversion functions	CBool, CByte, CChar, CDate, CDbl, CDec, CInt, CLng, CObj, CShort, CSng, CStr, Fix, Int
	These functions are compiled inline, which means that the conversion code is part of the code that evaluates the expression. Execution is faster because there is no call to a procedure to accomplish the conversion. Each function coerces an expression to a specific data type. CBool(expression) CByte(expression) CChar(expression) CDate(expression) CDbl(expression) CDec(expression) CInt(expression) CLng(expression) CObj(expression) CShort(expression) CSng(expression) CStr(expression)
Intrinsic data types	Boolean, Byte, Char, Date, Decimal, Double, Integer, Long, Object(default), Short, Single, String
	Boolean variables are stored as 16-bit (2-byte) numbers, but they can only be True or False. Use the keywords *True* and *False* to assign one of the two states to Boolean variables. When numeric data types are converted to Boolean values, 0 becomes False and all other values become True. When Boolean values are converted to numeric types, False becomes 0 and True becomes -1.
	Integer variables are stored as signed 32-bit (4-byte) integers ranging in value from -2,147,483,648 through 2,147,483,647.
	String variables are stored as sequences of unsigned 16-bit (2-byte) numbers ranging in value from 0 through 65535. Each number represents a single Unicode character. A string can contain up to approximately two billion (2×10^{31}) Unicode characters.
	The first 128 code points (0–127) of Unicode correspond to the letters and symbols on a standard U.S. keyboard. These first 128 code points are the same as those defined by the ASCII character set. The second 128 code points (128–255) represent special characters, such as Latin-based alphabet letters, accents, currency symbols, and fractions. The remaining code points are used for a wide variety of symbols, including worldwide textual characters, diacritics, and mathematical and technical symbols. Appending the identifier type character $ to any identifier forces it to the String data type.

(Continued)

Function or Data Type	Examples
Table 7-4	**Variable Conversion Functions, Intrinsic Data Types, and Verifying Data Type Functions** *(continued)*
	Date Data Type See also Data Type Summary | DateTime Structure | Double Data Type | Type Conversion Functions | Conversion Summary | Efficient Use of Data Types Date variables are stored as IEEE 64-bit (8-byte) integers that represent dates ranging from January 1 of the year 1 through December 31 of the year 9999, and times from 0:00:00 (midnight) through 11:59:59 P.M. Date values must be enclosed within number signs (#) and be in the format m/d/yyyy, for example, #5/31/1993#. If you convert a Date value to the String type, the date is rendered according to the short date format recognized by your computer, and the time is rendered according to the time format (either 12-hour or 24-hour) in effect on your computer.
Data verification functions	IsArray, IsDate, IsDbNull, IsError, IsNothing, IsNumeric, IsReference
	IsDate Function See also IsArray Function | IsDBNull Function | IsError Function | IsNothing Function | IsNumeric Function | IsReference Function | Object Data Type | Date Data Type | TypeName Function Returns a Boolean value indicating whether an expression can be converted to a date
	IsNumeric Function See also IsArray Function | IsDate Function | IsDBNull Function | IsError Function | IsNothing Function | IsReference Function | Object Data Type | TypeName Function Returns a Boolean value indicating whether an expression can be evaluated as a number

Tip It is a good habit to close code and designer windows if they are not needed at the moment. This reduces the potential for confusion that having too many screens displayed at once might cause.

4 Choose **File | Save All**.

5 Test the application. Check the chkClosed check box to make it display a check mark, and then click the Process button and verify that a message appears like the example below. If you clear the check box and click the Process button, a different message should appear.

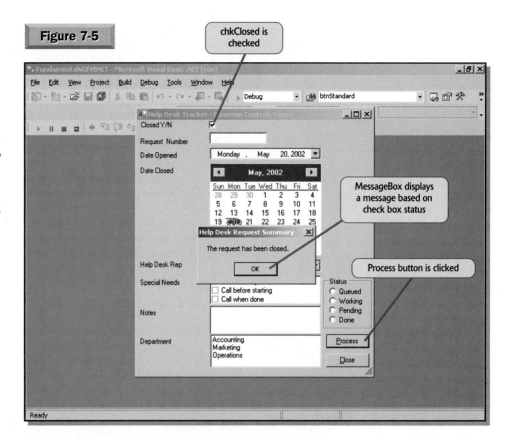

Figure 7-5

chkClosed is checked

MessageBox displays a message based on check box status

Process button is clicked

Tip

The most important consideration in naming a variable is that the name should fully and accurately describe the entity the variable represents. An effective technique for creating a good name is to state in words what the variable represents. It is easy to remember because the name is similar to the concept.

A variable that contains the current interest rate is better if named Rate or interestRate rather than r or x. A good mnemonic name generally speaks to the problem rather than the solution. A good name tends to express the *what* more than the *how*.

Using Constants

Some variables do not change value during the execution of a program. These are *constants* that appear many times in your code. If the program performs mathematical computations with the value of pi (3.14159...), this value is best represented with a constant named pi.

Constants are declared in the same way as variables, and the rules for their names are also the same: 255 characters, first character a letter, and then any combination of letters, underscores, and numerals. A named constant is like a variable except that you can't change the constant's value once you've assigned it, since it is a read-only type of variable. It is recommended that constants be named using capital letters and underscores.

For example,

Const pi = 3.14159

Area = 2*pi*Radius

Rather than

Area = 2*3.14159*Radius

Tip

Named constants enable you to refer to fixed quantities such as the maximum number of tickets by a name rather than a number. For example, use MAXIMUM_TICKETS rather than 1000. A constant's scope is the same as that of a variable declared in the same location. To create a constant that exists within the scope of a particular procedure, declare it inside that procedure. To create a constant that is available throughout an application, declare it using the Public keyword in the Declarations section of the class.

As we proceed through the remaining tasks in this project, we will start adding buttons to the Switchboard form for each coding example. Finally, sample code from some of these buttons will be copied into the Visual Basic .NET Toolbox. Once code is stored within the Toolbox, it is available to other Visual Basic .NET projects. We will learn more about using common code and the Toolbox later in this project.

Task 3:
To Use Constants

1 Double-click the *Switchboard.vb* form and type **656, 328** for the Size property.

2 Click the Close **X** button and then choose **Edit | Copy** and then **Edit | Paste** to add a new button. Position the new button to the right of the top button.

3 Choose **Edit | Paste** 16 more times to add 16 more buttons and arrange the buttons into three columns.

4 Complete the control properties as shown in Table 7-5.

Figure 7-6

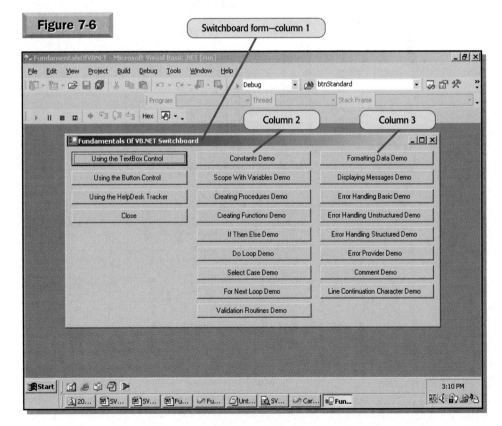

Table 7-5   Button Control Properties

Control Name	Size	Location	Text
btnTextBoxControl	200, 24	8, 8	Using the TextBox Control
btnButtonControl	200, 24	8, 40	Using the Button Control
btnHelpDeskTracker	200, 24	8, 72	Using the Help Desk Tracker
btnClose	200, 24	8, 104	Close
btnConstantsDemo	200, 24	224, 8	Constants Demo
btnScopeWithVariablesDemo	200, 24	224, 40	Scope With Variables Demo
btnCreatingProceduresDemo	200, 24	224, 72	Creating Procedures Demo
btnCreatingFunctionsDemo	200, 24	224, 104	Creating Functions Demo
btnIfThenElseDemo	200, 24	224, 136	If Then Else Demo
btnDoLoopDemo	200, 24	224, 168	Do Loop Demo
btnSelectCaseDemo	200, 24	224, 200	Select Case Demo
btnForNextLoopDemo	200, 24	224, 232	For Next Loop Demo
btnValidationRoutinesDemo	200, 24	224, 264	Validation Routines Demo
btnFormattingDataDemo	200, 24	440, 8	Formatting Data Demo
btnDisplayingMessagesDemo	200, 24	440, 40	Displaying Messages Demo
btnErrorHandlingBasicDemo	200, 24	440, 72	Error Handling Basic Demo
btnErrorHandlingUnstructuredDemo	200, 24	440, 104	Error Handling Unstructured Demo
btnErrorHandlingStructuredDemo	200, 24	440, 136	Error Handling Structured Demo
btnErrorProviderDemo	200, 24	440, 168	Error Provider Demo
btnCommentsDemo	200, 24	440, 200	Comment Demo
btnLineContinuationCharacterDemo	200, 24	440, 232	Line Continuation Character Demo

5 Double-click the Constants Demo button to view code.

6 Type the code provided in Figure 7-7.

7 Choose **File | Save All**.

Figure 7-7

btnConstantsDemo_Click event—Constants Demo button

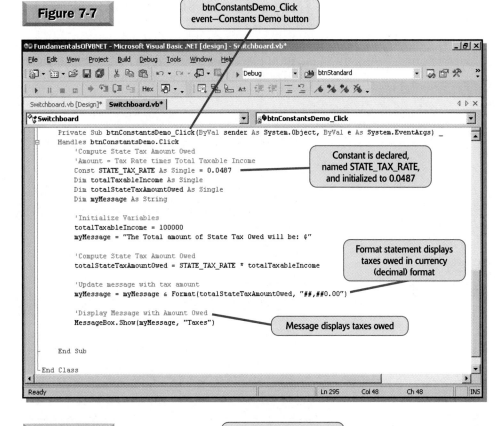

```
Private Sub btnConstantsDemo_Click(ByVal sender As System.Object, ByVal e As System.EventArgs) _
Handles btnConstantsDemo.Click
    'Compute State Tax Amount Owed
    'Amount = Tax Rate times Total Taxable Income
    Const STATE_TAX_RATE As Single = 0.0487
    Dim totalTaxableIncome As Single
    Dim totalStateTaxAmountOwed As Single
    Dim myMessage As String

    'Initialize Variables
    totalTaxableIncome = 100000
    myMessage = "The Total amount of State Tax Owed will be: $"

    'Compute State Tax Amount Owed
    totalStateTaxAmountOwed = STATE_TAX_RATE * totalTaxableIncome

    'Update message with tax amount
    myMessage = myMessage & Format(totalStateTaxAmountOwed, "##,##0.00")

    'Display Message with Amount Owed
    MessageBox.Show(myMessage, "Taxes")

End Sub
End Class
```

Constant is declared, named STATE_TAX_RATE, and initialized to 0.0487

Format statement displays taxes owed in currency (decimal) format

Message displays taxes owed

8 Choose **Debug | Start**, click the Constants Demo button, and then verify that the message appears as "The Total amount of State Tax owed will be: $4,870.00."

Figure 7-8

Constants Demo button on Switchboard form

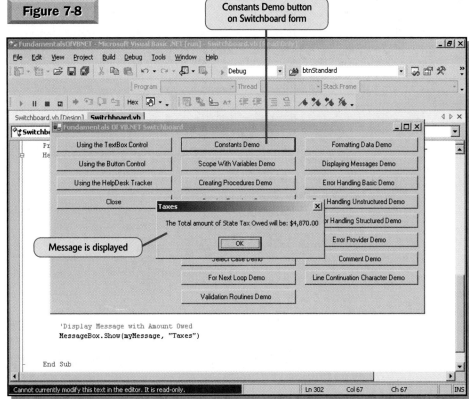

Using the TextBox Control	Constants Demo	Formatting Data Demo
Using the Button Control	Scope With Variables Demo	Displaying Messages Demo
Using the HelpDesk Tracker	Creating Procedures Demo	Error Handling Basic Demo
Close		Handling Unstructured Demo

Taxes

The Total amount of State Tax Owed will be: $4,870.00

OK

Message is displayed

Using Scope with Variables

In addition to its type, a variable also has scope. The scope of a variable represents the section of the application that can see and manipulate it. The next four tasks will focus on setting local, module-level, and public variables.

Setting Local Variables

If a variable is declared within a procedure, it is considered a *local variable* and only the code in the specific procedure has access to that variable. In the following example, all even numbers from 1 to 100 are added together and then a message displays the total amount.

Task 4:

To Set a Local Variable

 Double-click the Scope With Variables Demo button to view code.

 Type the code provided in Figure 7-9.

3 Choose **File | Save All**.

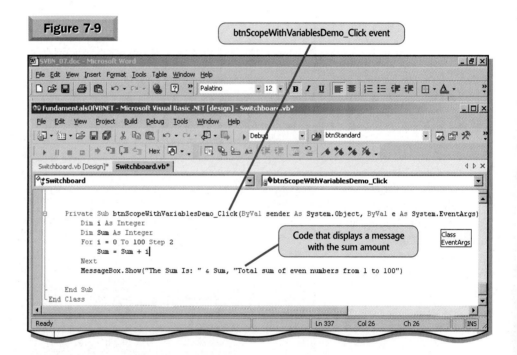

Figure 7-9

btnScopeWithVariablesDemo_Click event

```
Private Sub btnScopeWithVariablesDemo_Click(ByVal sender As System.Object, ByVal e As System.EventArgs)
    Dim i As Integer
    Dim Sum As Integer
    For i = 0 To 100 Step 2
        Sum = Sum + i
    Next
    MessageBox.Show("The Sum Is: " & Sum, "Total sum of even numbers from 1 to 100")

End Sub
End Class
```

Code that displays a message with the sum amount

> **Tip**
>
> The variables Sum and i are local to the btnScopeWithVariablesDemo_ Click event procedure. If you attempt to set the value of the Sum variable from within another procedure, Visual Basic .NET creates another Sum variable and uses it. This will not affect the variable Sum in the btnScopeWithVariablesDemo_Click event procedure.

> **Tip**
>
> Local variables are sometimes referred to as procedural variables.

4 Choose **Debug | Start** and verify the message. The amount should be **2550**.

5 Choose **Debug | Stop Debugging**.

Figure 7-10

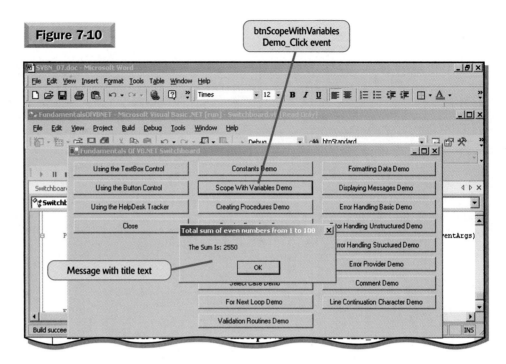

Setting Form and Class-level Variables

Within a form or Visual Basic .NET class we use the Private keyword to declare variables that are in scope for any function, procedure or sub procedure within the respective form or class. The Public keyword should never be used within a form or class.

Setting Module-Level Variables

There are times when you need to have a variable that is available to all procedures within the same project. These *module-level variables* can be accessed from within all procedures in any form, class, or module. A module will be added to the Fundamentals project to centralize code and variables that will be shared across the project. This reduces code redundancy, (copies of the same code in several places). Duplicate code should be avoided to reduce maintenance effort and improve the reliability, quality, and consistency of the code.

Tip

Within a module, if you declare a variable using the Public keyword, it becomes available to all procedures throughout the project. If you declare a variable using the Private keyword, it is only available to procedures within the module.

Task 5:
To Set a Form-Level Variable

1 Double-click the btn ScopeWithVariables Demo button to view code.

2 Select **Switchboard** from the left object drop-down list and then select **Declarations** from the right events drop-down list.

3 Type **Private CurrentDay as String**.

4 Modify the btnScope WithVariablesDemo_ Click event code as shown in Figure 7-11.

5 Choose **File | Save All**.

Figure 7-11

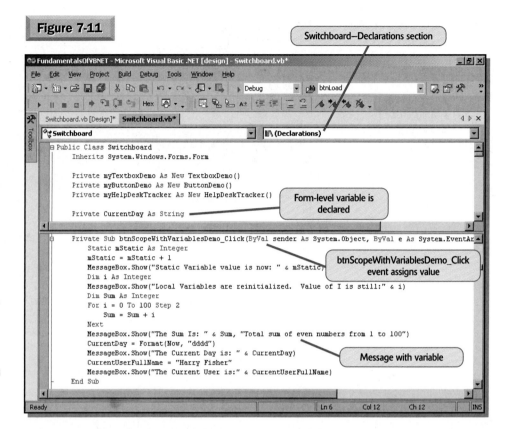

The Format statement found in the btnScopeWithVariablesDemo_Click event reads the current date and time using the system function Now, and then displays the day of the week using the "dddd" formatting. Other useful functions are given in Table 7-6.

Table 7-6	Useful Functions in btnScopeWithVariablesDemo_Click
Function	**Description**
IsArray	Returns True if the parameter is an array
IsDate	Returns True if the parameter is recognizable as a date
IsNumeric	Returns True if the parameter is recognizable as a number
IsObject	Returns True if the parameter is some object type
TypeName	Returns the name of the data type of the parameter—for example, TypeName(sFirstName) would return "String"
Now	Returns the current date and time
Today	Returns the current date, with the time set to 0:00:00 a.m. (midnight)

6 Choose **Debug | Start** and verify that two messages appear in sequence: **2550** and the day of the week.

7 Choose **Debug | Stop Debugging**.

Figure 7-12

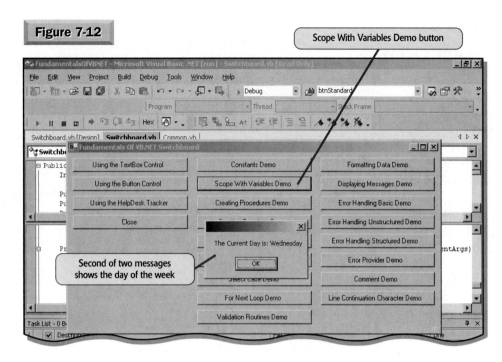

More on Public Variables

In situations where a variable must be accessible to the entire application, the variable must be declared as public. *Public variables* have a global scope (they are visible from any part of the application). To declare a public variable, use the Public statement in place of the Dim or Private statement.

 Tip Caution: Public variables may not be declared inside procedures. They must be declared as form variables or in a module.

 Tip In professional practice, private variables should be declared in a form or class while public variables should only be declared in modules. Although it is possible to declare public variables within a form or class, it is considered bad programming practice.

Task 6:
To Set Public Variables in a Module

1 Choose **Project | Add Module**, name it *Common.vb*, and then click the Open button.

2 Type Public Current UserFullName as String.

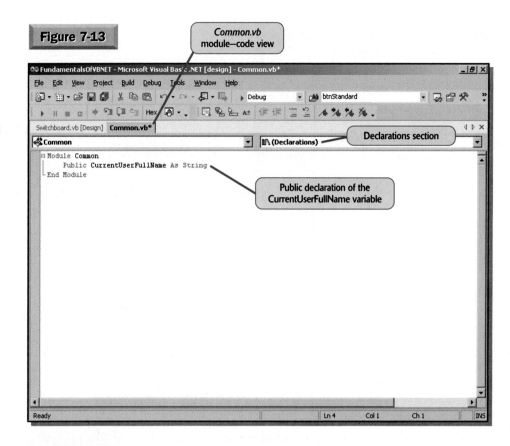

Figure 7-13

Common.vb module—code view

Declarations section

Public declaration of the CurrentUserFullName variable

3 Choose **View | Solution Explorer** and then double-click the Switchboard form.

4 Modify the btnScope WithVariablesDemo_ Click event code as shown in Figure 7-14.

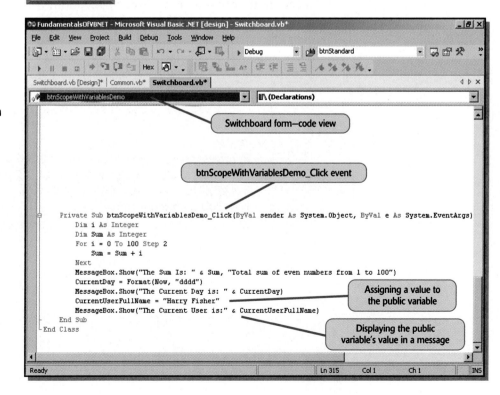

Figure 7-14

Switchboard form—code view

btnScopeWithVariablesDemo_Click event

Assigning a value to the public variable

Displaying the public variable's value in a message

5 Choose **File | Save All**, choose **Debug | Start**, and verify that the message appears as shown in Figure 7-15.

6 Choose **Debug | Stop Debugging**.

Figure 7-15

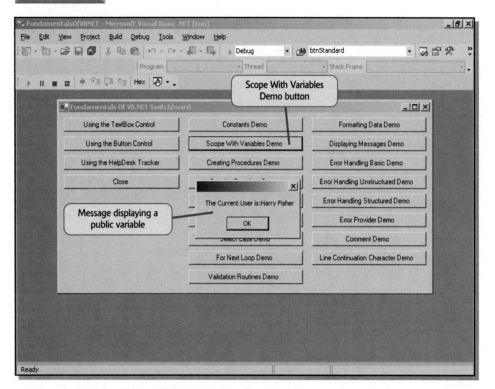

Tip Minimize scope. The more information you can hide, the less you have to keep in mind at one time. The less you have to keep in mind, the smaller the chance that you will make an error because you forgot one of the details you needed to remember. Do not assign a value to a variable until just before the value is used. The more you can do to clarify where a variable receives its value, the better. Global variables are accessible anywhere in a program. The term *global* is also sometimes used sloppily to refer to variables with a broader scope than local variables. Most programmers have concluded that using global variables is riskier than using local variables.

Setting the Lifetime of a Variable

In addition to type and scope, variables have a lifetime. This is the period during which they retain their value. Variables declared as public exist for the lifetime of the application. Local variables, declared within procedures with the Dim or Private statement, exist for as long as the procedures in which they were declared. When the procedure finishes, the local variables cease to exist, and the allocated memory is returned to the system.

In Task 4, the local variables Sum and i were declared in the click event. Once the code in this click event processes the End Sub statement, the variables Sum and i will no longer be defined. In Task 5, if we referenced the module level variable named CurrentDay from a different form, it would also be undefined since it was declared as private rather than public. In addition, if the Switchboard form were closed, the module-level variable would become undefined. In Task 6, the public variable will retain its value as long as the application is running.

Tip It is helpful to prefix variables by their scope. e.g. a local variable for name might be declared as Private lName as String. A public variable might be defined as Public pName as String.

Using Static Variables

Static variables retain their values between procedure calls. The advantage of using static variables is that they help minimize the total number of variables in the application. All you need is the running average, and the RunningAverage() function provides the value. The variables are not visible to any other procedure, so there is no risk that other procedures will change their values. We will explore the RunningAverage function in the next task.

Task 7:
To Use a Static Variable

1 Double-click the Scope With Variables Demo button to view code.

2 Modify the btnScope WithVariablesDemo_ Click event code as shown in Figure 7-16.

Declaration of static variable inside a procedure

Local variable is reinitialized each time the procedure runs

Figure 7-16

Switchboard.vb form

btnScopeWithVariablesDemo_Click event

Static variable value is incremented retaining previous value

Message displays current value of the static variable

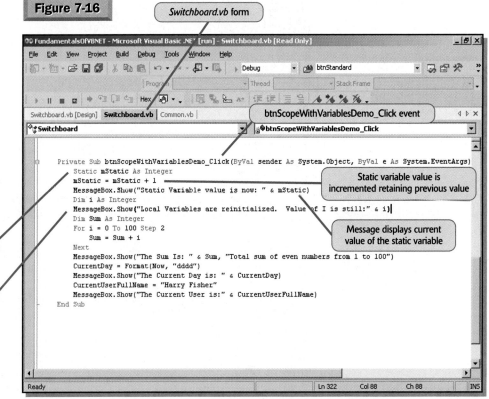

3 Choose **File | Save All**.

Figure 7-17

4 Choose **Debug | Start**, click the Scope With Variables Demo button, and then verify that the first message containing the static variable is initialized to 1.

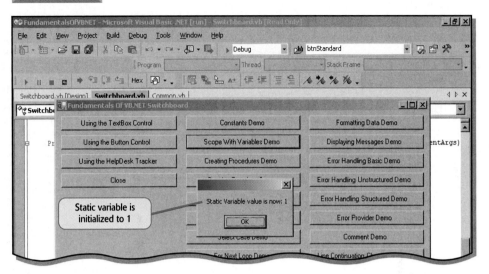

5 Click the OK button and then verify that the second message containing the local variable is reinitialized to 0. Click OK until all the messages have disappeared.

Figure 7-18

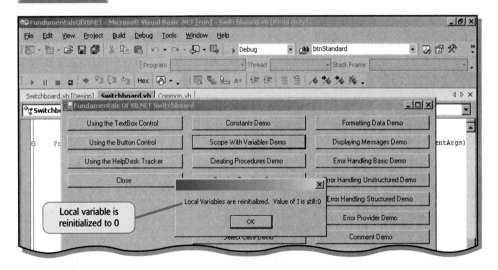

6 Click the Scope With Variables Demo button to repeat the variable testing and then verify that the first message containing the static variable has incremented from 1 to 2 as expected.

Figure 7-19

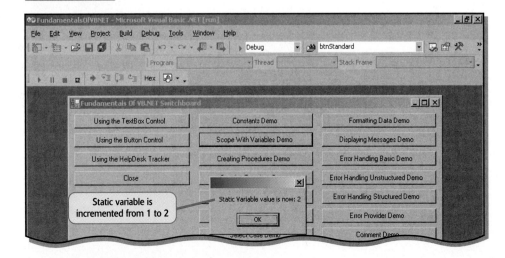

7 Click the OK button and then verify that the second message containing the local variable is reinitialized to 0 as expected.

8 Choose **Debug | Stop Debugging**.

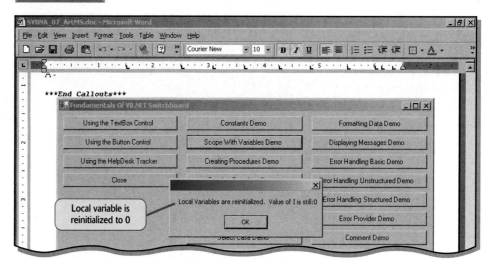

Figure 7-20

Creating Procedures and Functions

Although the built-in functions are useful, there will always be a time when you need to create your own routines. Two types of routines are used in Visual Basic .NET. A *procedure* performs a task, and is not required to return a value. However, a procedure can be programmed to return none, one or more arguments. A *function* performs a task and is required to return a single value. Examples of each type of routine will be provided in the next two tasks.

Creating Procedures

A procedure is a block of Visual Basic .NET code that performs some task but is not required to return a value to the routine that called it. To execute a procedure you can just place the name of the procedure into the code. It is also common to use the word *Call* followed by the procedure name to help differentiate the procedure from a variable or comment statement.

Tip You are not required to use the Call keyword when calling a procedure; however, if you use the Call statement to call any intrinsic, DLL, or user-defined function, the function's return value is discarded. It is good practice to use the call keyword when calling procedures because it helps make your code more readable.

Task 8:
To Create a Procedure

1 Double-click the *Common.vb* file in the Solution Explorer to view code.

2 Type **Public Sub DisplayCurrentTime** and then press [Enter].

3 Type the code provided in Figure 7-21.

> **Tip** To create a procedure in Visual Basic .NET you must use the Sub keyword. "Sub" is short for subroutine and represents a small modular set of instructions.

4 Choose **View | Solution Explorer** and then double-click the Creating Procedures Demo button to view code.

Figure 7-21

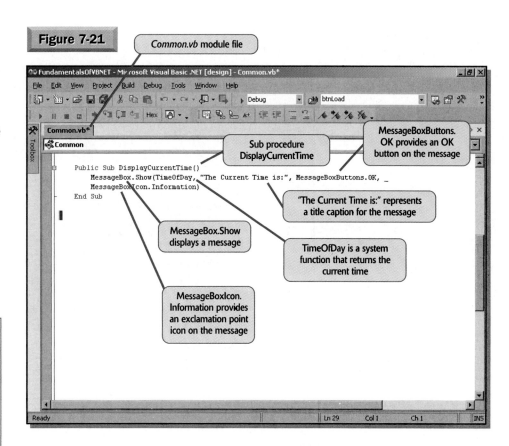

Common.vb module file

Sub procedure DisplayCurrentTime

MessageBoxButtons. OK provides an OK button on the message

"The Current Time is:" represents a title caption for the message

MessageBox.Show displays a message

TimeOfDay is a system function that returns the current time

MessageBoxIcon. Information provides an exclamation point icon on the message

Figure 7-22

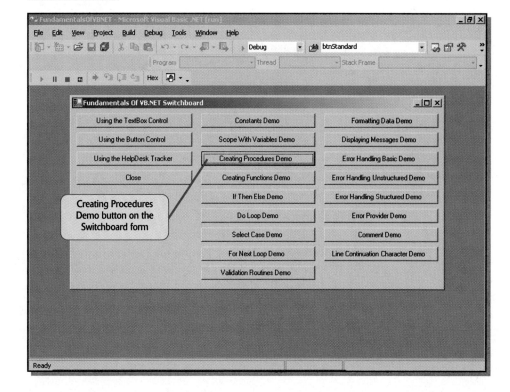

Creating Procedures Demo button on the Switchboard form

5   Type the code provided in Figure 7-23.

6   Choose **File | Save All**.

Figure 7-23

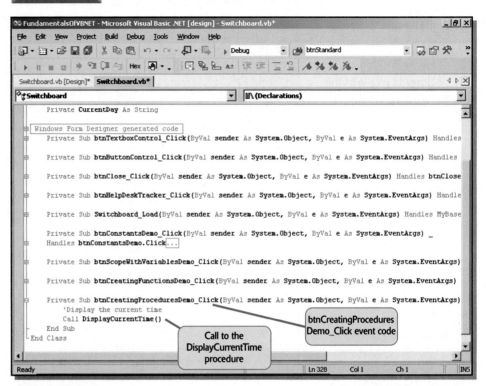

7   Choose **Debug | Start** and then click the Creating Procedures Demo button. Verify that the message appears with the current time.

8   Choose **Debug | Stop Debugging**.

Figure 7-24

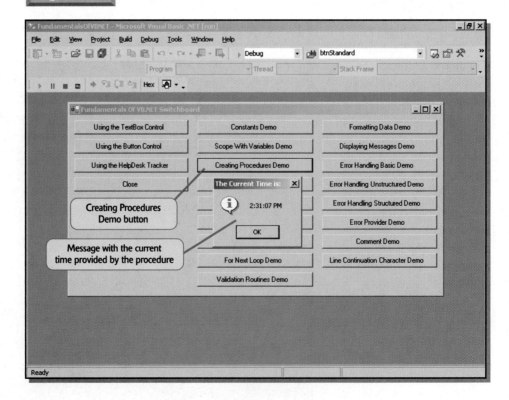

Tip

It is often helpful to create a breakpoint behind a button click event and walk through the code to ensure that the process is running as expected. To set a breakpoint in code, from the Code View window, click the left mouse button in the gray left margin next to the code where you want the system to wait. The line with the breakpoint appears with red highlighting. As the code runs, a yellow line appears on the line of code before it runs. Once the code is paused, press the [F8] key to step through the program one line at a time. Continue pressing the [F8] key as you move from the Switchboard form into the common module where the message is presented, and then see the Switchboard Code View window reappear. To remove the breakpoint, just click again in the gray left margin where the breakpoint currently is located and the red highlighting will disappear.

Figure 7-25

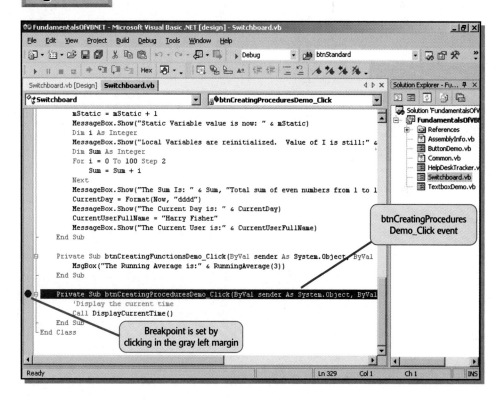

Creating Functions

The easiest way to start a function or a subroutine in the code window is to go someplace inside the module that is not already inside a sub or function and then start typing. The moment you press [Enter] after typing the header of the function or sub, the IDE editor adds the End statement of the correct type. In this example, we will create a function that returns the Running Average based on a number you type in. The function will be created in the *Common.vb* code module. A breakpoint will be used for testing once the code has been written.

Task 9:
To Create a Function

1 Choose **View |
Solution Explorer**,
double-click *Switchboard.vb*
to view code, and then
double-click the btnCreating
FunctionDemo button to
enter source code.

Tip
When creating
either a proce-
dure or a function, you
must type the function
declaration somewhere
above the End Class
statement at the
bottom of the Code
View window.

2 Type the code provided
in Figure 7-26.

Figure 7-26

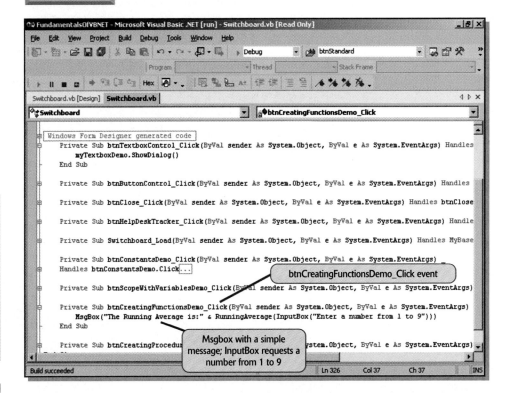

btnCreatingFunctionsDemo_Click event

Msgbox with a simple
message; InputBox requests a
number from 1 to 9

Tip
The Msgbox (*Message Box*) statement displays a message in a dialog
box, waits for the user to click a button, and then returns an integer indicating which button the user clicked. The *InputBox* statement displays a
prompt in a dialog box, waits for the user to input text or click a button,
and then returns a string containing the contents of the text box.

Tip
The code in Figure 7-26 is the logic that will invoke the function. The
actual steps to create a function are shown in Figure 7-27.

3 Click the *Common.vb* tab at the top of the Code View window or choose **View | Solutions Explorer** and double-click the *Common.vb* code module to view code.

4 Type the code provided in Figure 7-27.

5 Choose **File | Save All**.

Figure 7-27

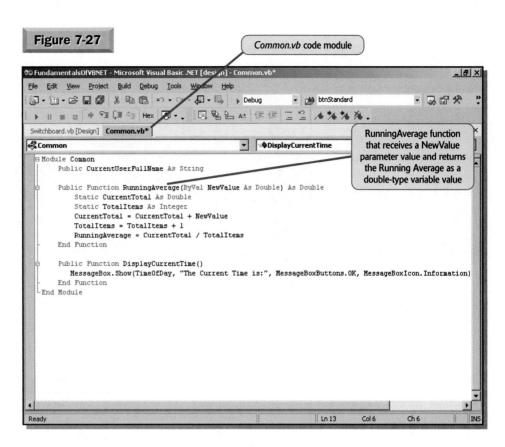

6 Choose **Debug | Start**, click the Create Functions Demo button, verify that a message prompt appears, type **2**, and then click the OK button.

Figure 7-28

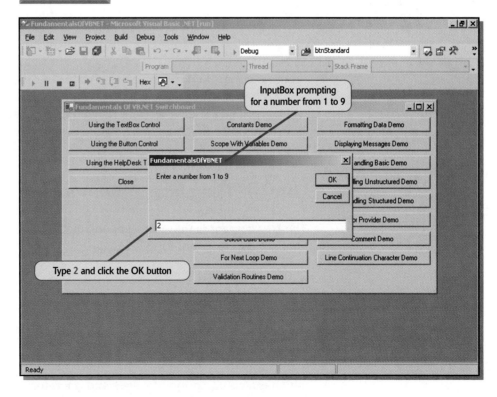

7 Verify that the Running Average is 2. Click the OK button to redisplay the Switchboard form.

8 Click the Create Functions Demo button again, type **4**, click OK, and verify that the Running Average is 3; then click the OK button.

9 Choose **Debug | Stop Debugging**.

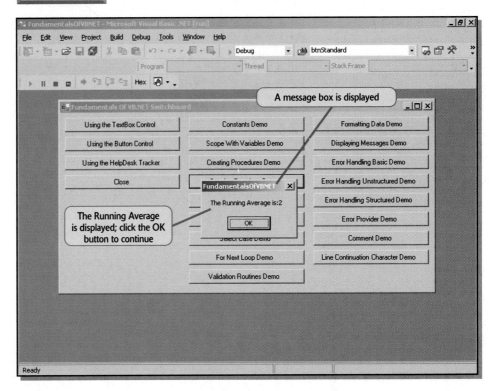

Figure 7-29

Control Statements

Control statements are parts of a programming language that exist only to determine what other parts of the program get executed. The determination occurs because the value of some variable or other criteria allows the program to act differently depending on the situation. The following control statements will be reviewed in this section: If Then Else statements, Do loops, Select Case statements, and For Next loops.

Using If Then Else Statements

The If statement is the simplest control statement, and one that is common to almost every programming language.

> If <condition> Then
>
>> Code to execute if the condition is true
>
> End If

The condition is the key part of this statement; it determines whether the inner block of code is executed. The condition takes the form of an expression, which is a combination of values and operators that is evaluated at runtime to arrive at a single value that can be used in testing.

You can also add one or more Else statements. For example,

If <condition> Then

    Zero or more VB statements go here

Else

    Zero or more VB statements go here

End If

You can also add one or more ElseIf statements. For example,

If <condition A> Then

    Code goes here if condition A is evaluated as True

ElseIf <condition B>

    Code goes here if condition B is evaluated as True

ElseIf <condition C>

    Code goes here if condition C is evaluated as True

End If

Task 10:
To Use the If Then Else Statement

1 Choose **View | Solution Explorer**, double-click to view the Switchboard form, and double-click the If Then Else Demo button to view code.

2 Type the code provided in Figure 7-30.

3 Choose **File | Save All**.

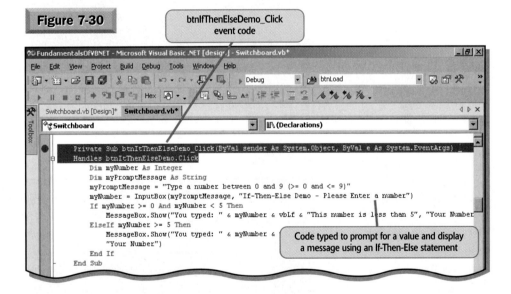

Figure 7-30

btnIfThenElseDemo_Click event code

Code typed to prompt for a value and display a message using an If-Then-Else statement

Tip Set a breakpoint in the btnIfThenElseDemo_Click event code. This is another opportunity to practice debugging code. When the code window appears, press the [F8] key to move one line at a time. Type **3** when prompted and then click the OK button. Press the [F8] key and watch how the program evaluates the number you typed and branches into the code and appropriate message.

④ Choose **Debug | Start**, type **3**, and click the OK button.

Figure 7-31

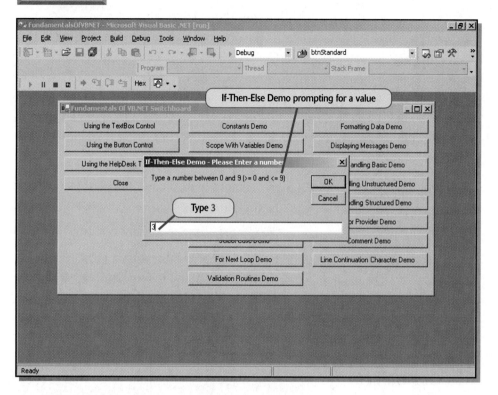

⑤ Verify that the message that appears is "You typed: 3. This number is less than 5." (Repeat Step 4, type **6**, and verify that the message that appears is "You typed: 6. This number is greater than 5.")

⑥ Choose **Debug | Stop Debugging** (or click the Close button on the Switchboard form).

Figure 7-32

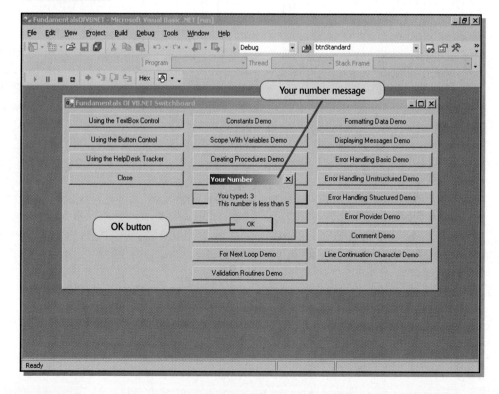

Using Do Loops

There are times when code needs to be repeated an indefinite number of times. *Do loops* provide this important feature. Loops often need to either keep on repeating an operation or not, depending on the results obtained within the loop. If your program needs to read all of the records in a disk file, you never know ahead of time how many records are in that file. The disk file could be empty. This type of programming problem requires an indefinite type of loop to read all of the records in the file, regardless of how many records are in it. There are two different types of Do loop structures: Do While and Do Until. The statements can be repeated either while the condition is True or until it becomes True.

Sometimes you need to check for a value other than equality. Relational operators are used in these situations (Table 7-7).

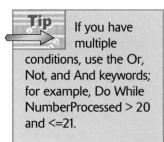

Tip If you have multiple conditions, use the Or, Not, and And keywords; for example, Do While NumberProcessed > 20 and <=21.

Table 7-7 Relational Operators

Operator	Definition
< >	Not equal to
<	Less than
<=	Less than or equal to
>	Greater than
>=	Greater than or equal to

Using a Do While Loop

The most common use for looping is while reading from a database and populating controls or performing a totaling function using data that has been received. During the reading process, the database is opened, the current record is positioned at the beginning of the data, and the process begins. In some cases, no records may be available. If no records are available, the program will exit the loop.

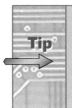

Tip You can always exit a Do loop or a For Next loop using the Exit Do or Exit For statement. Whenever Visual Basic .NET reads an Exit Do or Exit For statement, it immediately positions the code below the Loop or Next statement. The Exit Do statement transfers control immediately to the statement following the Loop statement.

Task 11:

To Use the Do While Loop

1 Choose **View | Solution Explorer**, double-click the Switchboard form, and then double-click the Do Loop Demo button to view code.

2 Type the code provided in Figure 7-33.

3 Choose **File | Save All**.

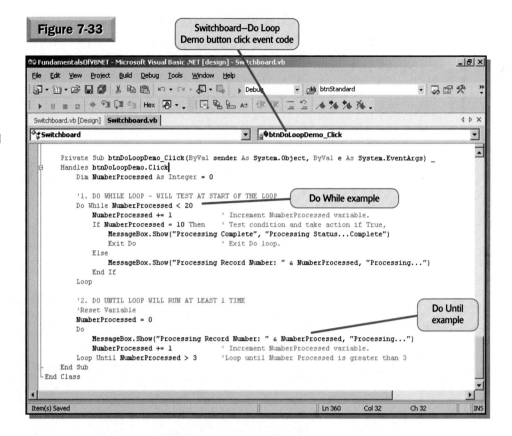

Figure 7-33

Switchboard—Do Loop Demo button click event code

```
Private Sub btnDoLoopDemo_Click(ByVal sender As System.Object, ByVal e As System.EventArgs) _
Handles btnDoLoopDemo.Click
    Dim NumberProcessed As Integer = 0

    '1. DO WHILE LOOP - WILL TEST AT START OF THE LOOP
    Do While NumberProcessed < 20                          ← Do While example
        NumberProcessed += 1            ' Increment NumberProcessed variable.
        If NumberProcessed = 10 Then    ' Test condition and take action if True,
            MessageBox.Show("Processing Complete", "Processing Status...Complete")
            Exit Do                      ' Exit Do loop.
        Else
            MessageBox.Show("Processing Record Number: " & NumberProcessed, "Processing...")
        End If
    Loop

    '2. DO UNTIL LOOP WILL RUN AT LEAST 1 TIME
    'Reset Variable
    NumberProcessed = 0                                    ← Do Until example
    Do
        MessageBox.Show("Processing Record Number: " & NumberProcessed, "Processing...")
        NumberProcessed += 1            ' Increment NumberProcessed variable.
    Loop Until NumberProcessed > 3      'Loop until Number Processed is greater than 3
End Sub
End Class
```

Tip

Review the code in the top section of Figure 7-33. The **Dim NumberProcessed as Integer = 0** statement declares a variable named NumberProcessed that has an Integer data type and an initial value of 0. An integer-type variable must be a whole number; decimal values are truncated. The **Do While NumberProcessed < 20** statement control structure processes code between the Do While and the Loop statement until either the NumberProcessed is > 20 or an Exit Do statement occurs. The **NumberProcessed += 1** statement might be new to you, and is translated into English as "increment the NumberProcessed variable by using its current value and increment it by 1." When the NumberProcessed = 10 statement becomes True, the code between the If and End If is processed. The **MessageBox.Show("Processing Record Number: & NumberProcessed, Processing…")** statement displays a message each time the program loops with the current NumberProcessed variable value. Once the loop determines that the NumberProcessed = 10, the Exit Do statement repositions the current line of code to the Loop statement, and the code moves downward from that point.

4 Choose **Debug | Start** and then click the Do While Loop Demo button.

5 Verify that the messages perform as follows: "Processing Record Number 1…10" and then "Processing Complete"; then verify that the messages restart again with "Processing Record Number 1…3," and then the Switchboard form reappears.

6 Choose **Debug | Stop Debugging**.

Tip Review the code in the bottom section of Figure 7-33. The **NumberProcessed = 0** statement reinitializes the variable to 0 in preparation for looping again. The Do statement begins the loop and executes it at least once. The MessageBox and variable incrementing statements occurs as before, but the loop continues until the NumberProcessed is > 3.

Figure 7-34

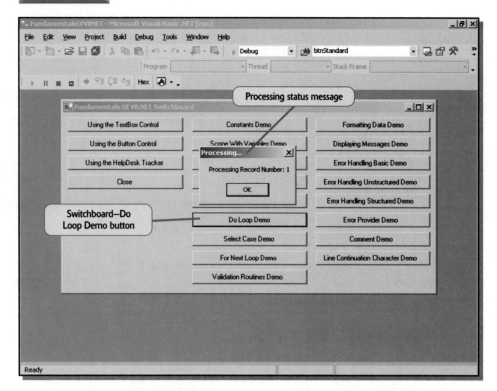

For additional practice debugging the code, insert a breakpoint next to the btnDoLoopDemo_Click event and press F8 after reaching the breakpoint to step through the code and watch how the program evaluates the test conditions. Try placing the mouse pointer over the CurrentNumber variable and notice how the current value appears in a ToolTip.

Other Ways

Using Select Case Statements

When you are comparing an expression with several different values, you can use *Select Case statements* as an alternative to If, If Then Else, and ElseIf statements. Although these statements can evaluate a different expression for each statement, this can result in a significant number of lines of logic that can confuse a programmer. This can be much more readable then a series of nested ElseIF statements. The Select statement evaluates a single expression only once and uses it for every comparison.

Visual Basic compares the value of the expression to the values in the Case statements in the order they appear in the Select Case code block. If it finds a match or a Case Else statement, it executes the corresponding statement block. In any case, it then executes the code following the End Select statement. You can have any number of Case statements, and you can include or omit a Case Else statement.

In this task, the Select Case statement is used to evaluate the number of customer orders so far, and determines the discounted price for this customer's next order.

Task 12:
To Use the Select Case Statement

1 Choose **View | Solution Explorer** and double-click the *Common.vb* code module.

2 Type the code provided in Figure 7-35.

Figure 7-35

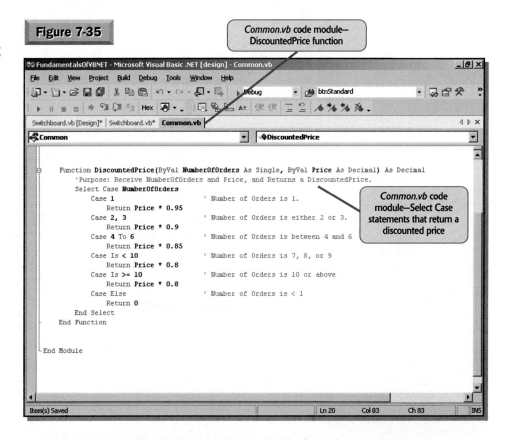

Common.vb code module— DiscountedPrice function

Common.vb code module—Select Case statements that return a discounted price

Tip A Case Else Statement only gets executed when none of the previous case conditions are met. It is good practice to always have a Case Else statement to catch any unexpected conditions.

3 Choose **View | Solution Explorer**, double-click the Switchboard form, and then double-click the Select Case Demo button to view code.

4 Type the code provided in Figure 7-36.

5 Choose **File | Save All**.

Figure 7-36

Switchboard form—Select Case Demo button click event code

Switchboard form—breakpoint in Code View window

Switchboard form—code that calls a function and displays a message

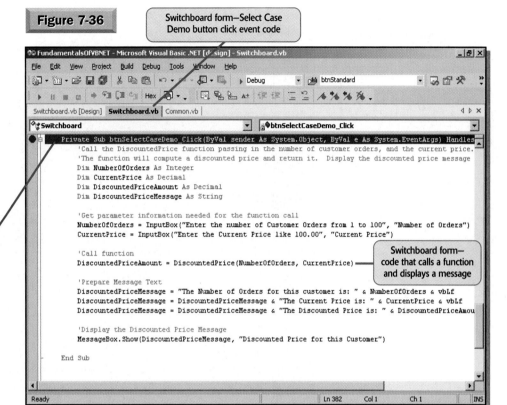

```
Private Sub btnSelectCaseDemo_Click(ByVal sender As System.Object, ByVal e As System.EventArgs) Handles
    'Call the DiscountedPrice function passing in the number of customer orders, and the current price.
    'The function will compute a discounted price and return it.  Display the discounted price message
    Dim NumberOfOrders As Integer
    Dim CurrentPrice As Decimal
    Dim DiscountedPriceAmount As Decimal
    Dim DiscountedPriceMessage As String

    'Get parameter information needed for the function call
    NumberOfOrders = InputBox("Enter the number of Customer Orders from 1 to 100", "Number of Orders")
    CurrentPrice = InputBox("Enter the Current Price like 100.00", "Current Price")

    'Call function
    DiscountedPriceAmount = DiscountedPrice(NumberOfOrders, CurrentPrice)

    'Prepare Message Text
    DiscountedPriceMessage = "The Number of Orders for this customer is: " & NumberOfOrders & vbLf
    DiscountedPriceMessage = DiscountedPriceMessage & "The Current Price is: " & CurrentPrice & vbLf
    DiscountedPriceMessage = DiscountedPriceMessage & "The Discounted Price is: " & DiscountedPriceAmou

    'Display the Discounted Price Message
    MessageBox.Show(DiscountedPriceMessage, "Discounted Price for this Customer")

End Sub
```

6 Choose **Debug | Start** and then click the Select Case Demo button. Type **5** for the Number of Orders prompt and click the OK button.

Figure 7-37

Number of Orders prompt

Switchboard Form— Select Case Demo button

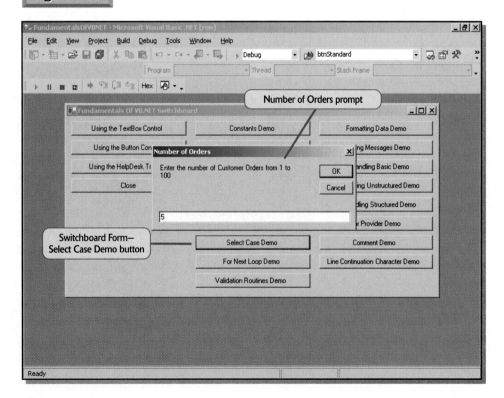

7 Type 100.00 for the
Current Price prompt
and then click the OK button.

Figure 7-38

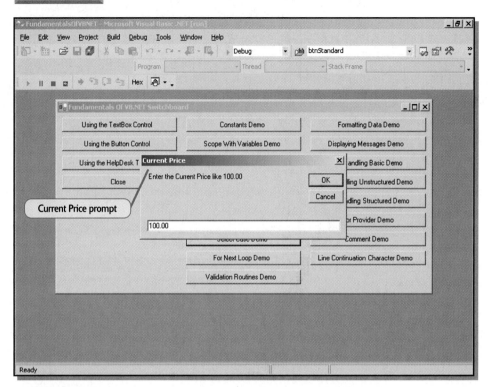

Current Price prompt

8 Verify that the
Discounted Price
is 85.

9 Click the Close button
(or choose **Debug |
Stop Debugging**).

Figure 7-39

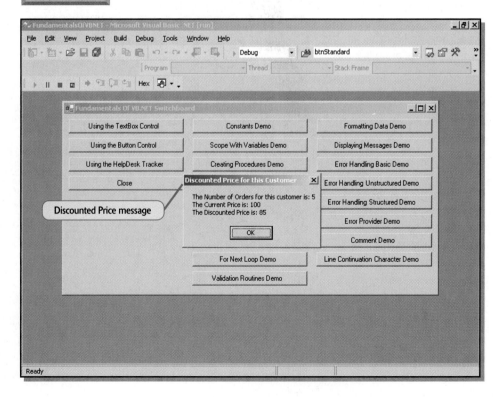

Discounted Price message

Using For Next Loops

For Next loops are performed a predetermined number of times. Visual Basic .NET sets the counter variable equal to the starting value and then determines whether the value for the counter is less than the ending value. If the value is greater than the ending value, Visual Basic .NET processes subsequent statements until it comes to the keyword Next. At that point, it defaults to adding 1 to the counter variable and starts the process again. This process continues until the counter variable is larger than the ending value. At that point, the loop is finished, and Visual Basic .NET moves past it.

You do not always have to add 1, the default. Sometimes it is necessary to count by twos, by fractions, or backwards. You can do this by adding the Step keyword to a For Next loop. The Step keyword tells VB.NET to change the counter by a specified amount. When you use a negative step, the body of the For Next loop is bypassed if the starting value for the counter is smaller than the ending value. This is most useful when deleting items from a list.

In the following task, you will create two loops: one that will count down using a -1 step value, and the second that will count up by the default step value of 1. After the loops reach either 0 for the first, or 10 for the second, they will move to the Next statement and continue downward.

Task 13:
To Use the For Next Loop

1 Choose **View | Solution Explorer**, double-click the *Switchboard.vb* file to display the form, and double-click the For Next Loop Demo button to view code.

2 Type the code provided in Figure 7-40.

3 Choose **File | Save All**.

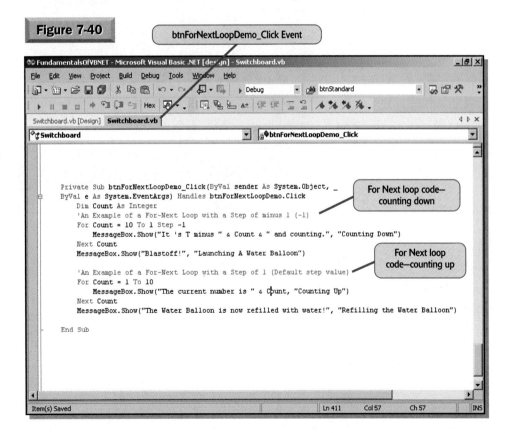

Figure 7-40

btnForNextLoopDemo_Click Event

For Next loop code—counting down

For Next loop code—counting up

```
Private Sub btnForNextLoopDemo_Click(ByVal sender As System.Object, _
ByVal e As System.EventArgs) Handles btnForNextLoopDemo.Click
    Dim Count As Integer
    'An Example of a For-Next Loop with a Step of minus 1 (-1)
    For Count = 10 To 1 Step -1
        MessageBox.Show("It 's T minus " & Count & " and counting.", "Counting Down")
    Next Count
    MessageBox.Show("Blastoff!", "Launching A Water Balloon")

    'An Example of a For-Next Loop with a Step of 1 (Default step value)
    For Count = 1 To 10
        MessageBox.Show("The current number is " & Count, "Counting Up")
    Next Count
    MessageBox.Show("The Water Balloon is now refilled with water!", "Refilling the Water Balloon")

End Sub
```

Tip

Walk through the code. An integer-type variable named Count is declared to keep track of the For Next loop value needed as the basis for ending the loop. The **For Count = 10 to 1 Step -1** statement starts at 10 and counts down to 1, reducing the value by 1 each time. The Message Box.Show statement displays the current value. The Next statement loops the code pointer back up to the For statement while decrementing the value due to the -1 step parameter. Once the value reaches 1, the code pointer is positioned on the line of code below the Next statement, and then displays the final "Blastoff!" message.

4 Choose **Debug | Start** and then click the For Next Demo button to test the code.

5 Verify that the messages appear as expected with a value that is reduced after clicking the OK button or pressing Enter.

Figure 7-41

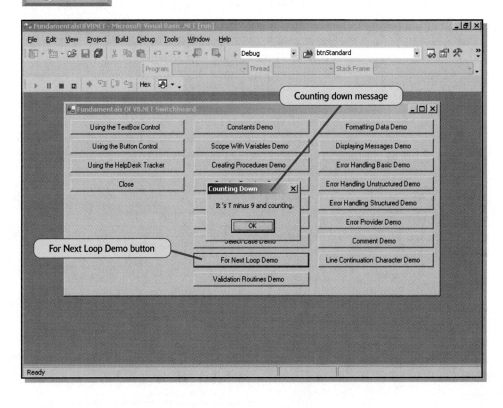

6 Verify that the message changes after the count reaches 1 and displays the "Blastoff!" message.

Tip This is another opportunity to place a breakpoint behind the For Next Loop Demo click event code. The code we have written demonstrates two different step values.

Figure 7-42

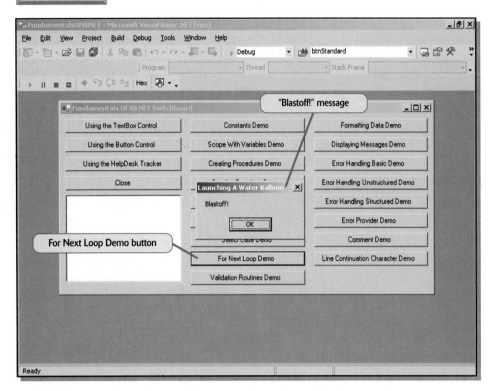

7 Verify that the message displayed is counting up starting at 1.

Figure 7-43

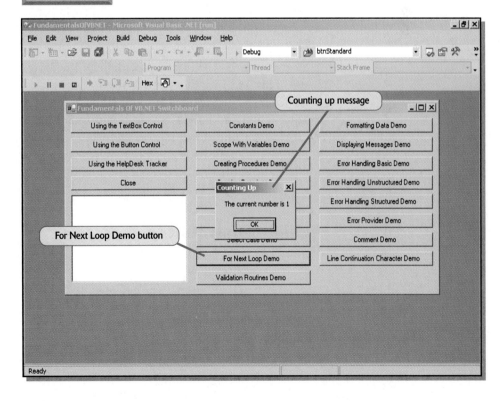

8 Click the OK button, or press Enter, to loop until reaching the value of 10 and then verify that the message changes to the "The Water Balloon is now refilled with water!" message. Click the OK button one more time to display the Switchboard form.

9 Click the Close button to end the application.

Figure 7-44

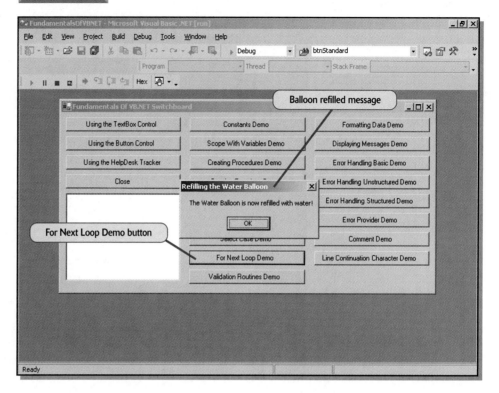

Adding Finishing Touches

At some point you will have to review code and fix it. Comments are highly recommended within code to identify the logical steps taken to solve a problem. This was first mentioned in a splash section at the beginning of the book. We will review how to comment code. When writing code, it is often helpful to be able to avoid having to scroll rightward to see code that might be too wide to see. The *line continuation character* enables you to write shorter lines of code that can all be seen at the same time. Finally, we will use the Tab Order Wizard to set the tab order for the Switchboard form.

Using Comments

As with any programming language, commenting your code is up to you. Comment statements are neither executed nor processed by Visual Basic .NET. As a result, they do not increase the size of your compiled code. There are two ways to indicate a comment. The usual way is with a single quote as shown in Figure 7-45.

Task 14:
To Use Comments

1 Choose **View | Solution Explorer** and double-click the *Switchboard.vb* file to display the form in design mode. Add a ListBox control to the Switchboard form and set the control properties as shown in Table 7-8.

2 Double-click the Comment Demo button to view code.

3 Type the code provided in Figure 7-45.

Figure 7-45

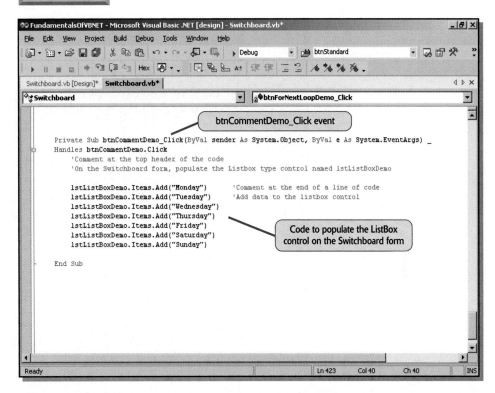

```
Private Sub btnCommentDemo_Click(ByVal sender As System.Object, ByVal e As System.EventArgs) _
Handles btnCommentDemo.Click
    'Comment at the top header of the code
    'On the Switchboard form, populate the Listbox type control named lstListBoxDemo

    lstListBoxDemo.Items.Add("Monday")        'Comment at the end of a line of code
    lstListBoxDemo.Items.Add("Tuesday")       'Add data to the listbox control
    lstListBoxDemo.Items.Add("Wednesday")
    lstListBoxDemo.Items.Add("Thursday")
    lstListBoxDemo.Items.Add("Friday")
    lstListBoxDemo.Items.Add("Saturday")
    lstListBoxDemo.Items.Add("Sunday")

    End Sub
```

btnCommentDemo_Click event

Code to populate the ListBox control on the Switchboard form

Table 7-8	Listbox Control Properties		
Control	**Size**	**Location**	**Property**
List Box	200, 147	8, 136	Name = lstListBoxDemo

4 Choose **File | Save All**.

5 Choose **Debug | Start** and then click the Comments Demo button.

6 Click the Close button.

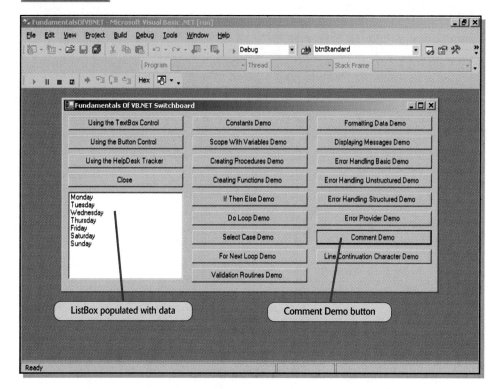

Figure 7-46

Using the Tab Order Wizard

When a form has multiple controls, users expect to be able to shift focus using the Tab key. Configuring the tab order for your set of controls requires that you understand two properties: TabStop and TabIndex. The TabStop property can be set to True or False. This value determines whether this control can be reached using the Tab key. Assuming that the TabStop property has been set to True for a control, the TabOrder property is then set to determine the order in which the controls will receive focus when the Tab key is pressed.

The Visual Basic .NET Interactive Development Environment (IDE) provides a *Tab Order Wizard,* which is activated by choosing **View | Tab Order**. Once the wizard is activated, the Tab Order value is displayed for each control on the form. To change these values, click each item in the order you choose. Notice that controls added to a GroupBox's control collection function as a collective. To exit Tab Order mode, choose **View | Tab Order** to toggle off the Tab Order Wizard.

Task 15:
To Use the Tab Order Wizard

1 Choose **View | Solution Explorer** and then double-click the Switchboard form to display it in design mode.

2 Choose **View | Tab Order**.

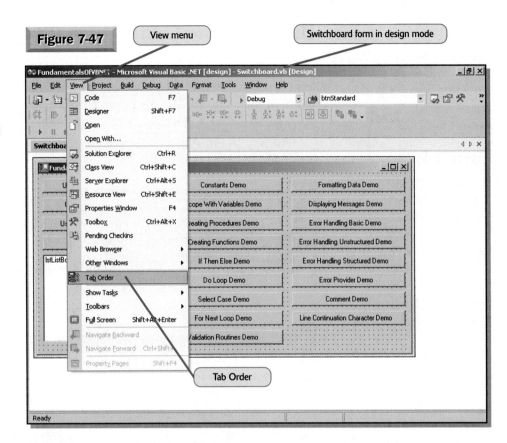

Figure 7-47

View menu

Switchboard form in design mode

Tab Order

3 Select the buttons in the following sequence: left column top-down, middle column top-down, right column top-down, and then the ListBox control.

4 Choose **File | Save All**.

5 Choose **View | Tab Order** to hide the Tab Order Wizard.

6 Choose **Debug | Start** and verify that the selected button is the top left button. Press Tab and verify that the selected buttons move as expected.

7 Click the Close button.

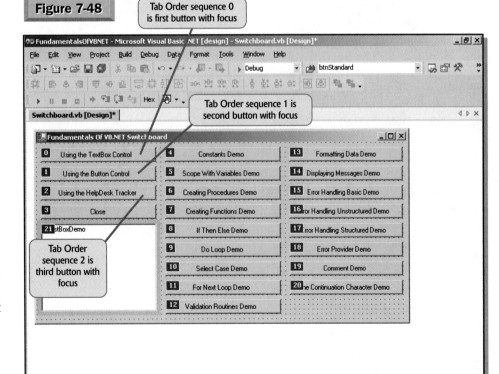

Figure 7-48

Tab Order sequence 0 is first button with focus

Tab Order sequence 1 is second button with focus

Tab Order sequence 2 is third button with focus

Using the Line Continuation Character

A single line of Visual Basic .NET code can be as many as 1,023 characters long, but for readability purposes, you are not advised to type beyond the width of the code window. By using the underscore (_) character, you can split a Visual Basic .NET statement onto more than one line.

Task 16:
To Use the Line Continuation Character

1 Choose **View | Solution Explorer**, double-click the Switchboard form to view it in design mode, and then double-click the Line Continuation Character Demo button to view code.

2 Type the code provided in Figure 7-49. Place a breakpoint in the left margin of the code window. Press F9, choose **Debug | New Breakpoint**, or press Ctrl + B.

3 Choose **File | Save All**.

4 Choose **Debug | Start** and verify that the code stops. Press F8 to step through the code one line at a time and verify that two code lines are highlighted for the second line of code.

5 Press F5 to run the program normally and then click the Close button when the Switchboard form reappears.

6 Press F5 or choose **Debug | Start** to run the program, and click the Line Continuation Character Demo button.

7 Click the Close button.

Figure 7-49

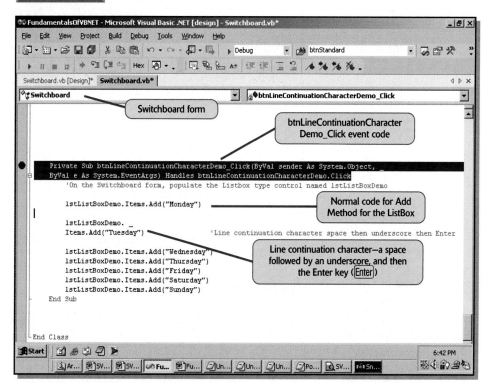

- Switchboard form
- btnLineContinuationCharacter Demo_Click event code
- Normal code for Add Method for the ListBox
- Line continuation character—a space followed by an underscore, and then the Enter key (Enter)

Tip You must put a space after the lstListBoxDemo.Item statement followed by the underscore (_) character. Nothing can follow the line continuation character; just press Enter to move down a line and continue typing your code.

Linking Code to the Payroll Transaction System Toolbox

As a programmer builds a series of successful code programs, it is often more efficient to organize the code patterns for reuse later. The Toolbox provides that capability.

Task 17:

To Link Code Patterns to the Payroll Transaction System Toolbox

1 Choose **View | Solution Explorer**, double-click the Switchboard form, and then double-click the Comments Demo button to view code.

> **Tip** To widen the Toolbox, position the mouse pointer on the right side of the Toolbox, then click and drag rightward to make the Toolbox wider.

2 Choose **View | Toolbox** and then widen the Toolbox to about 2 inches.

3 Right-click in an empty area of the Toolbox and choose **Add Tab**; then type **CodeSnippets** and press Enter.

Figure 7-50

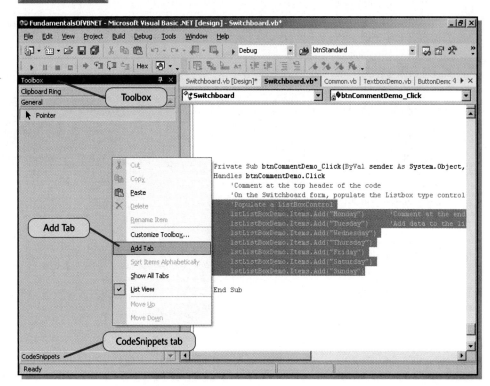

4 Type 'Populate a ListBox Control—see item D in Figure 7-51.

5 Select the text as shown in Figure 7-51.

6 Drag the highlighted text leftward over the CodeSnippets tab, and verify that the Toolbox displays "Populate a ListBox Control."

7 Choose **File | Save All**.

8 Click the Switchboard.vb (Design) tab across the top of the Code View window.

9 Double-click the Validation Routines Demo button. Click the CodeSnippets Toolbox tab to make it appear. Using the Toolbox, click and drag the Populate a ListBox Control item from the CodeSnippets tab over to the btnValidation RoutinesDemo_Click event code and then release the mouse button. Verify that the code appears without typing.

10 Choose **Edit | Undo** to remove the code just added, because it was just a demonstration of how we can create code snippets and reuse code.

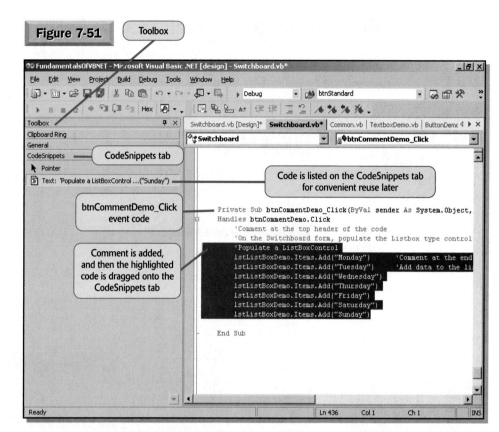

Figure 7-51 — Toolbox

CodeSnippets tab

Code is listed on the CodeSnippets tab for convenient reuse later

btnCommentDemo_Click event code

Comment is added, and then the highlighted code is dragged onto the CodeSnippets tab

Tip

Some Closing Thoughts...

If you are new to programming it might be wise to create code snippets for

- If then Else Statements
- Select Case Statements
- Populating a ListBox
- Nested If then ElseIf
- For Next Statements
- Do While Statements

These snippets will always be available anytime you are developing new code within your project. Using working patterns of code prevents us from having to "reinvent the wheel."

SUMMARY AND EXERCISES

SUMMARY

- Using ToolTips with controls provides a short popup message when the mouse hovers over the control.

- Variables can be local, module-level (Forms and Classes), public (In Modules), or static.

- Static variables retain their last value rather than reinitialize when used again.

- Procedures perform an action but do not return a value.

- Procedures can be programmed to return none, one, or multiple values.

- Functions perform one or more actions and must return a single value.

- Do loops repeat process code until an Exit Do or condition occurs that causes the loop to end.

- For Next loops are run a predetermined number of times.

- Line continuation characters are a space followed by an underscore. They permit a long line of code to appear readable on screen without scrolling for clarity.

- Comments help document the logic used to solve a problem and also helps maintenance programmers figure out the code written by others.

- Although comments can be prefaced with either REM of ' (a single quote), the single quote is the preferred method because it can be used in conjunction with the comment/uncomment buttons on the menu of the IDE.

- The Tab Order Wizard helps set the TabStop and TabOrder properties for many controls on a form.

- The Visual Basic .NET Toolbox can accept code that is highlighted and then dragged onto it. This code can be reused by all Visual Basic .NET projects on the development workstation.

KEY TERMS & SKILLS

KEY TERMS

assignment (p. 7-6)
constant (p. 7-10)
control statements
 (p. 7-28)
Do loops (p. 7-31)
For Next loops
 (p. 7-37)
functions (p. 7-22)
hover (p. 7-3)
If Then Else statements
 (p. 7-29)

InputBox (p. 7-26)
line continuation
 character (p. 7-40)
local variables (p. 7-14)
module-level variables
 (p. 7-15)
Message Box (p. 7-26)
procedures (p. 7-22)
public variables
 (p. 7-17)

reserved words
 (p. 7-6)
Select Case statements
 (p. 7-33)
standard naming
 conventions (p. 7-5)
Tab Order Wizard
 (p. 7-46)
ToolTips (p. 7-3)
variables (p. 7-6)

SKILLS

Create a function (p. 7-26)
Create a procedure (p. 7-23)
Declare a variable (p. 7-7)
Link code to the Payroll Transaction
 System Toolbox (p. 7-45)
Set a local variable (p. 7-14)
Set a module-level variable (p. 7-16)
Set a public variable (p. 7-18)
Use a static variable (p. 7-20)
Use comments (p. 7-41)

Use constants (p. 7-11)
Use the Do While loop (p. 7-32)
Use the For Next loop (p. 7-37)
Use the If Then Else statement
 (p. 7-29)
Use the line continuation character
 (p. 7-44)
Use the Select Case statement (p. 7-34)
Use the Tab Order Wizard (p. 7-42)
Use ToolTips with controls (p. 7-4)

STUDY QUESTIONS

MULTIPLE CHOICE

1. In this project, reusable code was placed onto what part(s) of the Interactive Design Environment?
 a. Toolbox
 b. Common Module
 c. both a and b
 d. controls

2. What type of control displays a popup help message when the mouse pointer hovers over a control?
 a. Label
 b. Textbox
 c. ToolTip
 d. Toolbar

3. When displaying a message, which reserved word provides a new line?
 a. vbcrlf
 b. NewLine
 c. vblf
 d. both a and c

4. Which of the following uses the standard naming convention for a constant?
 a. firstName
 b. FirstName
 c. firstname
 d. FIRST_NAME

5. Which of the following is NOT a function of Visual Basic .NET?
   a. IsDate
   b. Today
   c. Yesterday
   d. Now

6. Which of the following types of variables has a global scope?
   a. public
   b. private
   c. local
   d. module-level

7. Which of the following types of variables has a lifetime that lasts only as long as the procedure in which it was declared?
   a. public
   b. private
   c. local
   d. module

8. Which of the following control statements are valid?
   a. If Then Else
   b. Do While
   c. For Next
   d. all of the above

9. When multiple conditions are needed, which of the following are valid within an If Then statement?
   a. and
   b. or
   c. not
   d. all of the above

10. Which of the following relational operators represents Does Not Equal?
   a. >=
   b. <>
   c. ><
   d. <=

SHORT ANSWER

1. What is the name of the control that prompts you for an answer and returns the text you typed?
2. What function key is used to advance a debugging session one line at a time?
3. If you have multiple conditions, what keywords might you use?
4. How does one exit a Do loop quickly?
5. What type of control statement runs a predetermined number of times?
6. What parameter of the For Next loop allows code to count down?
7. Which control enables you to see multiple lines of code without scrolling?
8. Do comments increase the size of your compiled code?
9. What feature provided with Visual Basic .NET enables you to quickly set tab order properties?
10. What character is used for the line continuation character?

FILL IN THE BLANK

1. The _____ control provides a small floating window that displays a helpful message when the mouse pointer hovers over a control.
2. _____ components are added to the tray below the Windows Form Designer in the development environment so they are easily accessible without cluttering the visual design space.
3. _____ _____ conventions help identify the type of control being used and the associated properties available.

4. You cannot use words reserved by Visual Basic .NET for variable names unless you surround them with _____.

5. A named constant is like a variable except that you cannot change the constant's value once you've assigned it, since it is a _____ type of variable.

6. The _____ of a variable is the section of the application that can see and manipulate it.

7. If a variable is declared within a procedure, it is considered a _____ variable, and only the code in the specified procedure has access to that variable.

8. Centralized code reduces _____ redundancy.

9. The _____ formatting characters (four characters) provide the day of the week when used with the Now keyword.

10. Public variables should not be declared inside procedures; they must be declared as _____ variables or in a _____ to follow good programming practices.

FOR DISCUSSION

1. When would a Select Case statement be preferred over If Then statements?

2. Why would it be better to construct a Do loop where the condition appears at the top of the Do loop?

3. Why do some programmers conclude that using public variables with global scope is riskier than using local variables?

4. When would a function be preferred over a procedure?

5. Why is setting a breakpoint helpful for debugging code?

P R O J E C T 8

More Programming Fundamentals with Visual Basic .NET

hile it is desirable to write programs that work perfectly, this is seldom possible. As applications interact with other systems and databases, the number of places where code can break increases. Although we cannot always prevent an error from occurring, it is possible to manage errors gracefully. We will explore several error-handling strategies and the Error Provider provided with Visual Basic .NET to improve our ability to manage errors should they occur.

Tip

The *Fundamentals.sln* file can be found at
\\vb.net_brief\vb.net_datafiles\08\Students\FundamentalsOfVBNET\.

The *PayTransactionSystem.sln* file can be found at
\\vb.net_brief\vb.net_datafiles\08\Students\HR\PayTransactionSystem.

e-selections **Running Case**

The Pay Transaction System project is progressing well and soon we will be able to generate paychecks. Since payroll is probably the most sensitive information, and paychecks in general should be carefully processed, validation routines and error handling will be needed.

PROJECT 8

More Programming Fundamentals with Visual Basic .NET

The Challenge

Mr. Traylor has decided to standardize how error handling is implemented at the e-Selections division of Selections, Inc. Having so many developers at first was beneficial and work was generated at a record pace. Unfortunately, since each developer wrote code differently, it has become difficult to maintain and support the code they wrote. It is time to learn how to create code that can be shared and standardized within Visual Basic .NET.

The Solution

Validation routines will be implemented that check for valid data during data entry. Visual Basic .NET has an *Error Provider* facility that provides extensive error-handling features. We will finalize the Fundamentals program to learn how this facility is used, and then return to the Pay Transaction System in the next project to create forms that are linked to a database.

Figure 8-1

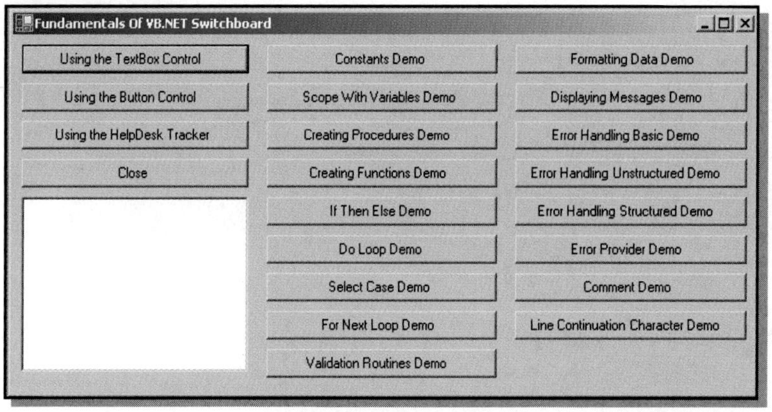

Fundamentals Of VB.NET Switchboard

Using the TextBox Control	Constants Demo	Formatting Data Demo
Using the Button Control	Scope With Variables Demo	Displaying Messages Demo
Using the HelpDesk Tracker	Creating Procedures Demo	Error Handling Basic Demo
Close	Creating Functions Demo	Error Handling Unstructured Demo
	If Then Else Demo	Error Handling Structured Demo
	Do Loop Demo	Error Provider Demo
	Select Case Demo	Comment Demo
	For Next Loop Demo	Line Continuation Character Demo
	Validation Routines Demo	

Using the Error Provider

Your Windows Forms application will need to validate user input. This is especially true with dialog boxes, as you should inform users if they make a processing error before continuing forward. The Error Provider can be used to provide a visual cue of a user input error. In Task 1, you will edit properties (Table 8-1) of the HelpDeskTracker data entry form to use the Error Provider.

Table 8-1	HelpDeskTracker Properties
Property	**Description**
CausesValidation	Indicates whether selecting this control causes conditions on the controls requiring validation
Validated	Occurs when the control is finished performing its validation logic
Validating	Occurs when the control is validating user input (that is, when the control loses focus)

Using Validation Routines

Forms or dialog boxes are often used to enable users to enter data. Visual Basic .NET provides a model for coding validation of information that is entered. Given a data entry form with a button, the user clicks the button when finished, and the validation code runs to ensure that the data is valid. A Cancel button will avoid validation.

The CausesValidation property and the Validating/Validated events exist on every control. To provide input validation, set the CausesValidation property to True on every data entry control, such as a text box, radio button, or combo box, and also on any button that causes the data to be used or saved, such as OK, Save, Continue, and Next. On buttons such as Help, Cancel, Previous, or other buttons where you do not care whether the data is valid when the button is clicked, set the CausesValidation property to False. Next, place the code to check whether the field data is valid in the validating event. When the user attempts to switch the focus to a control where CausesValidation is True, then the Validating event will be raised on each of the edit controls that have received focus since the last time you pressed a control where CausesValidation is True.

In the following example, we will add validation code to the HelpDeskTracker form.

Task 1:

To Use a Validation Routine

1 Choose **View | Solution Explorer** and double-click the *HelpDesk Tracker.vb* file to view the form in design mode.

2 Click the Request Number field (txtRequestNumber) to select it.

3 Choose **View | Properties** and then verify that the Causes Validation property is True.

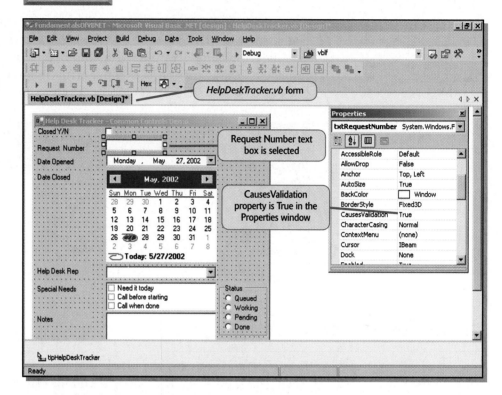

Figure 8-2

HelpDeskTracker.vb form

Request Number text box is selected

CausesValidation property is True in the Properties window

4 Select the Date Opened control (dtpDateOpened) and verify that the CausesValidation property is also set to True.

5 Click the Close **X** button and change the CausesValidation property to False. Double-click the Close button and type me.close.

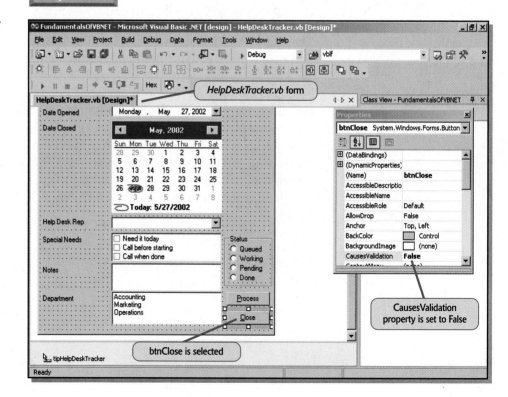

Figure 8-3

HelpDeskTracker.vb form

CausesValidation property is set to False

btnClose is selected

6 Double-click the Request Number (txtRequestNumber) field to view code, select the txtRequestNumber control from the top left drop-down list, and then select the Validating event from the top right drop-down list. Type the code provided in Figure 8-4 into the txtRequest Number_Validating event.

7 Choose **File | Save All**.

Figure 8-4

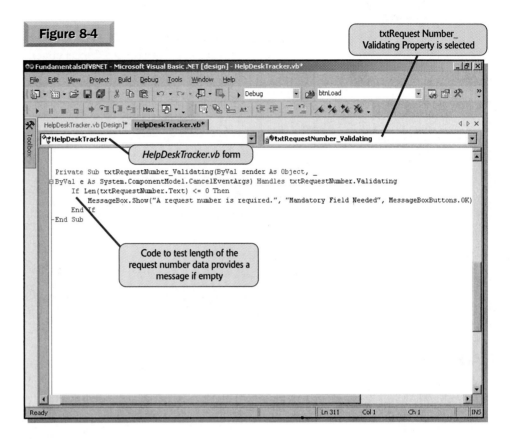

txtRequest Number_ Validating Property is selected

HelpDeskTracker.vb form

```
Private Sub txtRequestNumber_Validating(ByVal sender As Object, _
ByVal e As System.ComponentModel.CancelEventArgs) Handles txtRequestNumber.Validating
    If Len(txtRequestNumber.Text) <= 0 Then
        MessageBox.Show("A request number is required.", "Mandatory Field Needed", MessageBoxButtons.OK)
    End If
End Sub
```

Code to test length of the request number data provides a message if empty

8 Press F5 and the Tab key until the focus leaves the Request Number field; then verify that a warning appears indicating that the Request Number is required. Click the OK button to continue. You can also choose **Debug | Start** to run the program.

9 Click the Close button and verify that no warning appears and the Switchboard form reappears as expected.

10 Click the Close button.

Figure 8-5

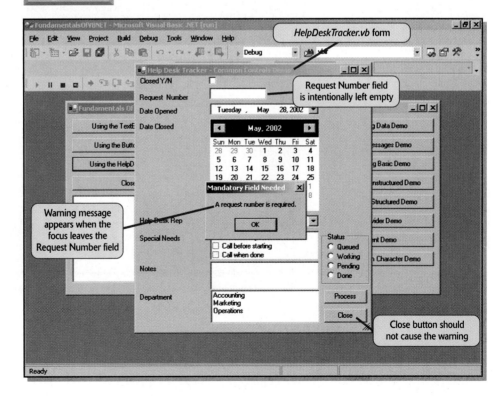

HelpDeskTracker.vb form

Request Number field is intentionally left empty

Warning message appears when the focus leaves the Request Number field

Close button should not cause the warning

> **Tip** Check for valid data only when the user clicks the OK button. This permits users to exit if they click the Cancel button without having to complete the form.

Formatting Data

The Format command is one of the most powerful commands for easily and quickly generating output in a desired format. We will return to the Switchboard form and display samples of formatted code.

> **Tip** *FormatCurrency* is a specialized formatting command for easily and quickly generating output in a currency format. *FormatDateTime* returns a string formatted in a specified date and time format.

Task 2:
To Format Data

1 Choose **View | Solution Explorer** and then double-click the *Switchboard.vb* file to view the form in design mode. Double-click the Formatting Data Demo button to view code.

Figure 8-6

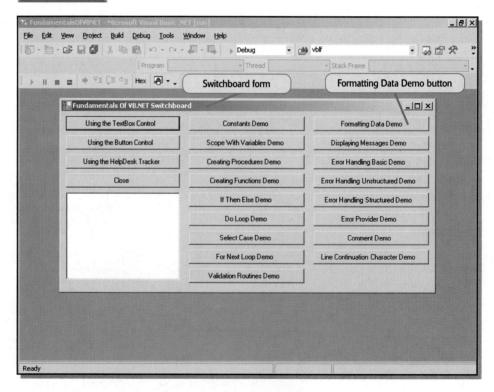

2 Type the code provided in Figure 8-7.

3 Choose **File | Save All**.

Figure 8-7

Formatting Data Demo button click event

Sample code to display information with different formatting options

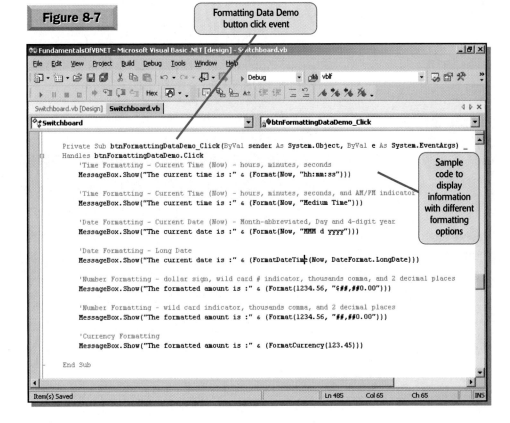

```
Private Sub btnFormattingDataDemo_Click(ByVal sender As System.Object, ByVal e As System.EventArgs) _
Handles btnFormattingDataDemo.Click
    'Time Formatting - Current Time (Now) - hours, minutes, seconds
    MessageBox.Show("The current time is :" & (Format(Now, "hh:mm:ss")))

    'Time Formatting - Current Time (Now) - hours, minutes, seconds, and AM/PM indicator
    MessageBox.Show("The current time is :" & (Format(Now, "Medium Time")))

    'Date Formatting - Current Date (Now) - Month-abbreviated, Day and 4-digit year
    MessageBox.Show("The current date is :" & (Format(Now, "MMM d yyyy")))

    'Date Formatting - Long Date
    MessageBox.Show("The current date is :" & (FormatDateTime(Now, DateFormat.LongDate)))

    'Number Formatting - dollar sign, wild card # indicator, thousands comma, and 2 decimal places
    MessageBox.Show("The formatted amount is :" & (Format(1234.56, "$##,##0.00")))

    'Number Formatting - wild card indicator, thousands comma, and 2 decimal places
    MessageBox.Show("The formatted amount is :" & (Format(1234.56, "##,##0.00")))

    'Currency Formatting
    MessageBox.Show("The formatted amount is :" & (FormatCurrency(123.45)))

End Sub
```

4 Press F5 and verify that the messages display different formats.

5 Click the Close button.

Figure 8-8

Formatting Data Demo button

Message with formatted time

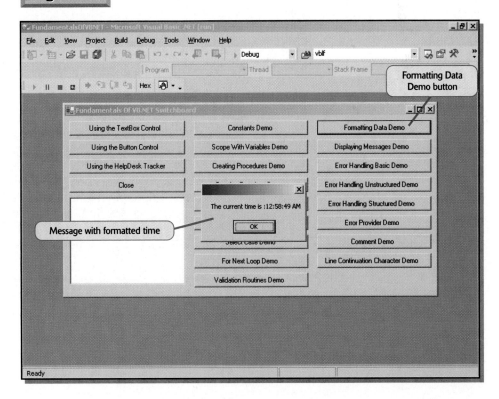

Displaying Messages

The *MessageBox class* provides a way to display simple dialog boxes that show a message and/or ask the user to make a choice from a fixed set of options (Yes/No, OK/Cancel, Abort/Retry/Ignore).

Task 3:
To Display Messages

1 Choose **View | Solution Explorer**, double-click the Switchboard form, and then double-click the Display Messages Demo button to view code in the click event.

2 Type the code provided in Figure 8-9.

3 Choose **File | Save All**.

Figure 8-9

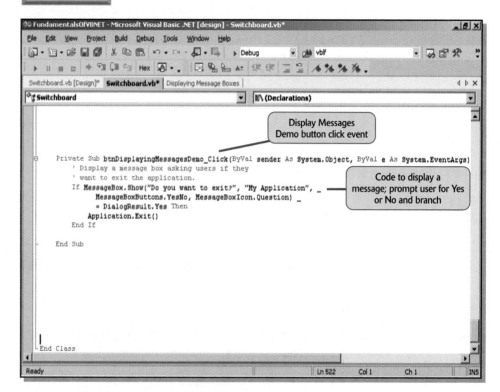

Display Messages Demo button click event

Code to display a message; prompt user for Yes or No and branch

```
Private Sub btnDisplayingMessagesDemo_Click(ByVal sender As System.Object, ByVal e As System.EventArgs)
    ' Display a message box asking users if they
    ' want to exit the application.
    If MessageBox.Show("Do you want to exit?", "My Application", _
        MessageBoxButtons.YesNo, MessageBoxIcon.Question) _
        = DialogResult.Yes Then
        Application.Exit()
    End If

End Sub
```

Tip Message boxes can also receive input. The Show method of the MessageBox class returns a value that can be used to determine a choice made by the user. You can store this value in an integer or compare the value returned when you display the message box using an If statement. The Style parameter of the Show method can be set to display the proper buttons to ask a user for information. In this example, we have provided a message, provided two buttons for either Yes or No, and displayed an image of a question mark character. When the No button is clicked, the code exits without changes. When the Yes button is clicked, the application ends.

4 Press F5 and verify that a message appears. Click the No button and verify that the message disappears. Click the Displaying Messages Demo button and then click the Yes button and verify that the application ends as expected.

> **Tip** In Visual Basic .NET, using *Msgbox* to create a message is still supported although it is legacy Visual Basic 6 code. The new syntax MessageBox.Show is preferred to make sure your code will work in the future releases of Visual Basic .NET.

Figure 8-10

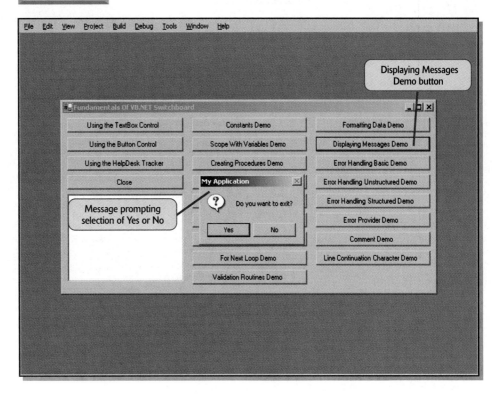

Error Handling

> **Tip** Log or somehow notify the user of the problem, let the user save his or her work if appropriate, and let the user gracefully exit the program if necessary.

The overall purpose of *error handlers* is to allow the program to gracefully recover when things don't go as expected. This is especially important when dealing with relational databases where multiple layers of technology are involved and there are many places that an application can break. In the remaining tasks, you will explore in detail basic error handling, unstructured error handing, structured error handling, and how to use the new Error Provider that comes with Visual Basic .NET.

Understanding Basic Error Handling

Handle errors in such a way that programs just don't stop in midstream. The error handling structure we will set up in this task will define an error handler and the On Error GoTo statement. The error handler is where you handle the exception when it occurs. The key is to retain control in the program no matter what happens. The On Error GoTo statement tells Visual Basic .NET where to redirect the code when an error occurs. We will add code into the click event of the Error Handling Basic Demo button on the Switchboard form and then set a breakpoint and walk through the code.

Task 4:

To Understand Basic Error Handling

1 Choose **View | Solution Explorer**, double-click to display the Switchboard form, and then double-click the Error Handling Basic Demo button to view code.

2 Type the code provided in Figure 8-11 and create a breakpoint at the Private Sub btnErrorHandlingBasicDemo _Click code statement.

3 Choose **File | Save All**.

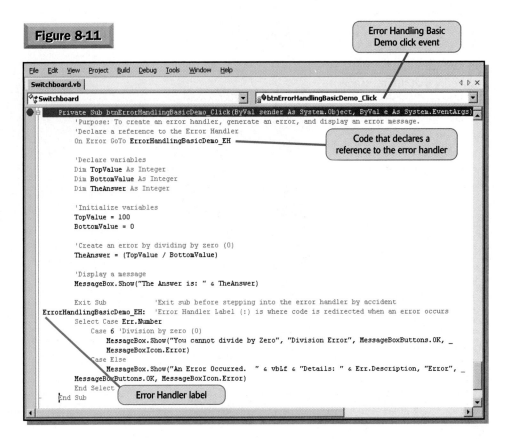

Figure 8-11

Error Handling Basic Demo click event

```
File  Edit  View  Project  Build  Debug  Tools  Window  Help

Switchboard.vb
Switchboard                                          btnErrorHandlingBasicDemo_Click

    Private Sub btnErrorHandlingBasicDemo_Click(ByVal sender As System.Object, ByVal e As System.EventArgs)
        'Purpose: To create an error handler, generate an error, and display an error message.
        'Declare a reference to the Error Handler
        On Error GoTo ErrorHandlingBasicDemo_EH          Code that declares a
                                                         reference to the error handler
        'Declare variables
        Dim TopValue As Integer
        Dim BottomValue As Integer
        Dim TheAnswer As Integer

        'Initialize variables
        TopValue = 100
        BottomValue = 0

        'Create an error by dividing by zero (0)
        TheAnswer = (TopValue / BottomValue)

        'Display a message
        MessageBox.Show("The Answer is: " & TheAnswer)

        Exit Sub          'Exit sub before stepping into the error handler by accident
    ErrorHandlingBasicDemo_EH:  'Error Handler Label (:) is where code is redirected when an error occurs
        Select Case Err.Number
            Case 6 'Division by zero (0)
                MessageBox.Show("You cannot divide by Zero", "Division Error", MessageBoxButtons.OK, _
                MessageBoxIcon.Error)
            Case Else
                MessageBox.Show("An Error Occurred.  " & vbLf & "Details: " & Err.Description, "Error", _
                MessageBoxButtons.OK, MessageBoxIcon.Error)
        End Select          Error Handler label
    End Sub
```

Tip

Two types of errors can be trapped by error-handling procedures: runtime errors and logic errors. Runtime errors are usually caused by mistakes in addressing resources, such as attempting to access missing files or reading past the bounds of an array. Logic errors are often the most difficult to find, and error logging is very helpful in locating these errors.

Tip

Basic and unstructured Error Handling are simple approaches that have roots in Visual Basic 6.0. If you are not familiar with these approaches, you may wish to skip to the structured error handling section which is the preferred and superior method for managing errors in Visual Basic .NET.

4 Press F5 and verify that the breakpoint stops the code; then press F8 and watch as an error occurs and finally see the error message appear.

5 Click the Close button or choose **Debug | Stop Debugging**.

6 Click the Close button.

Figure 8-12

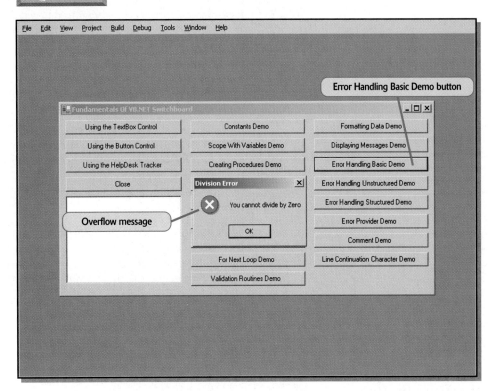

Tip

Since the On Error Goto ErrorHandlerBasicDemo_EH statement is at the top of the code window, and the error occurred somewhere below that statement, the code steps into the error handler and displays a message. We need to place an Exit Sub statement before the error handler; otherwise the error handler code will be executed.

In Visual Basic .NET you must use the On Error GoTo statement to enable an error handler and this line does not have a colon. The ErrorHandlingBasicDemo_EH: *label* below contains a colon (:). The colon appears at the end of the line to indicate that this is a label. The code following the label is the actual code of the error handler—that is, the code that is executed if an error occurs in the procedure.

Using Unstructured Error Handling

In *unstructured error handling*, an On Error statement placed at the beginning of a block of code handles any errors occurring within that block. When an error is found in a procedure after the On Error statement executes, the program branches to the line argument specified in the On Error statement. The line argument, which is a line number or line label, indicates the error handler location.

Sometimes a call is made from the original procedure to another procedure, and an error occurs in the called procedure. In such cases, if the called procedure does not handle the error, the error propagates back to the calling procedure, and execution branches to the line argument.

Once Visual Basic .NET jumps to the code in your error handler, you have several choices as to what to do next. For example, you can end the program by coding an Exit Sub statement within the error handler or just let the program reach the End Sub statement. You can instruct Visual Basic .NET to continue running the program at the same line of code that caused the error to begin with. You do this by coding a Resume statement. It is possible that the condition that caused the error may have been corrected. "Please insert a diskette" is an example of a message that might remind a user to insert a diskette and then click a button to continue saving a file. In the following task we will create another simple error handler and provide the user two choices: Resume or Resume Next. Resume will retry the validation statement again. Resume next will skip the validation condition and continue to the next instruction in the code sequence.

The On Error GoTo 0 statement disables error handling in the current procedure. It doesn't specify line 0 as the start of the error-handling code, even if the procedure contains a line numbered 0. Without an On Error GoTo 0 statement, an error handler is automatically disabled when a procedure is exited.

Tip

Task 5:

To Use Unstructured Error Handling

1 Choose **View | Solution Explorer**, double-click the Switchboard form, and then double-click the Error Handling Unstructured Demo button to view code.

2 Type the code provided in Figure 8-13 and then set a breakpoint at the Private Sub btnError HandlingUnstructuredDemo_ Click code statement.

3 Choose **File | Save All**.

Figure 8-13

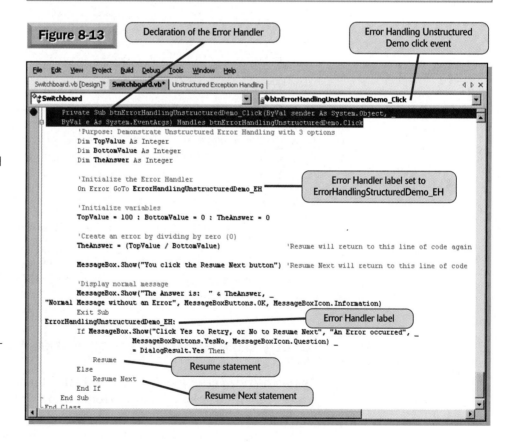

Declaration of the Error Handler

Error Handling Unstructured Demo click event

Error Handler label set to ErrorHandlingStructuredDemo_EH

Error Handler label

Resume statement

Resume Next statement

```
Private Sub btnErrorHandlingUnstructuredDemo_Click(ByVal sender As System.Object, _
    ByVal e As System.EventArgs) Handles btnErrorHandlingUnstructuredDemo.Click
    'Purpose: Demonstrate Unstructured Error Handling with 3 options
    Dim TopValue As Integer
    Dim BottomValue As Integer
    Dim TheAnswer As Integer

    'Initialize the Error Handler
    On Error GoTo ErrorHandlingUnstructuredDemo_EH

    'Initialize variables
    TopValue = 100 : BottomValue = 0 : TheAnswer = 0

    'Create an error by dividing by zero (0)
    TheAnswer = (TopValue / BottomValue)                'Resume will return to this line of code again

    MessageBox.Show("You click the Resume Next button")  'Resume Next will return to this line of code

    'Display normal message
    MessageBox.Show("The Answer is:  " & TheAnswer, _
"Normal Message without an Error", MessageBoxButtons.OK, MessageBoxIcon.Information)
    Exit Sub
ErrorHandlingUnstructuredDemo_EH:
    If MessageBox.Show("Click Yes to Retry, or No to Resume Next", "An Error occurred", _
                MessageBoxButtons.YesNo, MessageBoxIcon.Question) _
                = DialogResult.Yes Then
        Resume
    Else
        Resume Next
    End If
End Sub
End Class
```

4 Press F5, click the Error Handling Unstructured Demo button, and then press F8 at the breakpoint and verify that a message appears with two options: Yes or No. You can also choose **Debug | Start** to run the program.

5 Click the Yes button to Resume, and verify that the Resume message reappears.

Figure 8-14

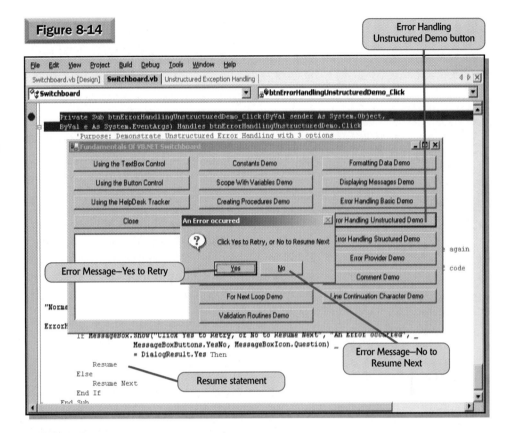

6 Click the No button to Resume Next, and verify that the Resume Next message appears. Click the OK button and the Switch-board form reappears.

7 Click the Close button.

Figure 8-15

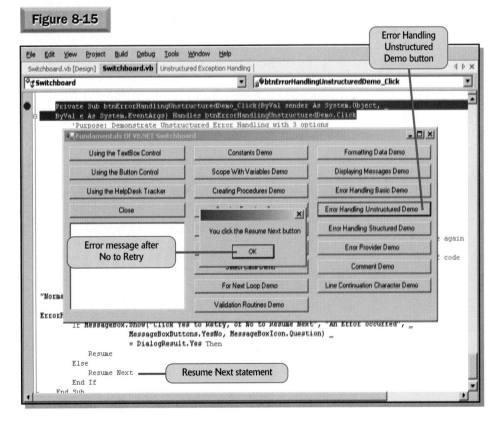

Using Structured Error Handling

Visual Basic .NET continues to support error trapping using On Error Resume Next, but it also has additional methods of managing errors known as *structured error handling* which is more common in languages such as Java and C++.

When an error occurs, the system moves backward using the *calling chain* until an error handler is found. If the program does not contain an error handler, Visual Basic .NET receives the error and the user is prompted to quit the application.

Careful attention to error-handling code is critical to an application, service, or component to prevent an abnormal ending. Using controls such as the DateTimePicker to obtain dates in valid formats and the MaskedEdit control to restrict entry of nonnumeric data can reduce or eliminate some need for custom validation code.

Try, Catch, and *Finally* are the basis of the new structured error handling (Table 8-2) in Visual Basic .NET. Other languages, including Java and C++ support it. This allows a program to intercept multiple error types as well as perform conditional execution based on an expression. In its simplest form, the Catch keyword can be used without any processing code to simply ignore the error.

Table 8-2	Structured Error Handling
Parts	**Description**
Catch	Optional. Multiple Catch blocks are permitted. If an error occurs while processing the Try block, each Catch statement is examined in textual order to determine whether it handles the error.
End Try	Terminates the Try...Catch...Finally structure
Exit Try	Optional. Keyword that breaks out of the Try...Catch...Finally structure. Execution resumes with the code immediately following the End Try statement. Not allowed in Finally blocks.
Finally	Optional. A Finally block is always executed when execution leaves any part of the Try statement.
When	Optional. A Catch statement with a When clause will only catch errors when *expression* evaluates to True. A When clause is only applied after checking the type of the error, and *expression* may refer to the identifier representing the error.

Tip The MaskedEdit control provides restricted data input as well as formatted data output. This control supplies visual cues about the type of data being entered or displayed. The DateTime Picker control allows the user to select a single item from a list of dates or times. When used to represent a date, it appears in two parts: a drop-down list with a date represented in text, and a grid that appears when you click on the down arrow next to the list. The grid looks like the Month Calendar control, which can be used for selecting multiple dates.

Task 6:

To Use Structured Error Handling

1 Choose **View | Solution Explorer**, double-click Switchboard form, and then double-click the Error Handling Structured Demo button to view code.

2 Type the code provided in Figure 8-16 and then set a breakpoint at the Private Sub btnError HandlingSstructuredDemo_ Click code statement.

3 Choose **File | Save All**.

4 Press F5 and F8 to step through the code.

5 Choose **Debug | Stop Debugging**.

Figure 8-16

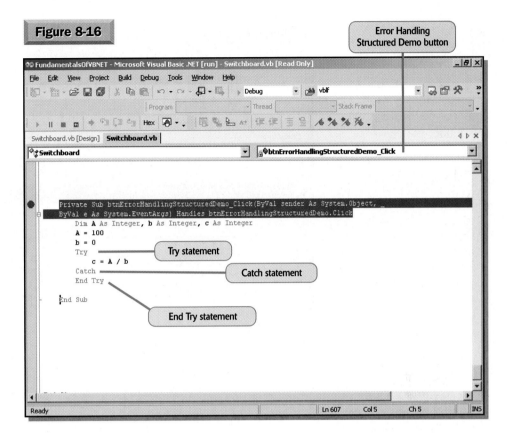

 Without the Try code, a message box would display an error message such as "An unhandled exception of type system.overflowException occurred in VBWinText.exe" and the program would exit.

 To implement an error handler, the Try, Catch, and Finally clauses must contain code that reacts to the error that is generated. A structured handling routine encapsulates a block of code in a way similar in appearance to an If Then Else structure. To begin adding actual error handling, you need to receive the information provided by the error.

6 Type the code provided in Figure 8-17.

7 Press F5 and F8 until the message appears, and then click the OK button.

Tip Like the Err object of unstructured error handling, objects created from the *Exception class* contain information about the error that occurred. In the Exception object is information describing the location in the code where the error occurred, the error type, and the causes of the error. Table 8-3 presents the properties of the Exception object.

Figure 8-17

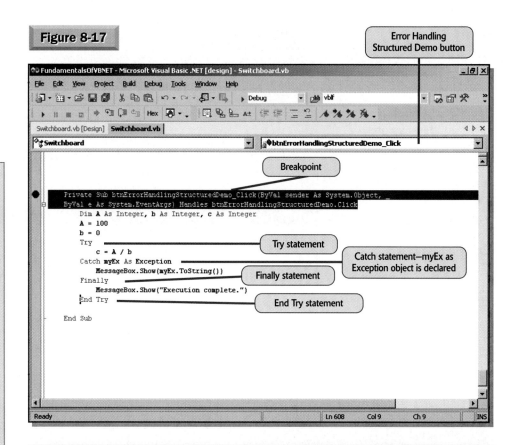

```
Private Sub btnErrorHandlingStructuredDemo_Click(ByVal sender As System.Object, _
ByVal e As System.EventArgs) Handles btnErrorHandlingStructuredDemo.Click
    Dim A As Integer, b As Integer, c As Integer
    A = 100
    b = 0
    Try
        c = A / b
    Catch myEx As Exception
        MessageBox.Show(myEx.ToString())
    Finally
        MessageBox.Show("Execution complete.")
    End Try

End Sub
```

Table 8-3	ExceptionObject Properties
Property	**Description**
HelpLink	Contains a link to the help file associated with the current error
Hresult	A unique numeric value assigned to the exception
Message	Hold the text message of the error
Source	Holds the name of the object in which the error occurred
StackTrace	Contains the list of methods on the call stack showing the method calls that lead to the error
TargetSite	Contains the method that caused the error

Tip To debug and step one line at a time, you may press the F8 button (or **Debug | Step into**). To debug and step over calls to code contained elsewhere in the project, you can press Shift + F8. For example, if the load event of a form provides a Call Populate_Form_Controls procedure statement, the F8 key would navigate from the form's load event code into the Populate_Form_Controls procedure code and then return to the form load event code and continue. If Visual Basic .NET is highlighting the Call Populate_Form_Controls statement in yellow and Shift + F8 is pressed, the code will move directly to the next line of code within the form load event rather then the Populate_Form_Controls procedure code. The program must be in break mode to debug in this manner.

SUMMARY AND EXERCISES

SUMMARY

- Using the Error Provider can give a visual cue of a user input error.
- The CausesValidation control property exists on every control and can determine whether a control will trigger the validating procedure event.
- When formatting data, the FormatDateTime and FormatCurrency commands can easily and quickly generate validated output in either date/time or currency formats.
- A message box provides a way to display simple dialog boxes that show a message and/or ask the user to make a choice.
- Message boxes can also receive input and branch within code like the If Then Else control structure.
- Error handling allows the program to gracefully recover when things don't go as expected.
- When an error occurs, log or somehow notify the user of the problem, let the user save his or her work, and let the user gracefully exit the program if necessary.
- The two types of errors that can occur are runtime errors and logic errors.
- Unstructured error handlers use the On Error Goto statement.
- Structured error handling uses the Try, Catch, and Finally statements.
- The Exception class contains information about the error, including the location in the code where the error occurred, the error type, and the causes of the error.

KEY TERMS & SKILLS

KEY TERMS

Catch (p. 8-14)
CausesValidation
   (p. 8-3)
calling chain (p. 8-14)
error handler (p. 8-9)
Error Provider (p. 8-2)
Exception class (p. 8-16)
Finally (p. 8-14)

FormatCurrency
   (p. 8-6)
FormatDateTime
   (p. 8-6)
label (p. 8-11)
MessageBox class
   (p. 8-8)
Msgbox (p. 8-9)

structured error
   handling (p. 8-14)
Try (p. 8-14)
unstructured error
   handling (p. 8-11)
Validated (p. 8-3)
Validating (p. 8-3)

SKILLS

Display messages (p. 8-8)
Format data (p. 8-6)
Understand basic error handling
   (p. 8-10)

Use a validation routine
   (p. 8-4)
Use unstructured error handling
   (p. 8-12)

STUDY QUESTIONS

MULTIPLE CHOICE

1. Which of the following are valid keywords for handling an error?
   a. Resume
   b. On Error GoTo 0
   c. Resume Next
   d. all of the above

2. What happens when an error occurs in a procedure that does NOT have an error handler?
   a. The code moves back up the calling chain to the procedure that called the code that contains the error.
   b. The application ends normally.
   c. The code locks up awaiting user interaction.
   d. Nothing happens.

3. Which of the following are valid structured error handling keywords?
   a. Try
   b. Catch
   c. Finally
   d. all of the above

4. A structured handling routine encapsulates a block of code in a way similar in appearance to which of the following?
   a. Select Case statement
   b. If Then Else statement
   c. Do While loop
   d. For Next loop

5. What is always executed when execution leaves any part of the Try statement of a structured error handling routine?
   a. Try
   b. Finally
   c. Catch
   d. End Try

6. Which of the following structured error handling statements terminates the Try Catch Finally structure?
   a. Finally
   b. End Try
   c. Exit Try
   d. When

7. Which of the following pieces of information are provided by the Exception object?
   a. the location in the code where the error occurred
   b. the error type
   c. the cause of the error
   d. all of the above

8. Which methods can be used to step one line within the current procedure when debugging code?
   a. the F8 key
   b. **Debug | Step Over** option
   c. Shift + F8 keys
   d. all of the above

9. Which methods can be used to step over a procedure call and remain within the current code during debugging?
   a. the F8 key
   b. **Debug | Step Into** option
   c. Shift + F8 keys
   d. all of the above

10. Checking for valid data only when the user clicks the OK button permits users to exit if they click
   a. the Cancel button.
   b. the Save button.
   c. the Help button.
   d. the control being validated.

SHORT ANSWER

1. What property exists on every control to provide input validation?
2. What two events exist on every control to enable validation?
3. On what three Button controls would you disable error handling?
4. Where do you handle errors?
5. What is the name of the line of error-handling code that ends with a colon?
6. What happens if you forget to include the Exit Sub statement before the error handler code?
7. What are two types of errors that can be trapped by error-handling procedures?
8. Which type of error is most difficult to find?
9. What is the name of the type of error handling that uses the On Error Goto statement?
10. What two words of code are always used to avoid entering the error handler unnecessarily?

FILL IN THE BLANK

1. Although we cannot always prevent an error from occurring, it is possible to _____ errors gracefully.
2. The _____ Provider can be used to give a visual cue of a user input error.
3. The _____ property of the Error Provider indicates whether selecting this control causes conditions on the controls requiring validation.
4. The _____ property of the Error Provider occurs when the control is finished performing its validation logic.

5. The _____ property of the Error Provider occurs when the control is validating user input.

6. The _____ format returns a string formatted in a specified date and time format.

7. The _____ format is a specialized formatting command for easily and quickly generating output in a currency format.

8. In previous versions of Visual Basic, the _____ command was used rather than the now preferred MessageBox.Show method.

9. The overall purpose of error handlers is to allow the program to _____ _____ when things don't go as expected.

10. When an error occurs is it important to _____ or _____ the user of the problem, let the user _____ his or her work, and let the user gracefully _____ the program if necessary.

FOR DISCUSSION

1. Why wouldn't you set the CausesValidation property of a Cancel button to True?

2. Why is error handling important?

3. If an error handler is not used, how will Visual Basic .NET respond?

4. When an error occurs in a called procedure that does not have an error handler, how does Visual Basic .NET manage that error?

5. What are a few ways to reduce the potential for errors without writing code?

P R O J E C T 9

Database Fundamentals: Building the Application Foundation

Many applications developed for corporations use a commercial database to manage information storage and retrieval. *Databases* enable us to create tables, views, and stored procedures (predefined queries) in a consistent manner. They are especially useful for multiuser systems in which various users may need to access the same information at the same time. Databases also provide password security, backup and recovery, and other useful utilities for querying the database. For this project, we will use a Microsoft Access database called *PayTrans.mdb* that has been supplied with the courseware.

Tip

A database is a set of data related to a particular topic or purpose. A database contains tables and can also contain queries and table relationships, as well as table and column validation criteria. In Visual Studio .NET, you use the *Server Explorer* to view and retrieve information from all of the databases installed on a server. You can list database tables, views, stored procedures, and functions in the Server Explorer; expand individual tables to list their columns and triggers; and right-click a table to choose the Table Designer from its shortcut menu.

Tip

The The *PayTrans.mdb* database and the *PayTransactionSystem.sln* file can be found at
\\vb.net_brief\vb.net_datafiles\09\Students\HR\PayTransactionSystem.

OBJECTIVES

After completing this project, you will be able to:

• Add a data connection through the Server Explorer

• Use the Data Form Wizard

• Test a form created with the Data Form Wizard

• Customize forms created with the Data Form Wizard

e-selections) Running Case

The programmers are finally starting to believe that Visual Basic .NET can do everything they need, including writing code. One aspect they need to see now is how to integrate a database into the project.

Documenting Programs

Creating Graphical User Interfaces along with Documentation for Future Reference and Support

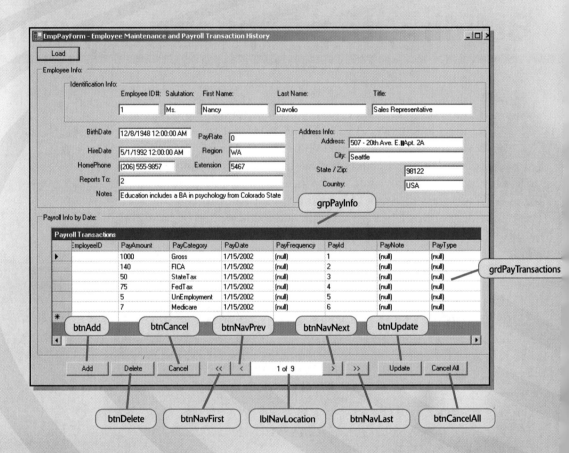

Most programmers do not like to document the programs they write after they are completed, but it is extremely helpful to map out the field name to the form image whenever possible.

Each project provides details about the construction of the necessary components.

Most corporate applications have a shelf life of well over 15 years, yet the programmers who work on a given project usually move on to another project or another organization every two years or so.

Think about how helpful it would be to have a visual map of the field sources as shown above if you were a new maintenance programmer charged with enhancing the form based on the latest user specifications. The Form Layout complemented with Use Case Diagrams/Descriptions and an Entity Relationship Diagram to depict the data model would allow you to get up and running quickly.

The alternative for many developers is to read the source code line by line in order to get a handle on what is going on in the application. This would have a negative effect on productivity and your comfort level.

Database Fundamentals: Building the Application Foundation

The Challenge

To demonstrate that Visual Basic .NET can provide robust data storage using a database and provide forms that can update the database easily, you will need to learn about the Server Explorer, which creates a link between our programming project and the database. A database will be provided to save you time. Review Figure 9-1 to identify some of the tables that will be used. More details will be provided as we complete the Pay Transaction System over the remaining projects. Finally, you will create a new form using the Data Form Wizard. This tool creates forms in minutes and generates code too. Although this sounds too good to be true, it actually is a great way to begin learning how to maintain data with Visual Basic .NET.

The Solution

The *PayTrans.mdb* database includes the tables needed for this project. In this project you will create a link from Visual Basic .NET and the Microsoft Access database. After a *connection* has been made, a new form will be created using the *Data Form Wizard*. This tool provided with Visual Basic .NET writes code and creates data-bound fields that update the database automatically. The Data Form Wizard is an excellent tool for creating prototype forms.

Tip The *data model* is called an *entity relationship diagram* (*ERD*) and is used to depict relationships from one table to another. The ERD in Figure 9-1 shows that one Employee can have many Pay transactions. The EmployeeID field relates the two tables. The ScheduledPayrolls table can have many Employees associated by PayType and many PayTransactions associated by a compound foreign key of PayDate and PayType. Finally, each PayTransaction has a PayCategory that must match a valid PayCategory in the PayCategory table. For the remainder of this project, we will focus on the tables shown in Figure 9-1.

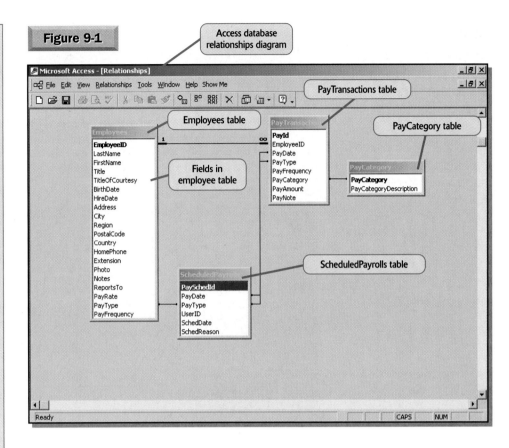

Figure 9-1

Creating a Data Connection through the Visual Basic .NET Server Explorer

Visual Studio .NET has a convenient interface called the Server Explorer that enables you to perform most of the functions necessary to work with existing databases. To start working with the *PayTrans.mdb* database we must first create a data connection.

Task 1:

To Create a Data Connection through the Server Explorer

1 Open *PayTransaction System.sln* and then choose **View | Server Explorer**.

Figure 9-2

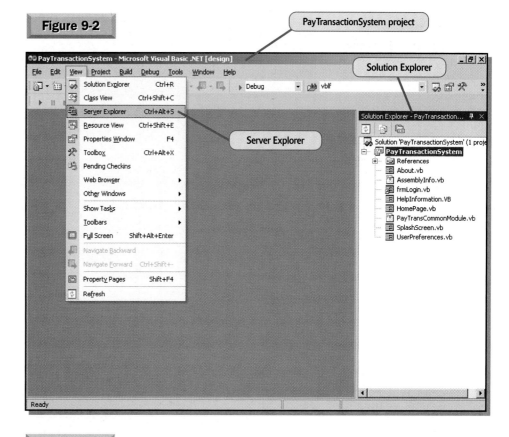

2 Within the Server Explorer, right-click **Data Connections** and choose **Add Connection**.

Figure 9-3

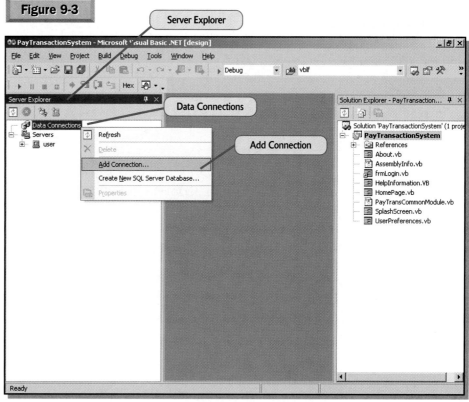

3 Verify that the Data Link Properties dialog box appears with the Connection tab selected on top.

Tip The Data Link Properties dialog box brings up the Connection tab by default. To use a Microsoft Access database such as *Pay Trans.mdb*, we must first fill out the correct information on the Provider tab. Visual Basic .NET assumes your provider is SQL Server unless you change it to another choice.

Figure 9-4

Data Link Properties—Provider tab

Data Link Properties—Connection tab

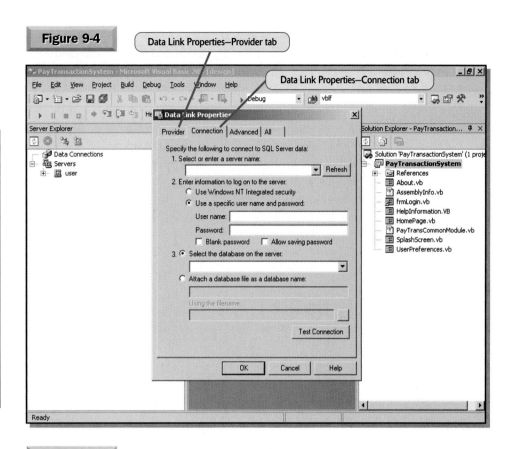

4 Click the Provider tab and verify that the list of data providers appears.

Tip As you can see, there are many available data providers including Oracle and SQL Server. The list includes all OLE DB providers detected on your computer.

5 Click **Microsoft Jet 4.0 OLE DB Provider**, click the Next button, and verify that the Connection tab appears.

Figure 9-5

Data Link Properties—Provider tab

Microsoft Jet 4.0 OLE DB Provider

Next button

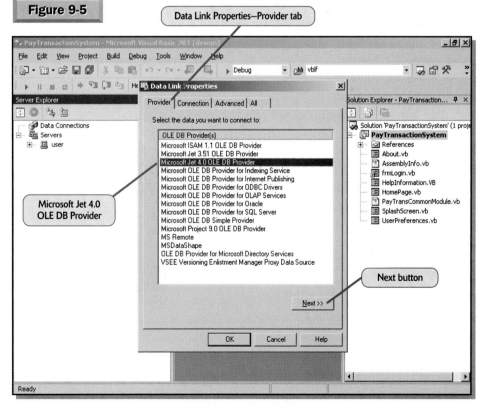

6 Click the Ellipse (...) button to display the Select Access Database dialog box.

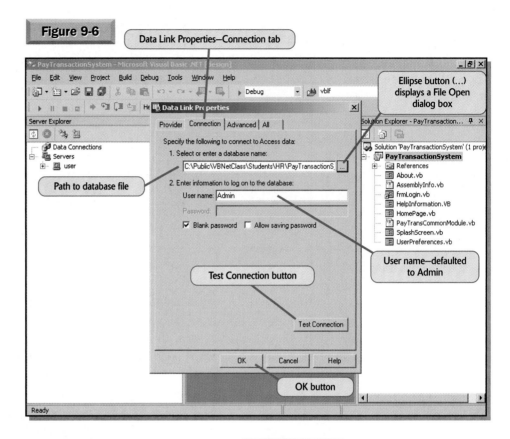

Figure 9-6

7 Verify that the Select Access Database dialog box appears. Enter the directory path and file name for the *PayTrans.mdb* Database file and then click the Open button. Enter a User name of Admin if it is not already the default and then check the **Blank password** check box if it is not already checked.

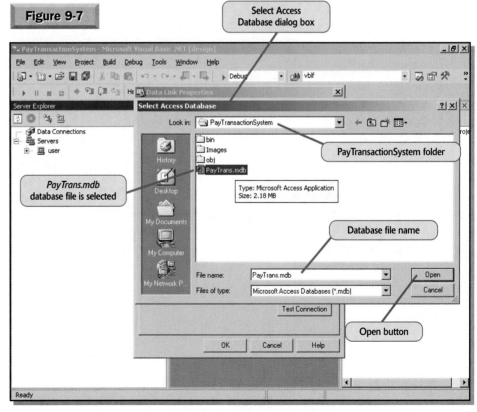

Figure 9-7

8 Click the Test Connection button and verify that the Test Connection Succeeded Message appears. Click the OK button in the Microsoft Data Link message box; then click the OK button to close the Data Link Properties dialog box and save your data connection information.

9 Choose **File | Save All**.

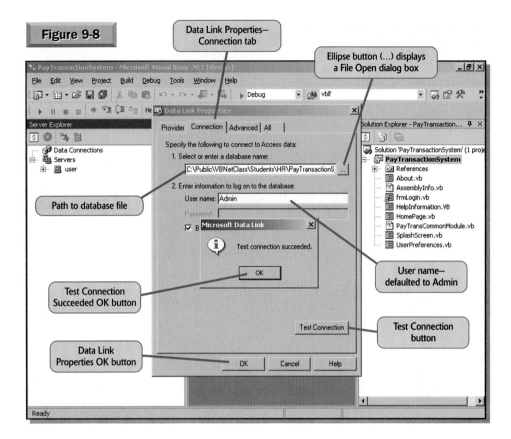

Figure 9-8

Now that the data connection is set up, you will verify the setup and rename the connection. If everything has been configured correctly, you will see your new connection for the PayTrans database in the Server Explorer window.

Task 2:

To Verify That the Data Connection Was Set Up in the Server Explorer

1 In the Server Explorer, click the plus sign (+) next to **Data Connections** and you will see Tables, Views, and Stored Procedures for the *PayTrans.mdb* database.

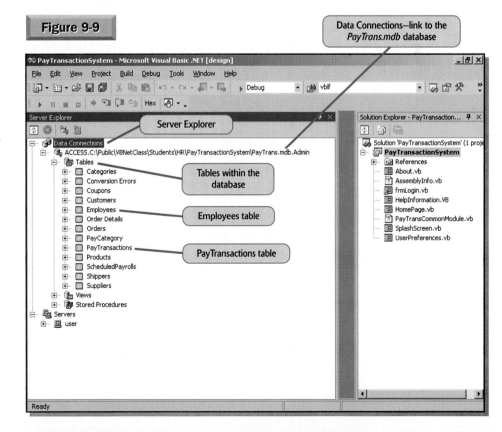

Figure 9-9

2 Right-click the Access database file name and then choose **Rename** as shown in Figure 9-10.

Figure 9-10

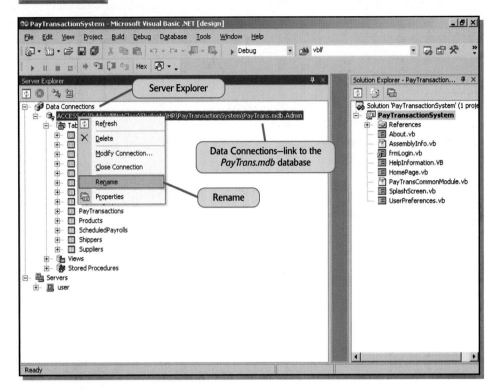

3 Type **PayTransaction Database** as the new database name and press Enter.

Figure 9-11

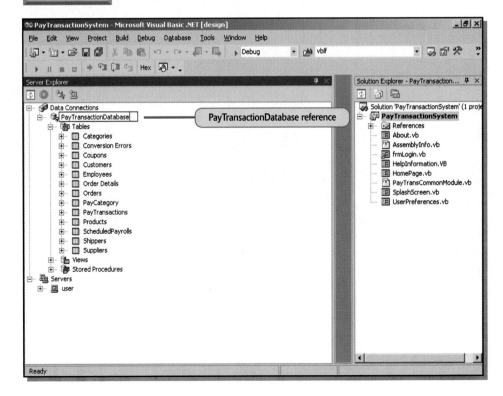

4 Right-click the Pay TransactionDatabase data connection and then choose **Properties**.

Figure 9-12

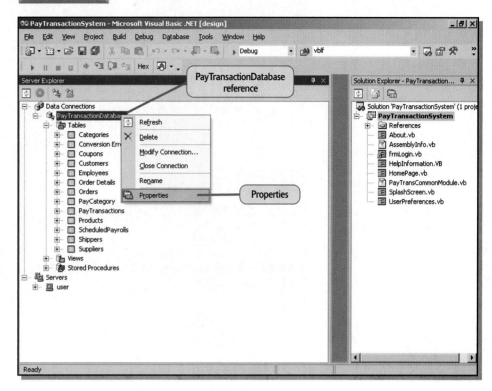

> **Tip** The Properties window will be displayed and look similar to Figure 9-13. The most important property that you will use later in your programming is ConnectString. You will not be able to write programs that use a database without a proper connect string. You can always use the Server Explorer to display the ConnectString and copy and paste the string into your programs. This will be discussed in more detail later.

5 Verify that the Properties window appears. The actual database path may be different based on the setup for your class.

6 Choose **File | Save All**.

Figure 9-13

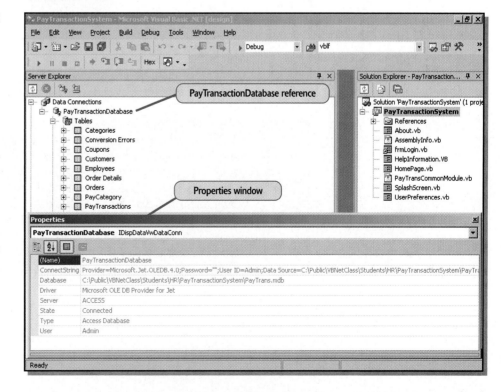

Congratulations! You are connected to the Payroll Transaction System database and are ready to start programming data-related forms. Depending on the database you are using, the Server Explorer may have more or fewer options to work with. For instance, with Microsoft Access, you can only use existing database objects such as tables, views, and stored procedures. If you right-click a table, view, or stored procedure, you can view the properties and refresh the list (for example, if you have added a table to the model after you started the Server Explorer and you want to see it in your list of tables).

Figure 9-14

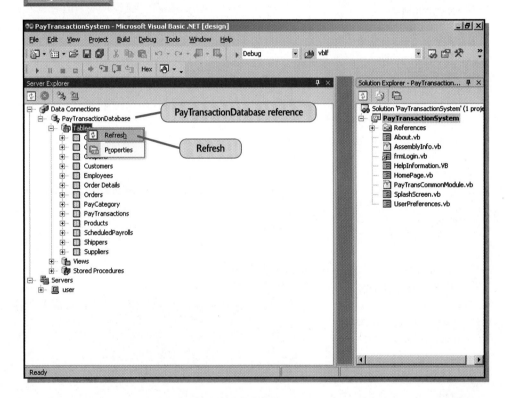

A SQL Server or Oracle 8i/9i database, on the other hand, has many more features available from the Server Explorer, such as creating Database Diagrams, Tables, Views, Store Procedures, Functions, Package Bodies. When you right-click these objects you will see a New menu option that is not available in Access databases. Visual Studio .NET is currently optimized to use SQL Server or Oracle 8i/9i, as you can perform virtually all of your database administration activities directly from the Visual Studio .NET Interactive Development Environment (IDE).

Using the Data Form Wizard

The Data Form Wizard is a productivity tool that helps you create Windows forms with data-bound controls without having to write the program from a blank slate. The wizard runs you through the entire process of creating the data-bound form that provides a completely functional Windows interface that loads and displays data, enables users to make changes to the data and save those changes back to the database.

To be productive in programming it is useful to have templates and patterns that you can use as a model to get something up and running quickly. In many business scenarios, time to market and productivity is extremely important. If you are new to programming or leaning a new language such as Visual Basic .NET, the benefits of using a wizard can be significant to your learning process, productivity and success.

We will use the Data Form Wizard to create a form that displays employee records and their related payroll transactions. From this form, you will be able to add new employees and maintain employee data as well as view, add, and maintain payroll transaction records. First we will generate the form and verify that it is in working order, and then we will customize the form to improve its appearance and functionality.

Task 3:
To Use the Data Form Wizard

1 In the Solution Explorer, right-click the PayTransactionSystem project and choose **Add | Add Windows Form**.

Figure 9-15

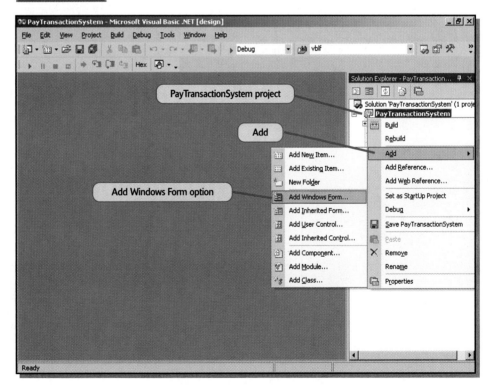

2 In the **Add New Item** dialog box, select the Data Form Wizard Template and type EmpPayForm.vb as the new form name.

Figure 9-16

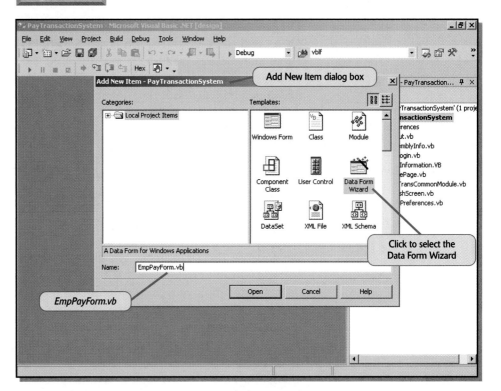

3 Verify that the Welcome to the Data Form Wizard dialog box appears and then click the Next button.

Figure 9-17

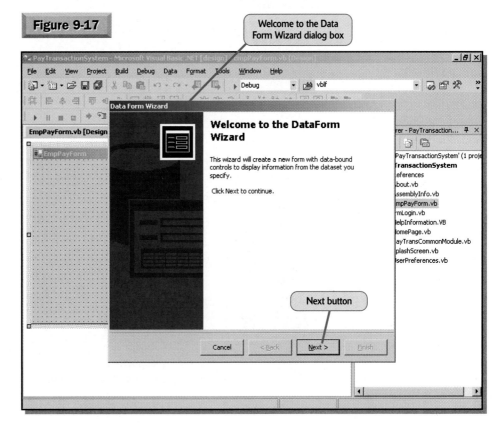

4 Select the **Create a new dataset named:** radio button and then type **EmpPay** for the dataset name. Click the Next button to continue.

Figure 9-18

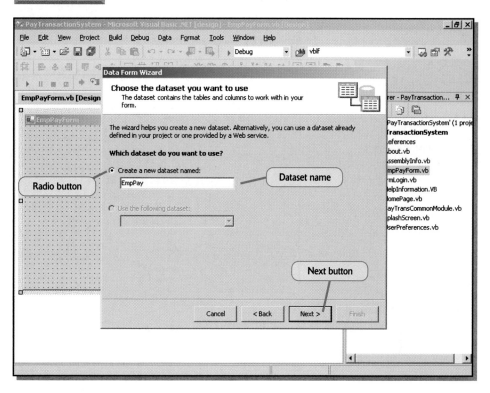

Tip If you have never created a dataset for your project previously, this dialog box will only enable you to select the **Create a new dataset named:** option. If your project already has one or more datasets, then the form will enable you to pick from a list of existing datasets.

5 Select **Pay TransactionDatabase** from the **Which connection should the wizard use?** drop-down list. Click the Next button to continue.

Figure 9-19

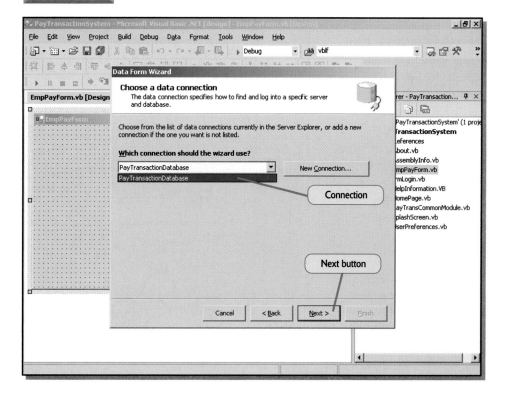

6 Verify that the **Choose tables or views** dialog box appears.

Tip When an item is selected and then added (or removed), it will move from one side to the other. For example, when the Employees table is added, it will first appear on the left, and after the > (Add) button is clicked, the Employees table will appear on the right in the **Selected item(s):** list. You may need to scroll to locate tables if they are not displayed.

Figure 9-20

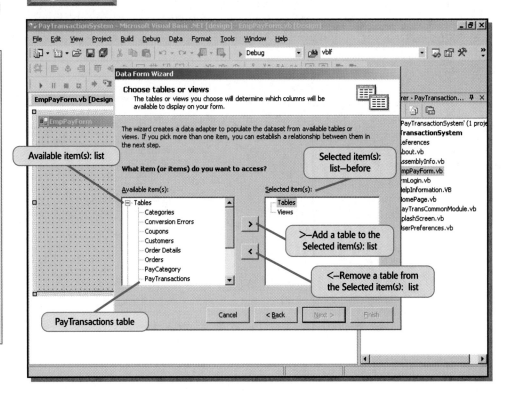

7 Select the Employees table in the **Available item(s):** list, and then click the > (Add) button in the center to add the Employees table to the **Selected item(s):** list.

8 Select the PayTransactions table in the **Available item(s):** list, and then click the > (Add) button to add the Pay Transactions table to the **Selected item(s):** list.

Tip When you click the Next button, Visual Basic .NET processes the information you have provided. This may take a moment.

Figure 9-21

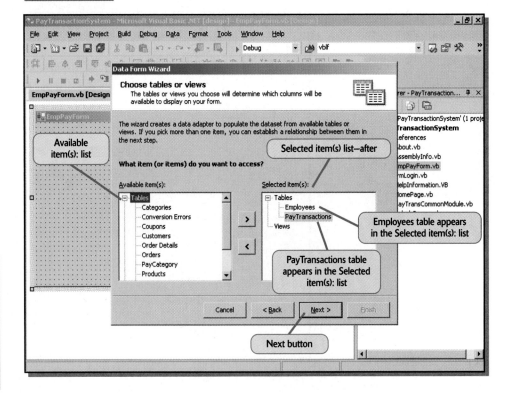

A relationship between tables identifies the Parent and Child of the table relationship as well as the column(s) that will link the records between the two tables. In the form below we created a relationship called EmpPay where Employees is identified as the Parent table and PayTransactions is identified as the Child table. The primary key of the Employees table is EmployeeID; it will link to the EmployeeID column in the PayTransactions table, where EmployeeID is a foreign key to the Employees table.

A *primary key* is a column or combination of columns that uniquely identifies a row in a table. It cannot allow null values and must always have a unique value. A primary key is used to relate a table to foreign keys in other tables.

A *foreign key* is a column or combination of columns whose values match the primary key of some other table. A foreign key does not have to be unique. Foreign key values should be copies of the primary key values; no value in the foreign key except NULL should ever exist unless the same value exists in the primary key.

9 Verify that the **Create a relationship between tables** dialog box appears. Type **EmpPay** in the Name field and select Employees for the Parent table, PayTransactions for the Child table, EmployeeID from the Keys (Parent), and EmployeeID from the Keys (Child). Then click the > (Add) button to add to the Relations: list.

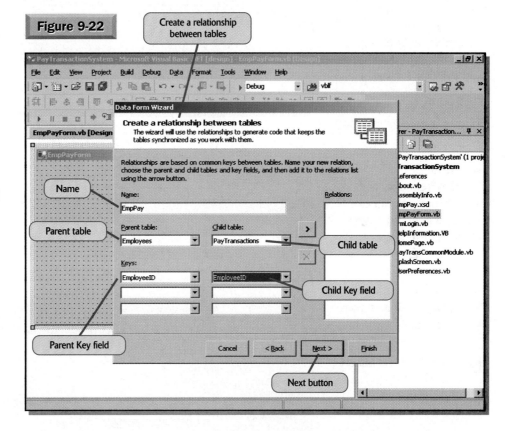

Figure 9-22

Create a relationship between tables

Name

Parent table

Parent Key field

Child table

Child Key field

Next button

Once you have completed the **Create a relationship between tables** dialog box, click the > (Add) button. This will move the EmpPay relationship from the left side of the form to the Relations: list box on the right, as shown in Figure 9-23.

10 Click the Next button.

Tip If the form had more tables and/or relations to describe, you could enter them now. Since we do not have any more relations to define, we can click the Next button to continue. We will now select the columns that will be displayed on the form.

It is very important to take your time when filling out this form; there are limitations (bugs) that will prevent the data form from being generated successfully if you are not careful.

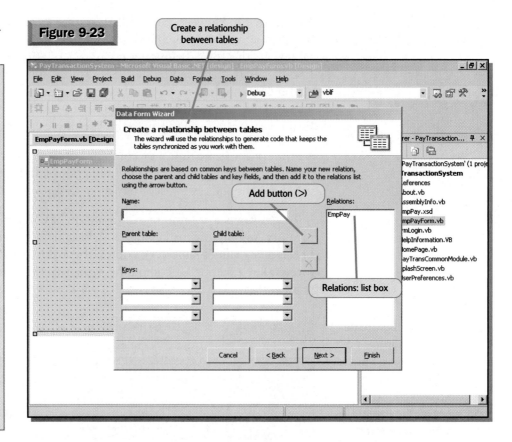

Figure 9-23

Create a relationship between tables

11 Clear the PayFrequency and PayTypePhoto check boxes in the Columns: list for the Master table (Employees) on the left side, and then clear the EmployeeID check box in the Columns: list for the Detail table (PayTransactions) on the right side.

12 Click the Next button.

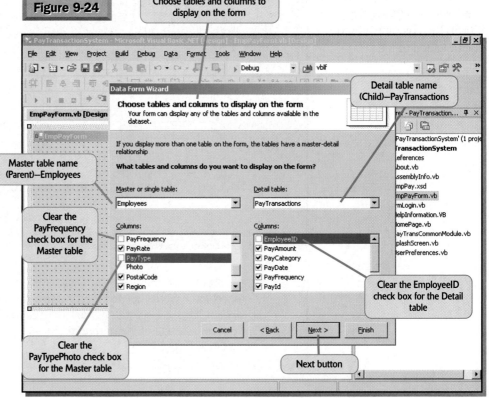

Figure 9-24

Choose tables and columns to display on the form

Troubleshooting If columns with the same name are shared between tables and you do not clear the check box for one of the tables so that the column names are unique, the resultant form that is generated will be useless. When duplicate column names do exist, you may receive a message box similar to the one shown in Figure 9-25. This message box will not be displayed until several forms later when you are at the final step of Data Form Wizard generation. Avoid using duplicate column names.

Figure 9-25

13 In the **Choose the display style** dialog box, select **Single record in individual controls** and then click the Finish button.

Figure 9-26

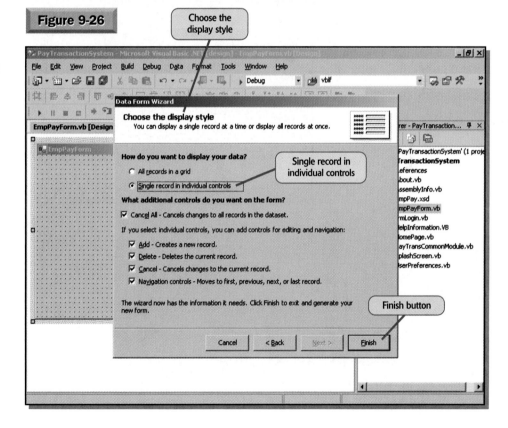

Tip

Make sure you select **Single record in individual controls** for this option and check off all additional controls prior to pressing on the Finish button to start the form generation process.

When you click the Finish button, the program pauses. It will take several moments for the EmpPayForm form to be generated. Once it is generated, the EmpPayForm looks like Figure 9-27. Since this is the first time we have seen a data form generated by the wizard, we will take a few moments to explain what you are seeing.

Figure 9-27

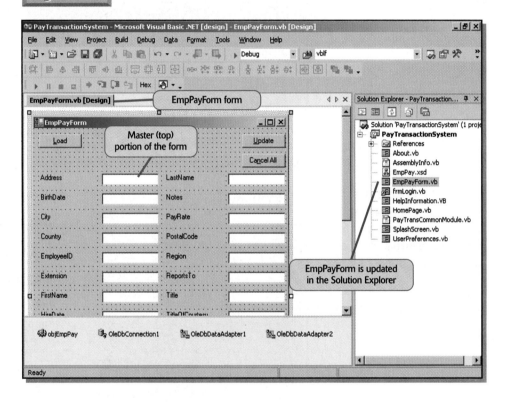

Tip

You might be asking yourself, "Where is the PayTransaction data I was expecting to see in a grid?" The grid is actually there, but you cannot see it until you scroll down as shown in Figure 9-28.

14 Choose **File | Save All**.

Figure 9-28

Tip

When you scroll down within the Form Designer, you can see some additional command buttons and the grid with the PayTransaction data.

What are those icons at the bottom of the form? Visual Basic .NET Windows Forms can have many objects attached to them that are used internally for their operation but not displayed on the form (Table 9-1).

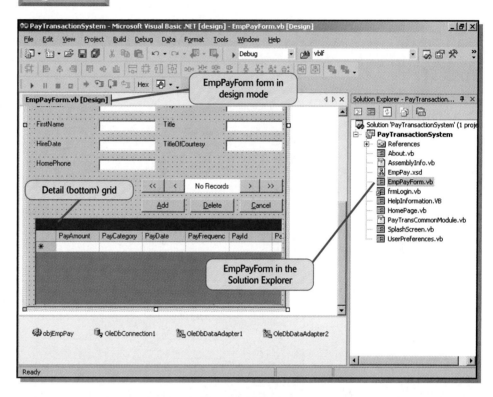

Table 9-1	Visual Basic .NET Windows Forms Objects
Object	**Explanation**
objEmpPay	The name of the dataset used by the form. A dataset is the container that holds the data used by the form. A dataset can have one or more tables and a form can have one or more datasets.
OleDbConnection1	The database connection that identifies the connection string and methods used to communicate with the database. There is usually one connection per physical database.
OleDbDataAdapter1	The data adapter for the Employees table. Think of a *data adapter* as a bridge that links your database and connection to the dataset.
OleDbDataAdapter2	This is the data adapter for the PayTransactions table.

Testing a Form Created with the Data Form Wizard

The Data Form Wizard produces a form that is very functional but usually is not very aesthetically pleasing in appearance. You will want to change the layout of the form once you have verified that it is functioning correctly with the database. Verifying that the form is working correctly is an important time saver so that you do not spend significant time modifying the form and its code only to find out later that the form never worked correctly in the first place. The following are suggested steps for testing the *EmpPayForm.vb* form.

Task 4:

To Test a Form Created with the Data Form Wizard

1 Right-click the PayTransactionSystem project in the Solution Explorer and choose **Properties**.

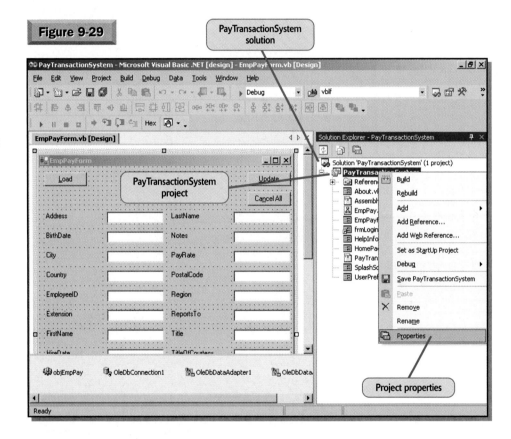

Figure 9-29

PayTransactionSystem solution

PayTransactionSystem project

Project properties

2 Select **EmpPayForm** from the **Startup object:** drop-down list to change the project startup object.

3 Choose **File | Save All**.

> **Tip**
> It is a good idea to save your project before running your application in the IDE. The debugging process requires a significant amount of memory, and you are more likely to freeze/lock up your workstation during these types of activities. "Better safe than sorry" is our motto from lessons learned the hard way.

4 Choose **Debug | Start** to begin debugging.

Figure 9-30

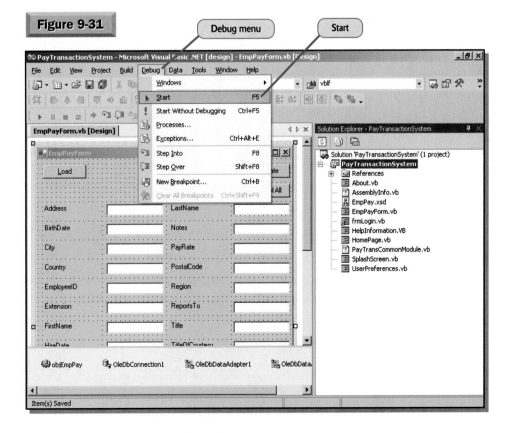

Figure 9-31

5 Verify that the EmpPayForm form appears without data.

> **Tip** When you run the form it will appear as shown and you may be surprised to see that no data is displayed on the form. The Data Form Wizard generates a program that requires you to click the Load button before querying the database and displaying the data on the form.

Figure 9-32

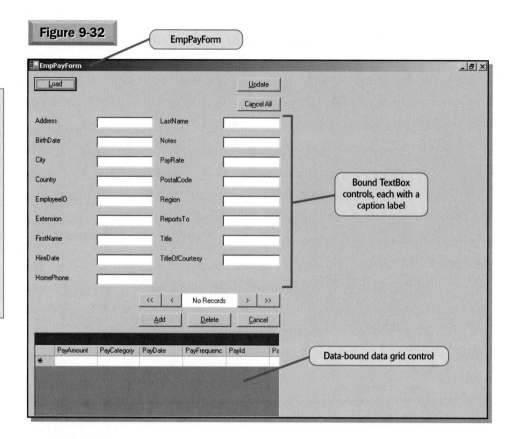

EmpPayForm

Bound TextBox controls, each with a caption label

Data-bound data grid control

6 Click the Load button and verify that the form is populated with data.

7 Choose **Debug | Stop Debugging**.

> **Tip** As you can see in Figure 9-33, the form is very functional but could use some improvement in the layout of various fields in a more meaningful way. We will work through modifying the form and customizing some of the code in our next set of tasks.

Figure 9-33

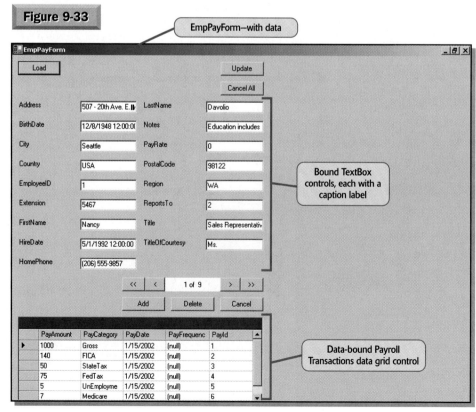

EmpPayForm—with data

Bound TextBox controls, each with a caption label

Data-bound Payroll Transactions data grid control

Customizing Forms Created with the Data Form Wizard

We will use some of the fundamentals learned earlier to modify the EmpPayForm to have a professional look and make it usable in an end user environment. In the next task, we will modify the form generated by the wizard to look like Figure 9-34 with virtually no additional programming. To complete this section, you will have six tasks: widening the EmpPayForm and creating the Address Info group, creating the Identification group, creating the Employee Info group, creating the Payroll Info by Date group, moving the command buttons and navigation location to the bottom of the form, and testing the program. Let's get started with the non-programming-related tasks to modify the form to look like Figure 9-34.

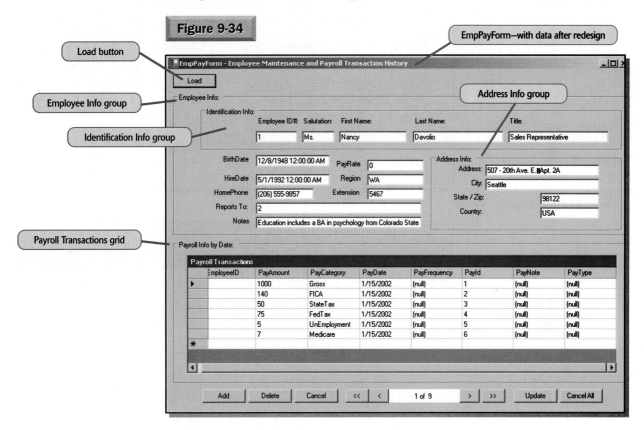

Figure 9-34

Widening the EmpPayForm and Creating the Address Info Group

To facilitate adding GroupBox controls and reorganizing the existing controls, we will widen the form.

Task 5:
To Widen the EmpPayForm and Create the Address Info Group

1 Double-click the EmpPayForm in the PayTransactionSystem in the Solution Explorer to display the form in design mode. Complete the properties as shown in Table 9-2.

2 Drag the right middle resize handle as wide as your display will allow so that you can see the whole width of the form at once without scrolling.

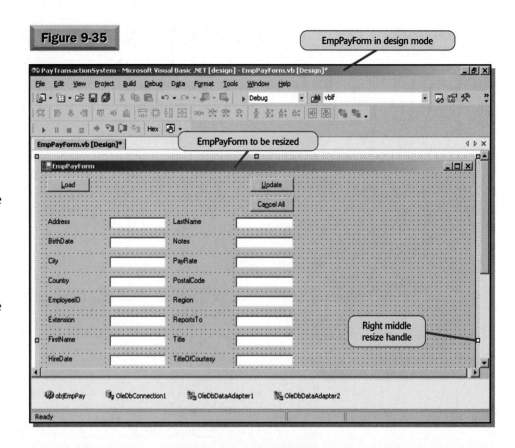

Figure 9-35

Table 9-2	EmpPayForm Properties
Property	**Value to Set**
Name	EmpPayForm
Location	0, 0
Size	812, 612

3 In the Toolbox, double-click the GroupBox control to add it to the EmpPayForm form and complete the GroupBox properties as shown in Table 9-3.

Figure 9-36

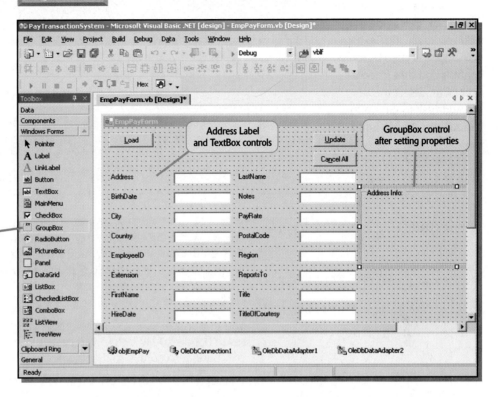

Toolbox—double-click the GroupBox control to add it to the EmpPayForm form

Table 9-3   Address Information GroupBox Properties

Property	Value to Set
Name	grpAddressInfo
Location	448, 104
Modifiers	Friend
Size	336, 128
Text	Address Info:

Tip To select more than one control, click to select the first control and then hold down the Shift key while clicking the next control. Once the controls you want to cut and paste are selected, you will use the **Edit | Cut** and **Edit | Paste** commands to move the controls so they appear within the Address Info group.

4 Cut and paste existing Address fields into the group box. Select the Address Label and TextBox (lblAddress and editAddress) controls and then choose **Edit | Cut**. Select the grpAddressInfo GroupBox control and choose **Edit | Paste**. Complete the Address properties as shown in Table 9-4.

Table 9-4   Address Properties

Type	Control	Property	Value to Set
Label	lblAddressInfo	Location	32, 16
		Modifiers	Friend
		Size	64, 23
TextBox	editAddress	Location	96, 16
		Modifiers	Friend
		Size	200, 20

Tip When you cut the controls, they are temporarily placed on the Windows Clipboard. Once there, they can be pasted elsewhere. When you select the grpAddressInfo GroupBox control, notice that the resize handles appear. When you paste the controls, both the label and the text box will reappear within the GroupBox control.

You must make sure you have the GroupBox control selected (it will have resize handles on it) before you paste the labels and text boxes into it. It is important to do this so that the labels and fields belong to the group.

5 Select the City Label and TextBox (lblCity and editCity) controls and then choose **Edit | Cut**. Select the grpAddressInfo GroupBox control and choose **Edit | Paste**. Complete the City properties as shown in Table 9-5.

Table 9-5   City Properties

Type	Control	Property	Value to Set
Label	LblCity	Location	32, 40
		Modifiers	Friend
		Size	64, 23
		Text	City:
TextBox	EditCity	Location	96, 40
		Modifiers	Friend
		Size	200, 20

6 Select the PostalCode Label and TextBox (lblPostalCode and editPostalCode) controls and then choose **Edit | Cut**. Select the grpAddressInfo GroupBox control and choose **Edit | Paste**. Complete the PostalCode properties as shown in Table 9-6.

Table 9-6	Postal Code Properties		
Type	**Control**	**Property**	**Value to Set**
Label	lblPostalCode	Location	32, 64
		Modifiers	Friend
		Size	64, 23
		Text	State / Zip (State will be added later)
TextBox	EditPostalCode	Location	192, 64
		Modifiers	Friend
		Size	104, 20

7 In the Toolbox, click the Label object and draw a label to the left of the editPostalCode text box.

Table 9-7	State Label Properties
Property	**Value to Set**
Name	lblState
Text	State
Location	144, 64
Modifiers	Friend
Size	40, 23

Tip

Although there is no State column in our Employee table, we will later add a lookup to a table that contains both postal codes and states/provinces. This can be optionally done during the programming customization that we will perform in the next project.

If you draw the Label object directly on the grpAddressInfo group box, it will automatically be part of the group box (Table 9-7).

8 Select the Country Label and TextBox (lblCountry and editCountry) controls and then choose **Edit | Cut**. Select the grpAddressInfo GroupBox control and choose **Edit | Paste**. Complete the Country properties as shown in Table 9-8.

Table 9-8	Country Label Properties		
Type	**Control**	**Property**	**Value to Set**
Label	lblCountry	Location	32, 88
		Modifiers	Friend
		Size	64, 23
TextBox	editCountry	Location	192, 88
		Modifiers	Friend
		Size	104, 20

9 Verify that the Address group box appears as shown in Figure 9-37.

10 Choose **File | Save All**.

Figure 9-37

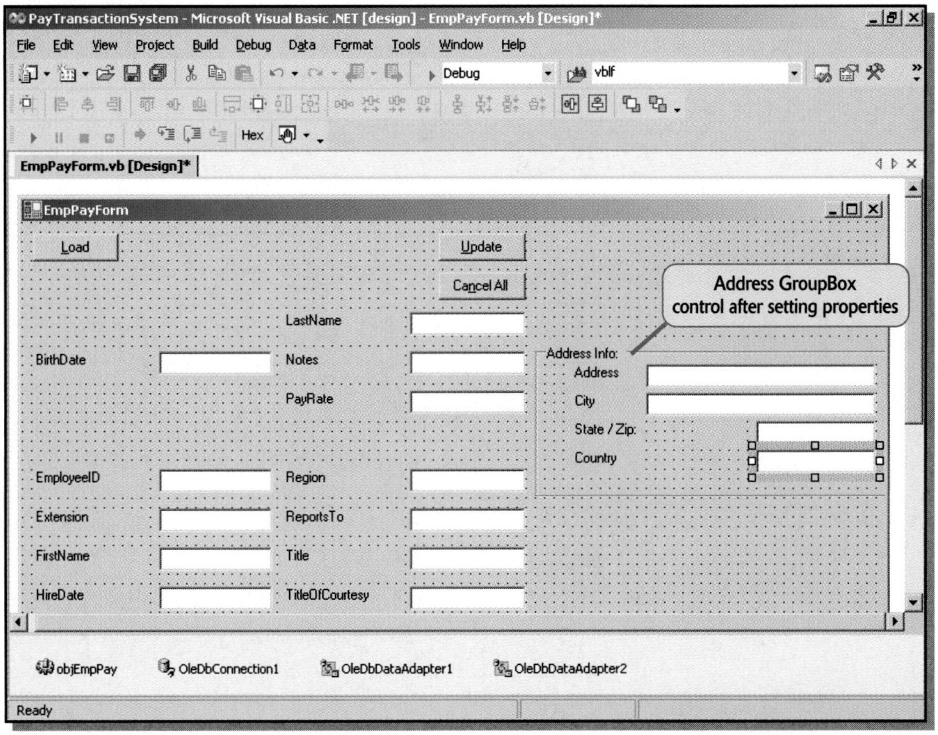

Creating the Identification Group

We will now create another group box called grpIdentificationInfo that looks similar to Figure 9-38 and contains the Employee ID, Salutation, First Name, Last Name, and Title.

Task 6:

To Create the Identification Info Group

1 Select the EmpPayForm.

Identification Info GroupBox control

Figure 9-38

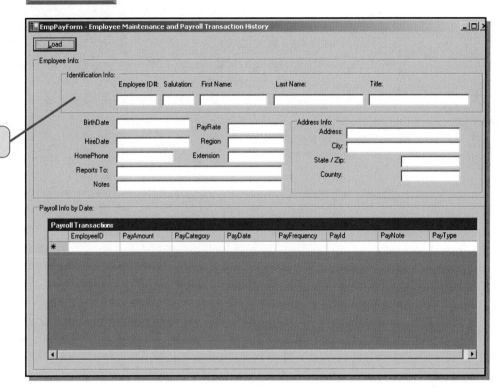

Tip It is important to select the form before adding the group box, to ensure that the GroupBox control will be attached to the form rather than inside the Address group box that previously had been selected. It would be helpful to move the Cancel All Button control to the top of the form on the same vertical alignment as the Load button, since the Identification Info group box will overlap this button.

2 In the Toolbox, double-click the GroupBox control to add it to the EmpPayForm form. Complete the GroupBox properties as shown in Table 9-9.

Table 9-9 GroupBox Properties

Property	Value to Set
Name	grpIdentification
Location	48, 24
Modifiers	Friend
Size	736, 72
Text	Identification Info:

③ Select the Label and TextBox controls for each item and choose **Edit | Cut**. Select the grpIdentification GroupBox control and choose **Edit | Paste**. Complete the properties for each label and text box within the grpIdentification group box as shown in Table 9-10.

④ Choose **File | Save All**.

Table 9-10	Identification Group Properties		
Type	**Control**	**Property**	**Value to Set**
Label	lblEmployeeID	Location	72, 16
		Modifiers	Friend
		Size	104, 23
		Text	Employee ID#
		TextAlign	TopRight
TextBox	editEmployeeID	Location	96, 40
		Modifiers	Friend
		Size	72, 20
Label	lblSalutation	Location	176, 16
		Modifiers	Friend
		Size	64, 23
		Text	Salutation:
		TextAlign	TopLeft
TextBox	editSalutation	Location	176, 40
		Modifiers	Friend
		Size	56, 20
Label	lblFirstName	Location	240, 16
		Modifiers	Friend
		Size	64, 23
		Text	First Name:
TextBox	editFirstName	Location	240, 40
		Modifiers	Friend
		Size	118, 20
Label	lblLastName	Location	360, 16
		Modifiers	Friend
		Size	72, 23
		Text	Last Name:
		TextAlign	TopRight

(Continued)

Table 9-10   Identification Group Properties *(continued)*

Type	Control	Property	Value to Set
TextBox	editLastName	Location	368, 40
		Modifiers	Friend
		Size	160, 20
Label	lblTitle	Location	536, 16
		Modifiers	Friend
		Size	100, 23
		Text	Title:
		TextAlign	TopLeft
TextBox	editTitle	Location	536, 40
		Modifiers	Friend
		Size	176, 20

Creating the Employee Info Group

The Employee Info group box will serve as a container for the Identification Info group, the Address group, and the remaining employee-related fields, not including the Payroll Transactions that appear in the grid at the bottom of the form.

Task 7:
To Create the Employee Info Group

1 Select the EmpPayForm form. In the Toolbox, double-click the GroupBox control to add it to the form. Complete the GroupBox properties as shown in Table 9-11.

Figure 9-39

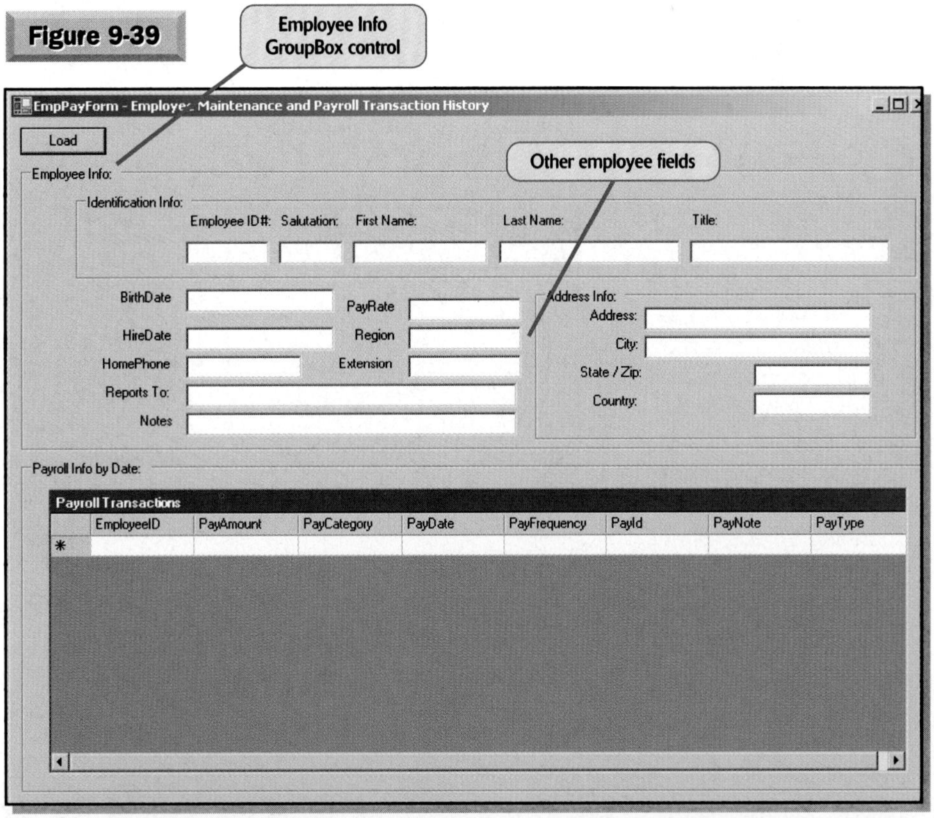

Tip Once you add the GroupBox control and set the properties, it will cover most of the top half of the EmpPayForm. As you migrate controls from the form into the Employee Info group box, you will need to move the Employee Info group box down temporarily. Once you cut and paste the controls you can finalize placement of the Employee Info groupbox.

2 Cut the grpIdentification GroupBox control and paste it into the grpEmployeeInfo group box.

3 Cut the grpAddressInfo GroupBox control and paste it into the grpEmployeeInfo group box.

Table 9-11	Employee Groupbox Properties
Property	**Value to Set**
Name	grpEmployeeInfo
Location	8, 40
Modifiers	Friend
Size	794, 240
Text	Employee Info:

4 Cut the Label and TextBox controls from the form and paste them into the grpEmployeeInfo group box. Complete the properties for each label and text box within the grpEmployeeInfo group box as shown in Table 9-12.

5 Choose **File | Save All**.

Tip Once an object such as a text box has become part of a group box, you can simply click the group box and cut and paste or drag the group box with all of its corresponding objects to a new location.

Table 9-12	Employee Group Properties		
Type	**Control**	**Property**	**Value to Set**
Label	lblBirthDate	Location	64, 104
		Size	72, 23
		Text	Birth Date:
		TextAlign	TopRight
TextBox	editBirthDate	Location	144, 104
		Size	128, 20
Label	lblHireDate	Location	64, 136
		Size	72, 23
		Text	Hire Date:
		TextAlign	TopRight
TextBox	editHireDate	Location	144, 136
		Size	128, 20
Label	lblHomePhone	Location	64, 160
		Size	80, 23
		Text	Home Phone:
		TextAlign	TopRight

(Continued)

Table 9-12   Employee Group Properties *(continued)*

Type	Control	Property	Value to Set
TextBox	editHomePhone	Location	144, 160
		Size	100, 20
Label	lblReportsTo	Location	72, 184
		Size	64, 23
		Text	Reports To:
		TextAlign	TopRight
TextBox	editReportsTo	Location	144, 184
		Size	292, 20
Label	lblNotes	Location	64, 208
		Size	72, 23
		Text	Notes:
		TextAlign	TopRight
TextBox	editNotes	Location	144, 208
		Size	292, 20
Label	lblPayRate	Location	256, 112
		Size	72, 23
		Text	Pay Rate:
		TextAlign	TopRight
TextBox	editPayRate	Location	336, 112
		Size	100, 20
Label	lblRegion	Location	256, 136
		Size	72, 23
		Text	Region:
		TextAlign	TopRight
TextBox	editRegion	Location	336, 136
		Size	100, 20
Label	lblExtension	Location	256, 160
		Size	72, 23
		Text	Extension:
		TextAlign	TopRight
TextBox	editExtension	Location	336, 160
		Size	100, 20

Creating the Payroll Info by Date GroupBox

The Payroll Info by Date GroupBox control will contain the data-bound grid that displays payroll information for the currently selected employee. Some employees may eventually have more rows of payroll information than the space allotted on the form. The grid displays vertical scroll bars once the number of rows exceeds the space available. Horizontal scroll bars also permit additional columns of data to be available, although some columns may be hidden until the user scrolls to the right to reveal them. In this task, the grid will be cut and pasted into the new Payroll Info by Date GroupBox control to improve the appearance of the form and make it consistent top and bottom. This is a Header/Detail-type form where the top displays a single employee record, and the bottom displays one or more associated payroll transaction records. This is a very typical scenario in business data entry form requirements.

Task 8:

To Create the Payroll Info by Date Group

1 Select the EmpPayForm form. In the Toolbox, double-click the GroupBox control to add it to the form. Complete the GroupBox properties as shown in Table 9-13.

Table 9-13	Pay Transaction GroupBox Properties
Property	**Value to Set**
Name	grpPayTrans
Location	8, 288
Modifiers	Friend
Size	794, 240
Text	Payroll Info by Date:

Tip In this task another GroupBox control will be added and the grid will be cut and pasted into it. Since some buttons will be hidden by the new grid and GroupBox control, they should be moved. Click on the buttons while holding down the [Shift] key to select multiple controls. Release the [Shift] key and drag the buttons to the bottom of the form. The buttons will be repositioned in the next task.

2 Cut and paste the grid onto the grpPayTrans group box. First, cut the grid containing the Payroll Transactions. Next, make sure you have the grpPayTrans group box selected (resize handles are visible) and then paste the grid directly onto the group box. Once the grid is pasted onto the group box, you can resize the grid so that it looks similar to Figure 9-40. Complete the Payroll Transactions properties as shown in Table 9-14.

3 Choose **File | Save All**.

Payroll Info by Date
GroupBox control

Figure 9-40

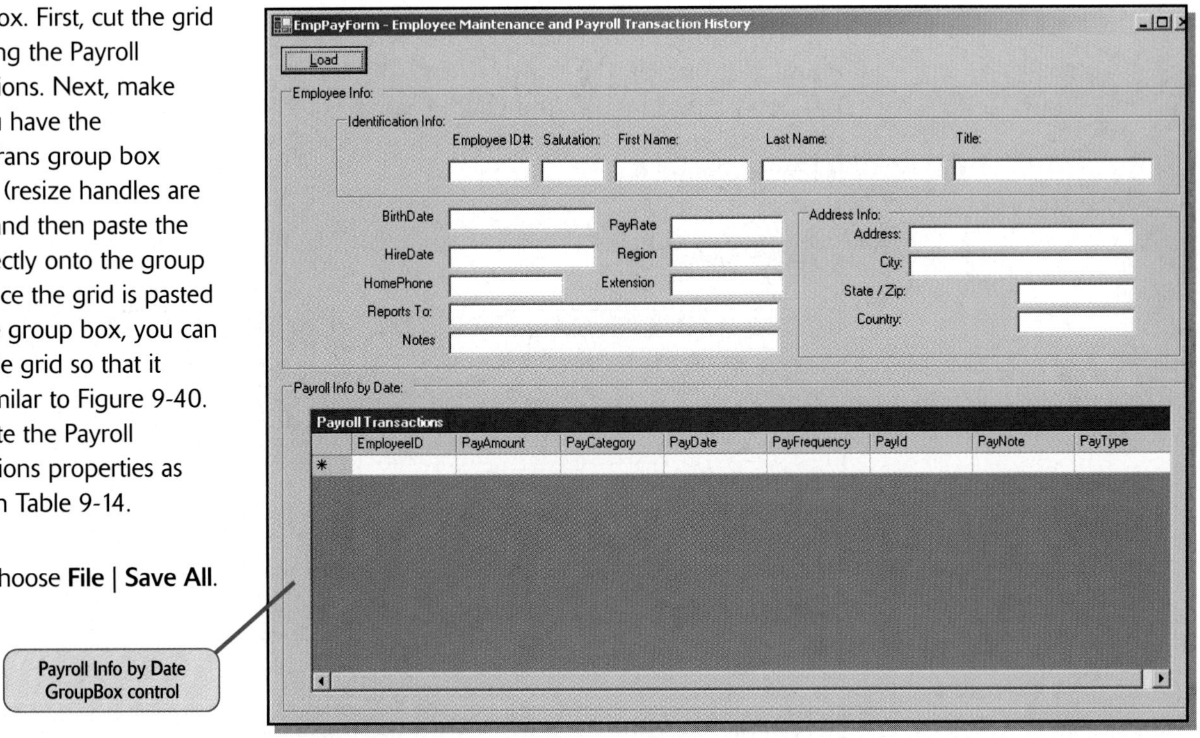

Table 9-14   **Payroll Transaction Grid Properties**

Property	Value to Set
Name	grdPayTransactions
AllowNavigation	False
CaptionText	Payroll Transactions
DataMember	Employee.EmpPay
DateSource	objEmpPay
Location	24, 24
Size	752, 200
Text	Payroll Info by Date:

Moving the Command Buttons and Navigation Location to the Bottom of the Form

It is common for corporate applications to use a consistent layout for command buttons at the bottom (or top for browser-based forms) of most Windows-based forms. You should move your command buttons and navigation location label down to the bottom of your form so it looks similar to the layout in Figure 9-41.

Figure 9-41

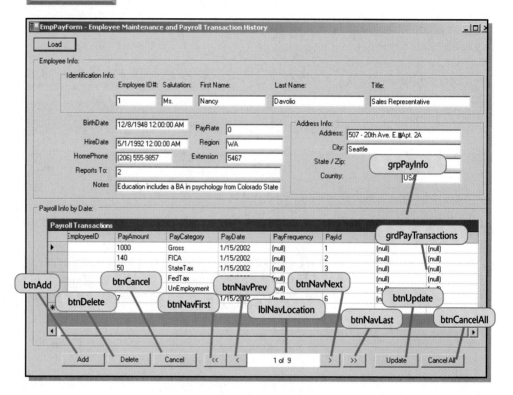

Tip

We do not want to use the cut-and-paste technique used for moving text boxes and labels from the form to a group box. There is programming logic behind each of the command buttons and we may lose the connection between the button and corresponding click event subprocedure if we use a cut-and-paste technique. It is better to move the command buttons one at a time, or to select a few at a time by clicking them while holding down the Shift key and dragging them to the desired location.

Task 9:

To Move the Command Buttons and Navigation Location to the Bottom of the Form

1 Choose **View | Properties**.

2 Click the control drop-down list at the top of the Properties window.

3 Select **btnAdd** from the control drop-down list and then complete the properties as shown in Table 9-15. Repeat for each button and label.

4 Choose **File | Save All**.

Figure 9-42

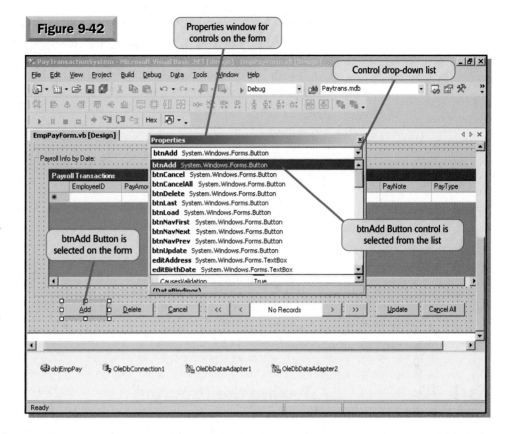

Table 9-15	Button Properties		
Type	**Control**	**Property**	**Value to Set**
Button	btnAdd	Location	59, 538
		Size	75, 23
Button	btnDelete	Location	139, 538
		Size	75, 23
Button	btnCancel	Location	219, 538
		Size	75, 23
Button	btnNavFirst	Location	307, 538
		Size	40, 23
Button	btnNavPrev	Location	347, 538
		Size	35, 23
Label	lblNavLocation	Location	379, 538
		Size	128, 23
Button	btnNavNext	Location	507, 538
		Size	35, 23

(Continued)

Table 9-15	Button Properties *(continued)*		
Type	**Control**	**Property**	**Value to Set**
Button	btnNavLast	Location	547, 538
		Size	40, 23
Button	btnUpdate	Location	603, 538
		Size	75, 23
Button	btnCancelAll	Location	683, 538
		Size	75, 23

 Tip　Congratulations! Your form should now have a professional look and feel to it and appear similar to the full-screen image displayed at the beginning of this section. At this point you should feel a tremendous sense of accomplishment and you are ready to test the fruits of your labor.

Task 10:

To Test the Program

1 Press F5 to start the debugger and test your program.

 **Tip**　You may have to make a correction or two if you had any typos in the names of the objects. Once all the bugs have been removed, your form should appear with data.

2 Click the btnNavNext button and notice that the data changes.

3 Click the btnNavPrev button and notice that the data changes and the grid repopulates.

Testing the Program

At this point, the controls have been repositioned and several GroupBox controls have been added. Since the controls were connected to the database prior to the rearrangement of the control, they should still populate with data when the project runs.

 Tip　You will notice that record 1 contains many rows of payroll information, and other records do not display any data in the grid. This merely indicates a typical situation in which certain employees have been with the company longer and therefore have additional records.

SUMMARY AND EXERCISES

SUMMARY

- Many applications developed for corporations use a commercial database to manage information storage and retrieval.
- Databases enable us to create tables, views, and stored procedures in a consistent manner.
- Databases provide password security, backup and recovery, and other useful utilities for querying the database.
- The data model is called an entity relationship diagram (ERD) and is used to depict relationships from one table to another.
- Visual Studio .NET has a convenient interface called the Server Explorer that enables you to perform most of the functions necessary to work with existing databases.
- The Data Form Wizard is a productivity tool that enables you to create Windows forms with data-bound controls without having to write the program from scratch.
- A primary key is a column or combination of columns that uniquely identifies a row in a table. It cannot allow null values and must always have a unique index.
- A foreign key is a column or combination of columns whose values match the primary key of some other table.
- The Data Form Wizard produces a form that is very functional but usually is not very aesthetically pleasing.
- GroupBox controls help organize related controls.

KEY TERMS & SKILLS

KEY TERMS

connection (p. 9-4)
database (p. 9-1)
data adapter (p. 9-21)
dataset (p. 9-15)
Data Form Wizard
  (p. 9-4)

data model (p. 9-5)
entity relationship diagram (ERD)
  (p. 9-5)
foreign key (p. 9-17)
primary key (p. 9-17)
Server Explorer (p. 9-1)

SKILLS   Create a data connection through the
Server Explorer (p. 9-6)
Create the Employee Info group
(p. 9-33)
Create the Identification Info group
(p. 9-31)
Create the Payroll Info by Date group
(p. 9-36)
Move the command buttons and
navigation location to the bottom of
the form (p. 9-39)

Test a form created with the Data
Form Wizard (p. 9-22)
Test the program (p. 9-40)
Use the Data Form Wizard
(p. 9-13)
Verify that the data connection was set
up in the Server Explorer
(p. 9-9)
Widen the EmpPayForm and create
the Address Info group
(p. 9-26)

STUDY QUESTIONS

MULTIPLE CHOICE

1. The dialog box that displays the Provider
and Connection tabs is
   a. Data Link Properties.
   b. Data Connection.
   c. Data Adapter.
   d. Data Form Wizard.

2. The list of data providers includes
   a. all OLE DB providers detected on
   your computer.
   b. all standard providers on the market.
   c. only ODBC-compliant data sources.
   d. Oracle.

3. Which of the following are different types
of database features?
   a. tables
   b. queries
   c. validation
   d. all of the above

4. Which of the following are characteristics
of a primary key?
   a. A column or combination of columns
   that uniquely identifies a row in a
   table.
   b. It cannot allow null values and must
   always be unique.
   c. A primary key is used to relate a table
   to foreign keys in other tables.
   d. all of the above

5. Before you can see data in a form generated by the Data Form Wizard, while the
program is running, which button must
you click?
   a. Run
   b. Start
   c. Load
   d. Save

6. To add controls to a GroupBox control
you can do all of the following except
   a. set focus to the group box, and then
   double-click a control in the Toolbox.
   b. click a control in the Toolbox to select
   it, and then draw the control on the
   group box to add it to the group.
   c. click the form, and then double-click a
   control in the Toolbox.
   d. cut an existing control and then paste
   it within the GroupBox control.

7. Databases are especially useful for
   a. password security.
   b. backup and recovery.
   c. querying the database.
   d. all of the above

8. All of the following are valid data-related objects in the Pay Transaction System except
   a. objEmpPay.
   b. OleDbConnection1.
   c. OleDbDataAdapter1.
   d. objDbData.

9. To select multiple controls you must hold down
   a. the [Alt] key.
   b. the [Shift] key.
   c. the [Ctrl] key.
   d. none of the above

10. Once an object such as a text box has become part of a group box, you can
    a. cut and paste the group box to a new location.
    b. drag the group box to a new location.
    c. copy and paste the group box with all of its corresponding objects to a new desired location.
    d. all of the above

SHORT ANSWER

1. What three things do databases enable us to create in a consistent manner?
2. What are three useful functions provided by a commercial database?
3. What tool is used to quickly generate data entry forms with data-bound controls?
4. What interface provided by Visual Basic .NET enables you to perform most of the functions necessary to work with existing databases?
5. The Data Link Properties dialog box provides what two tabs that must be set up correctly to link with a database?
6. Visual Studio .NET is currently optimized to use what two commonly available databases?
7. What tool creates a form with data-bound controls that can load and display data and enables users to make changes to the data and save those changes to the database?
8. What is the name of the term used to identify a Parent and Child link for tables and fields between tables?
9. What did we have to do in order to see the grid on our data entry form (EmpPayForm) created by the Data Form Wizard before the redesign of the form?
10. What is a data adapter?

FILL IN THE BLANK

1. A _____ is a set of data related to a particular topic or purpose.
2. The _____ Explorer creates a link between a programming project and the database.
3. The data model is called a _____ _____ _____ and is used to depict relationships from one table to another.

4. The _____ _____ Wizard is a productivity tool that helps you create Windows Forms with data-bound controls without having to write program code.

5. A _____ key is a column or combination of columns that uniquely identifies a row in a table.

6. A _____ key is a column or combination of columns whose values match the primary key of some other table.

7. The Data Form Wizard generates a program that requires you to click the _____ button prior to querying the database and displaying the data on the form.

8. The four most common navigation buttons are (hint: move where) _____, _____, _____, and _____.

9. A _____ control is commonly used to organize related controls on a form.

10. It is important to select the form before adding the _____ to ensure that the _____ control will be attached to the form rather than inside the previously selected tool on the form.

FOR DISCUSSION

1. When would you use the Data Form Wizard?
2. How does the Server Explorer provide data to the form?
3. What data providers are available when you are setting up the dataset?
4. What control might help ensure that a valid date is entered for the Hire Date field?
5. Why would a database be preferable to a flat file?

ON YOUR OWN

1 PROTECTING FIELDS

Protect the editEmployeeID text box so that it cannot be accidentally overwritten by an end user.

2 USING THE DATETIMEPICKER CONTROL

Change the EmpPayForm to use a DateTimePicker object for the Birth Date and Hire Date fields.

3 MATCHING DATA TO SELECTED RECORD

Change the Reports field to display the Last Name, First Name of the Employee whose EmployeeID matches the number in the editReportsTo text box.

Change the editTitle text box to be a combo box populated with a distinct list of Titles currently in use by the Employees table.

Adding the Finishing Touches with Custom Programming

I n this project, we will learn how to create and modify Visual Basic .NET source code for greater programming control and functionality.

> **Tip** The *PayTrans.mdb* database and the *PayTransactionSystem.sln* files can be found at
> \\vb.net_brief\vb.net_datafiles\10\Students\HR\PayTransactionSystem.

e-selections   **Running Case**

Having developed so much capability in such a short time, the programmers are ready to finalize this first release of the Pay Transaction System and begin to deploy it to a few key users.

OBJECTIVES

After completing this project, you will be able to:

- *Update the project startup object*

- *Add the Employee Payroll form to the menu*

- *Add a search group box*

- *Customize SQL statements*

- *Add a Close button*

- *Modify the EmpPay form to utilize color preferences*

- *Add the User Preferences form to the Sub Main*

- *Test the application*

- *Build the application*

Adding the Finishing Touches with Custom Programming

The Challenge

Demonstrate that Visual Basic .NET can provide an application that is easy to deploy and appears to be professionally refined.

The Solution

Adding a search capability to the Employee Payroll Form will make the form inherently more useful. Our objective is to allow a search directly by the EmployeeID if known or by any combination of the Last Name, First Name, and Title fields. Once search conditions are entered, users can click the Search button to retrieve one or more records that meet the search conditions.

Finally we will build an *.exe* file to distribute the application to end users. This will be an excellent ending point for our book, as we will have created a complete application from soup to nuts.

Our next book will focus on expanding the application to build business and validation services in a middle tier and to incorporate data services for a sophisticated relational database such as Microsoft SQL Server and/or Oracle 8i.

Figure 10-1

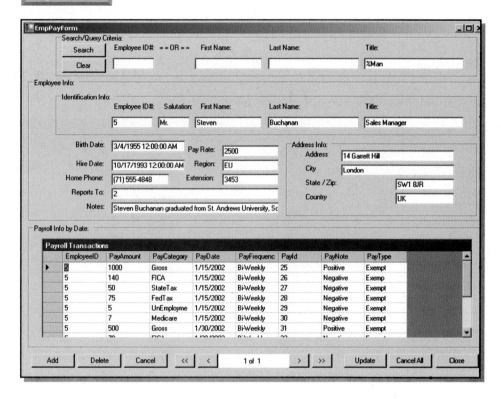

Changing the Project Startup Object from EmpPayForm to the PayTransCommonModule

We will now change the startup object to ensure that the process flows as designed. Rather than hard-coding the startup object to the form being tested, we will reset it to the PayTransCommonModule. This final change to this project property setting will ensure that the application begins by showing, in order, the splash screen, the login form, the User Preferences form, and finally the homepage.

Task 1:

To Change the Project Startup Object from the EmpPayForm to the PayTrans CommonModule

1 Right-click the PayTransactionSystem solution in the Solution Explorer and choose **Properties**. The Payroll Transaction System Properties page appears.

2 Choose **PayTrans CommonModule** from the **Startup object:** drop-down list and click the OK button.

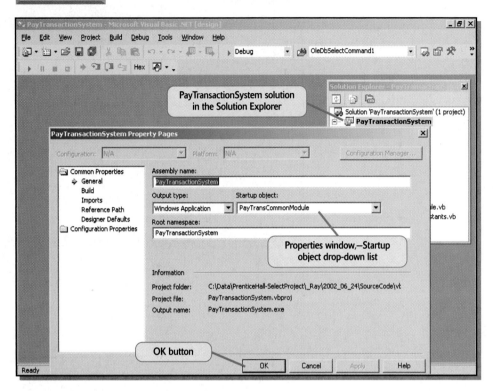

Figure 10-2

3 Modify the View menu to include the Employee Payroll Form. In the Solution Explorer, double-click *HomePage.vb* to display the form in design mode and then click the View menu on the *HomePage.vb* form to display the Menu Editor. Type Employee Payroll Form in the Type Here field under the View menu and then press [Enter].

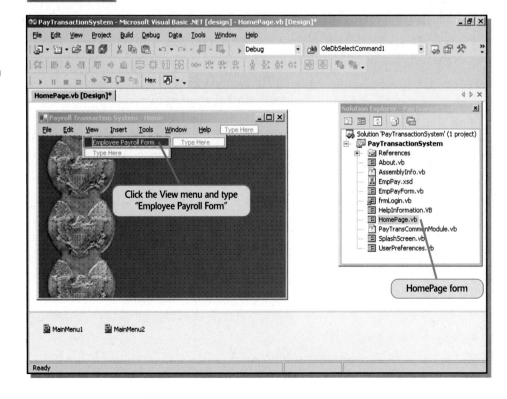

Figure 10-3

4 In the Properties window, change the Name property for the Employee Payroll Form menu item to **MenuItem_EmpPayForm**.

Figure 10-4

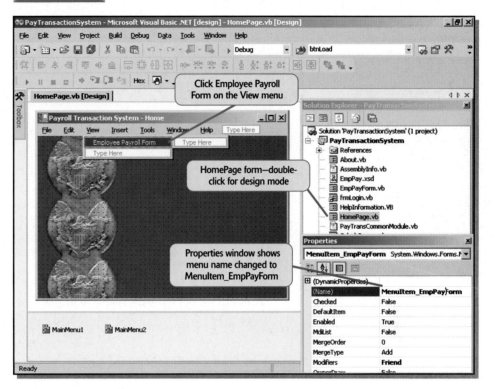

5 In the Solution Explorer, right-click the *HomePage.vb* form and choose **View Code** to display code for the form. Type **Public EmpPay as New EmpPayForm()** as shown in Figure 10-5. The code belongs in the Public Class HomePage section in the Declarations section of the source code.

Figure 10-5

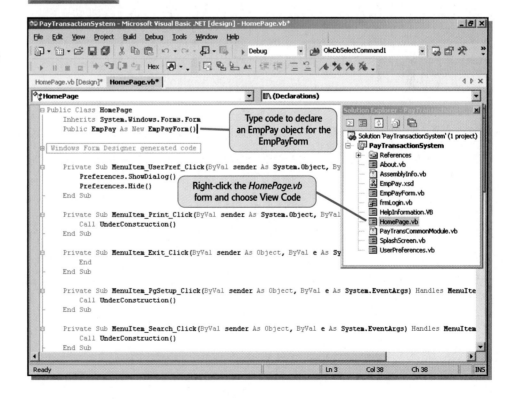

6 Double-click *HomePage.vb* in the Solution Explorer to display the form in design mode. Double-click the Employee Payroll Form menu item on the View menu to view the click event for the menu item. Type EmpPay.Show Dialog() in the click event as shown in Figure 10-6.

7 Choose **File | Save All**.

Figure 10-6

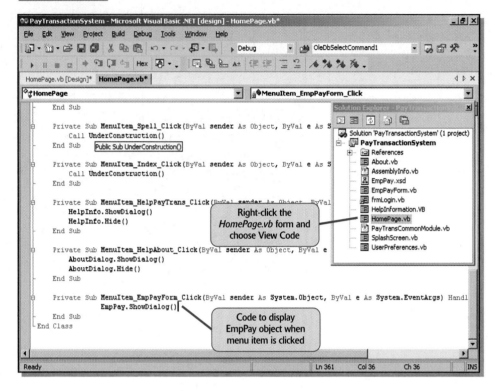

Adding a Search Group Box to the EmpPayForm

We will add an additional group box to the top of the form that looks similar to Figure 10-7. Two new buttons will be added: Search and Clear. Five labels and four text boxes will also be added to the group box to help facilitate search operations. Review Figure 10-1 to see the desired form layout with the new Search GroupBox control, resized Employee Info and Payroll Info by Date GroupBox controls, and the shortened Payroll Transactions grid.

Task 2:
To Add a Search Group Box to the Employee Payroll Form

1 Click the EmpPayForm to select it. In the Toolbox, double-click the GroupBox control to add it to the form.

2 Click the GroupBox control to select it. In the Toolbox, double-click the Button control to add a new button within the Search group box. Double-click the Button control again to add a new button within the Clear group box.

3 In the Identification Info GroupBox control, hold down the Shift key while clicking the left mouse button to select the following Label controls: EmployeeID, Salutation, FirstName, LastName, and Title. Choose **Edit | Copy** to temporarily copy the Label controls to the Clipboard. Click to select the Search GroupBox control and then choose **Edit | Paste** to paste copies of the controls into the Search GroupBox control. Align the labels with labels so they look similar to the layout of the labels found in the Identification Info group box.

Figure 10-7

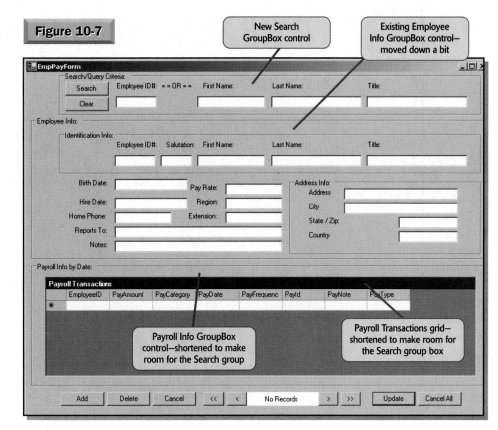

New Search GroupBox control

Existing Employee Info GroupBox control— moved down a bit

Payroll Info GroupBox control—shortened to make room for the Search group

Payroll Transactions grid—shortened to make room for the Search group box

Tip The existing Load button (btnLoad) will be temporarily ignored, as the new GroupBox control will cover it. Don't worry about this now as we will replace the bottom with a Search button shortly.

4 Repeat Step 3 for the TextBox controls. Hold down the Shift key while clicking the left mouse button to select the following TextBox controls: EmployeeID, Salutation, FirstName, LastName, and Title. Choose **Edit | Copy** to temporarily copy the TextBox controls to the Clipboard. Click to select the Search GroupBox control and then choose **Edit | Paste** to paste copies of the controls into the Search GroupBox control. Align the text boxes so they look similar to the layout of the text boxes found in the Identification Info group box.

5 Click each new text box within the Search GroupBox control one at a time; then delete the DataBindings Text property value. The DataBindings property can be found near the top of the Properties window. You can view the properties in alphabetical order by clicking the command button at the top of the Properties window. (This might be a good tip if you can not find the property you are looking for, the properties can be displayed by category.)

6 Complete the control properties as shown in Table 10-1.

7 Choose **File | Save All**.

Table 10-1 Pay Transaction Group Properties

Control Name	Location	Size	Property Setting (Action Taken)
grpPayTrans	8, 320	794, 208	Resized to shorten (action taken) Location and Size were changed
grpEmployeeInfo	8, 75	794, 240	Moved down on the form (action taken) Location and Size were changed
grdPayTransactions	24, 24	752, 168	Shortened grid needed for searching (action taken) Location and Size were changed
grpSearchCriteria (new)	56, 0	736, 72	Search/Query criteria:
btnSearch (new)	11, 16	75, 23	&Search
btnClear (new)	11, 42	75, 23	&Clear
lblSearchEmployeeID	96, 16	80, 23	Employee ID#: (TextAlign=TopRight)
lblSearchOr **(Copy of the Salutation label)**	176, 16	64, 23	= = OR = = (Space=Space=SpaceORSpace=Space=) (TextAlign=TopLeft)
lblSearchFirstName	248, 16	64, 23	First Name: (TextAlign=TopLeft)
lblSearchLastName	368, 16	72, 23	Last Name: (TextAlign=TopLeft)
lblSearchTitle	536, 16	100, 23	Title: (TextAlign=TopLeft)
searchEmployeeID	98, 40	72, 20	(Empty) DataBindings-Text=None
searchFirstName	240, 40	118, 20	(Empty) DataBindings-Text=None
searchLastName	368, 40	160, 20	(Empty) DataBindings-Text=None
searchTitle	536, 40	176, 20	(Empty) DataBindings-Text=None

Tip To delete the DataBindings Text property value, click the plus sign next to the DataBindings property and then select the existing Text property by holding down the left mouse button and dragging it over the existing text. Press the Delete key to delete the existing text and then press the Enter key to save the updated property value. A value of None should appear in the DataBindings Text property when you are finished. This unbinds the Search text boxes from the database. Repeat until all four text boxes have a value of None for this property.

Customizing the SQL Statements to Use the Values Entered in the Search Fields as a Filter for the Records That Will Be Displayed on the Form

To perform an employee search, we need to enter search criteria using the new Search group box and the associated TextBox controls, store the search criteria using variables into a new PublicVariablesAndConstants code module, add code behind the Search button, and finally execute the search using a query to populate the form. Code will be added to the Clear button to empty the search criteria controls.

Creating a PublicVariablesAndConstants Module for Code

A new module will be added to the PayTransactionSystem solution that will contain public variables used by the search feature of the Employee Payroll Form. We will add three new variables to store the search criteria needed for the database query. This query when executed will retrieve the desired employee records that match the search criteria entered.

Other Ways

In the next section you will be instructed to create a new module "PublicVariablesAndConstants." These variables could have easily been added to the "PayTransCommon" module. For a small project like ours, we chose to introduce a new module because in large enterprise systems it would be a good practice to separate common variables/constants from common procedures and functions.

Task 3:
To Create a PublicVariables AndConstants Module for Code

1 Choose **Project | Add Module**, type Public VariablesAndConstants for the name, and then click the Open button.

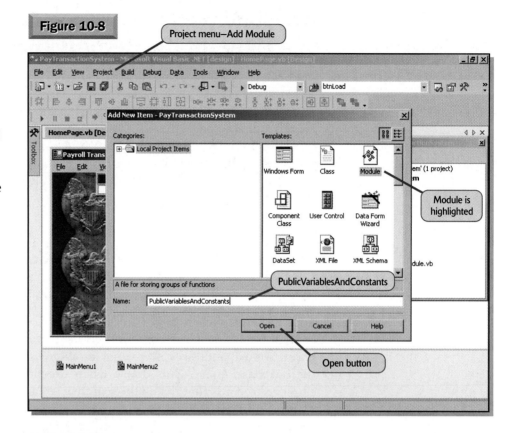

Figure 10-8

2 Type the variable declarations for three variables into the module as shown in Figure 10-9.

3 Choose **File | Save All**.

Tip The first variable, SQLstr, will be used to define the Employee query; the second variable, SQLstr2, will be used to define the Payroll Transaction query. The last variable, SQLSearchCriteria, will be used to create a common Where condition between the two tables in the dataset so that the parent/child relationships between the two tables are enforced and coordinated.

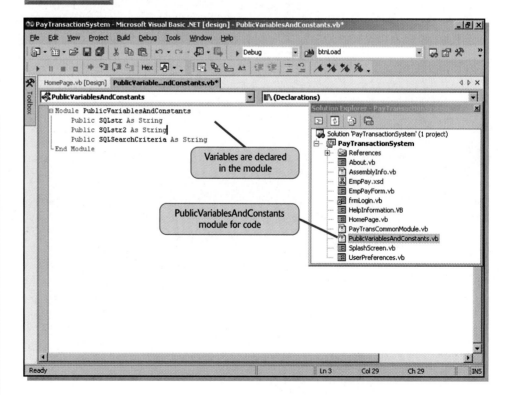

Figure 10-9

Adding Code behind the Search Button

Code will be added to assign values to the new variables when the Search button is clicked.

Task 4:
To Add Code behind the Search Button

1. In the Solution Explorer, double-click EmpPayForm to view the form in design mode.

2. Double-click the Search button on the EmpPayForm object to view code.

3. Type the code as shown in Figure 10-10.

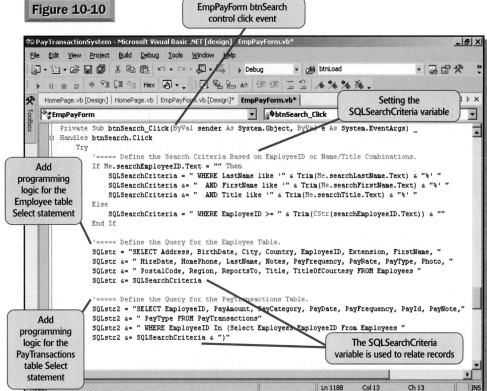

Figure 10-10

EmpPayForm btnSearch control click event

Setting the SQLSearchCriteria variable

Add programming logic for the Employee table Select statement

Add programming logic for the PayTransactions table Select statement

The SQLSearchCriteria variable is used to relate records

```
Private Sub btnSearch_Click(ByVal sender As System.Object, ByVal e As System.EventArgs) _
Handles btnSearch.Click
    Try
        '===== Define the Search Criteria Based on EmployeeID or Name/Title Combinations.
        If Me.searchEmployeeID.Text = "" Then
            SQLSearchCriteria = " WHERE LastName like '" & Trim(Me.searchLastName.Text) & "%' "
            SQLSearchCriteria &= "  AND FirstName like '" & Trim(Me.searchFirstName.Text) & "%' "
            SQLSearchCriteria &= "  AND Title like '" & Trim(Me.searchTitle.Text) & "%' "
        Else
            SQLSearchCriteria = " WHERE EmployeeID >= " & Trim(CStr(searchEmployeeID.Text)) & ""
        End If

        '===== Define the Query for the Employee Table.
        SQLstr = "SELECT Address, BirthDate, City, Country, EmployeeID, Extension, FirstName, "
        SQLstr &= " HireDate, HomePhone, LastName, Notes, PayFrequency, PayRate, PayType, Photo, "
        SQLstr &= " PostalCode, Region, ReportsTo, Title, TitleOfCourtesy FROM Employees "
        SQLstr &= SQLSearchCriteria

        '===== Define the Query for the PayTransactions Table.
        SQLstr2 = "SELECT EmployeeID, PayAmount, PayCategory, PayDate, PayFrequency, PayId, PayNote,"
        SQLstr2 &= " PayType FROM PayTransactions"
        SQLstr2 &= " WHERE EmployeeID In (Select Employees.EmployeeID From Employees "
        SQLstr2 &= SQLSearchCriteria & ")"
```

Tip

This code may not be clear, so the following will try to explain what we are doing.

The condition **If Me.searchEmployeeID.Text =** "" tests to see if the searchEmployeeID text box is empty. If it is, then we want a search criteria based on the combination of first name, last name, and title.

If the searchEmployeeID text box is not empty, the search condition will be based exclusively on the EmployeeID. Notice that the SQLSearchCriteria string is reused in both programs to ensure correct correlation of records across both tables.

Tip

You can concatenate strings with other strings using the **&=** statement. This is a shorter version of using **myString = myString & newString**. For example, given **myString = "Welcome to Visual Basic .NET"**, the following two programming constructs accomplish the same result: **myString = myString & "with UML Visual Modeling"** and **myString &= "with UML Visual Modeling"**.

Adding Programming Logic to Populate the Form Controls

Next we will add programming logic to execute the queries and populate the text boxes on the form. Since the TextBox and Grid controls are data-bound to the database, the code that is needed must update the data-retrieval-related properties.

Task 5:

To Add Programming Logic to Populate the Form Controls

1 Type code as shown in Figure 10-11.

2 Choose **File | Save All**.

Figure 10-11

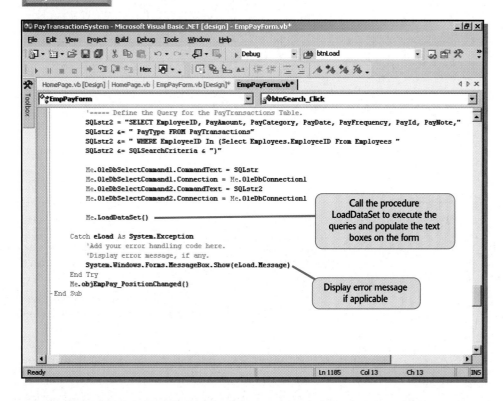

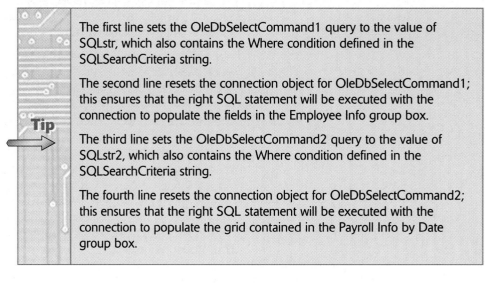

Tip

The first line sets the OleDbSelectCommand1 query to the value of SQLstr, which also contains the Where condition defined in the SQLSearchCriteria string.

The second line resets the connection object for OleDbSelectCommand1; this ensures that the right SQL statement will be executed with the connection to populate the fields in the Employee Info group box.

The third line sets the OleDbSelectCommand2 query to the value of SQLstr2, which also contains the Where condition defined in the SQLSearchCriteria string.

The fourth line resets the connection object for OleDbSelectCommand2; this ensures that the right SQL statement will be executed with the connection to populate the grid contained in the Payroll Info by Date group box.

Adding Code to the Clear Button to Empty Search Criteria

The Clear button provides a convenient means to empty search criteria that may be present in the Search TextBox controls. The Text property of each search-related text box is assigned an empty string value using two double quote characters without a space.

Task 6:

To Add Code to the Clear Button to Empty Search Criteria

1 In the EmpPayForm, double-click the Clear button to view code.

2 Type the code as shown in Figure 10-12.

3 Choose **File | Save All**.

Figure 10-12

btnClear_Click event

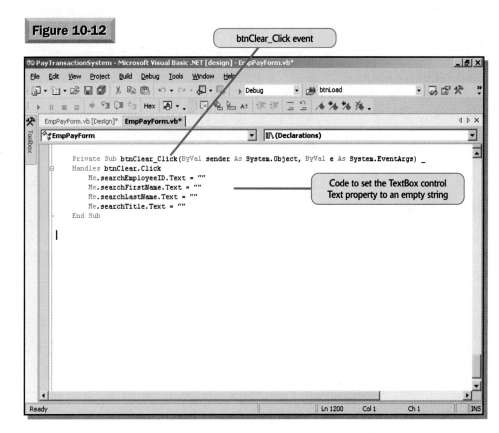

Code to set the TextBox control Text property to an empty string

Adding a Close Button to the Form

Users expect a button to close a form. Copying an existing button and setting the Name and Text properties will add a new button. To make it fit, the existing buttons across the bottom of the form will be shifted to the left. Rename the new button and set the text for the button caption.

Task 7:
To Add a Close Button to the Form

1 Click the Cancel All button to select it and then choose **Edit | Copy** and **Edit | Paste**. Name the new button btnClose and set the Text property to Cl&ose.

2 Complete the control properties as shown in Table 10-2.

3 Type the code as shown in Figure 10-13.

4 Choose **File | Save All**.

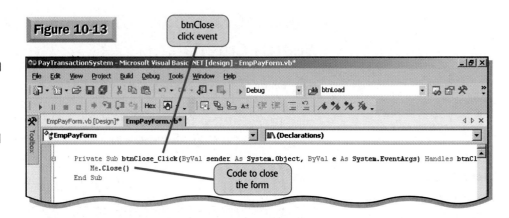

Figure 10-13

btnClose click event

Code to close the form

Table 10-2	Button and Label Properties
Control Name	**Location**
btnAdd	14, 538
btnDelete	94, 538
btnCancel	174, 538
btnNavFirst	262, 538
btnNavPrev	302, 538
lblNavLocation	334, 538
btnNavNext	462, 538
btnLast	502, 538
btnUpdate	558, 538
btnCancelAll	638, 538
btnClose	720, 538

Modifying the EmpPayForm Properties for Background Color and Label Text Color Based on the Settings in the User Preferences Form

The last piece of our example will be to incorporate color preferences into your form. In a production application, your preferences would usually be saved to a database or an *XML* file for later retrieval. In our example, these settings will be available from memory but we can use the same techniques to alter the appearance and behavior of our forms.

Task 8:

To Modify the EmpPayForm Properties for Background Color and Label Text Color Based on the Settings in the User Preferences Form

1 Double-click the EmpPayForm form background to view code in the EmpPayForm_Load event.

2 Type the code as shown in Figure 10-14.

3 Choose **File | Save All**.

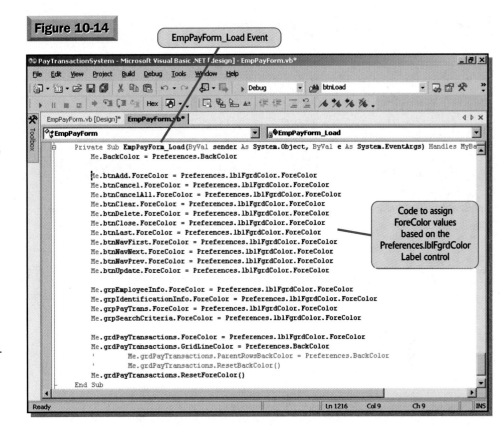

Figure 10-14

EmpPayForm_Load Event

Code to assign ForeColor values based on the Preferences.lblFgrdColor Label control

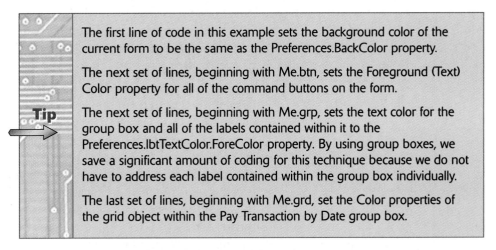

Tip

The first line of code in this example sets the background color of the current form to be the same as the Preferences.BackColor property.

The next set of lines, beginning with Me.btn, sets the Foreground (Text) Color property for all of the command buttons on the form.

The next set of lines, beginning with Me.grp, sets the text color for the group box and all of the labels contained within it to the Preferences.lbtTextColor.ForeColor property. By using group boxes, we save a significant amount of coding for this technique because we do not have to address each label contained within the group box individually.

The last set of lines, beginning with Me.grd, set the Color properties of the grid object within the Pay Transaction by Date group box.

Adding the User Preferences Form to the Sequence of Forms Loaded in the Sub Main Procedure

By adding Preferences.ShowDialog() before the Home.ShowDialog() statement, we will force users to set color preferences, and then use those preferences when displaying the Employee Payroll Form by choosing it on the View menu on the homepage.

Task 9:

To Add the User Preferences Form to the Sequence of Forms Loaded in the Sub Main Procedure

1 In the Solution Explorer, double-click the *PayTransCommon Module.vb* file to view code.

2 Revise the code in the Sub Main procedure as shown in Figure 10-15.

3 Choose **File | Save All**.

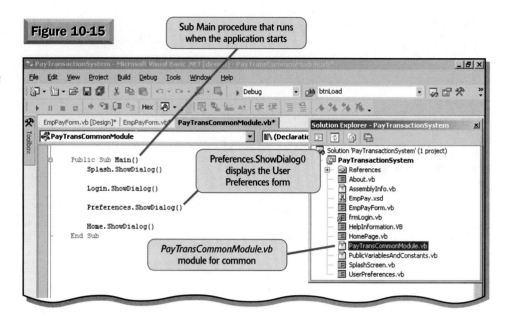

Figure 10-15

Sub Main procedure that runs when the application starts

Preferences.ShowDialog() displays the User Preferences form

PayTransCommonModule.vb module for common

Testing the Application

Click the Start button to initiate the debugger and test your program. You may have to make a correction or two if you had any typos in the names of any of the objects. Once all the bugs have been removed, your program should do the following:

- Display the splash screen and wait for the user to click it.
- Display the Login form and require the user to enter a valid user name and password. (Remember that the password is "password" unless you customized the code to something else.)
- Display the User Preferences form and wait for the user to set the desired background and foreground color preferences. When you are finished, exit the form by clicking the X in the upper right corner of the form (we never added a Close button to the User Preferences form).
- The homepage should appear next.

Task 10:

To Test the Application

1 Choose **Debug | Start**.

2 Click the splash screen when it appears.

3 Type password in the Login Password field and then click the OK button.

4 Select **Yellow** in the Text/Foreground Color ComboBox control; in the Background Color ComboBox control, select **Change Color**, select **Dark Green**, and then click the OK button.

5 Click the ☒ button in the top right corner to close the User Preferences form.

6 From the HomePage form, choose **View | Employee Payroll Form**.

7 Verify that the foreground and background colors match your User Preferences selections.

8 Click the Close button on the Employee Payroll Form and choose **File | Exit**.

Figure 10-16

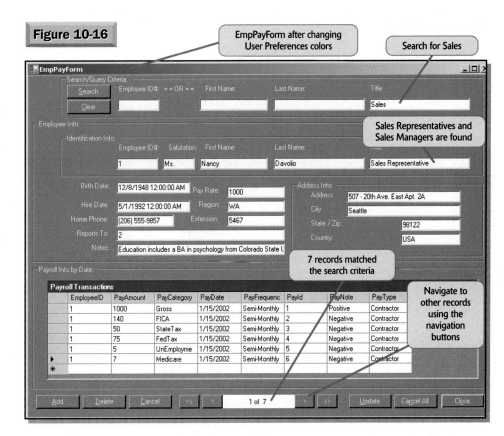

EmpPayForm after changing User Preferences colors

Search for Sales

Sales Representatives and Sales Managers are found

7 records matched the search criteria

Navigate to other records using the navigation buttons

Tip

Try the form out. Your new program has a search feature using the % wildcard character in the front—such as the %Man search condition, which finds all job titles with "man" in them, such as "Sales Manager." You also do not have to worry about upper and lower case mixes and do not have to put a wildcard at the end of your search, as the program does it for you. For example, in the Title a search condition of "Sales" will look for "Sales%" based on how the program builds the SQLSearchCondition string.

Some sample search conditions:

First and Last Name of A provides a list individuals that have first and last names beginning with the letter a.

Last Name of C provides a list of individuals that have a last name starting with c.

Title of Sales yields both Sales Representatives and Sales Managers when the search criteria entered is the word sales.

Title of %Rep yields just Sales Representatives

Building the Application So It Can Be Distributed to Another Workstation

This is really easy with Visual Basic .NET, as you do not have to create *setup.exe* installation programs. Many computers have had the .NET Framework, (found on the SDK provided by Microsoft or found on the Microsoft Web site), installed on them. In the past, distributing applications meant creating a setup program and identifying additional files that might be needed such as DLLs for controls used on a form. Now with the .NET framework preinstalled on a users workstation, program installations are simple. Installations are a two-step process. Install the .NET framework and copy the exe file. Note: Computers with Windows XP SP1 or Windows 2000 SP3 already have the .NET Framework installed, so you can just copy the EXE file.

Task 11:

To Build the Application So It Can Be Distributed to Another Workstation

1 Choose **Build** | **Build PayTransaction System**.

2 Choose **File** | **Save All**.

Figure 10-17

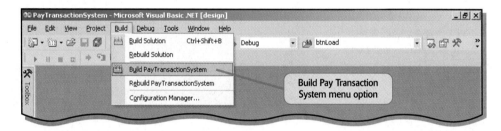

3 Verify that a *PayTransactionSystem. exe* file was created in a bin folder under the project folder.

4 Exit Visual Basic .NET by choosing **File | Exit**.

5 From the Windows Explorer, double-click the *PayTransactionSystem.exe* file and verify that the application runs in the compiled version.

6 Choose **File | Exit** on the homepage to exit the application.

Tip If everything goes well, you should be able to run your application as a stand-alone executable and send copies of it to end users (as long as they have the .NET SDK installed on their computers).

Figure 10-18

Figure 10-19

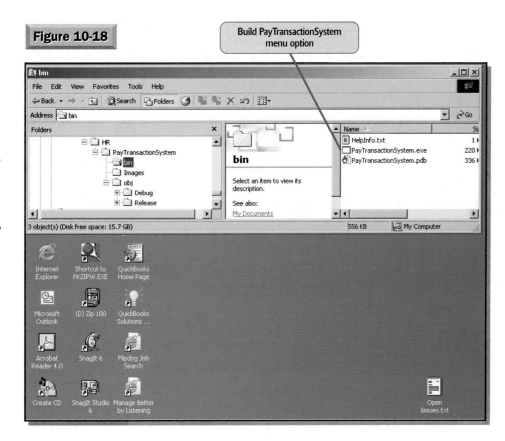

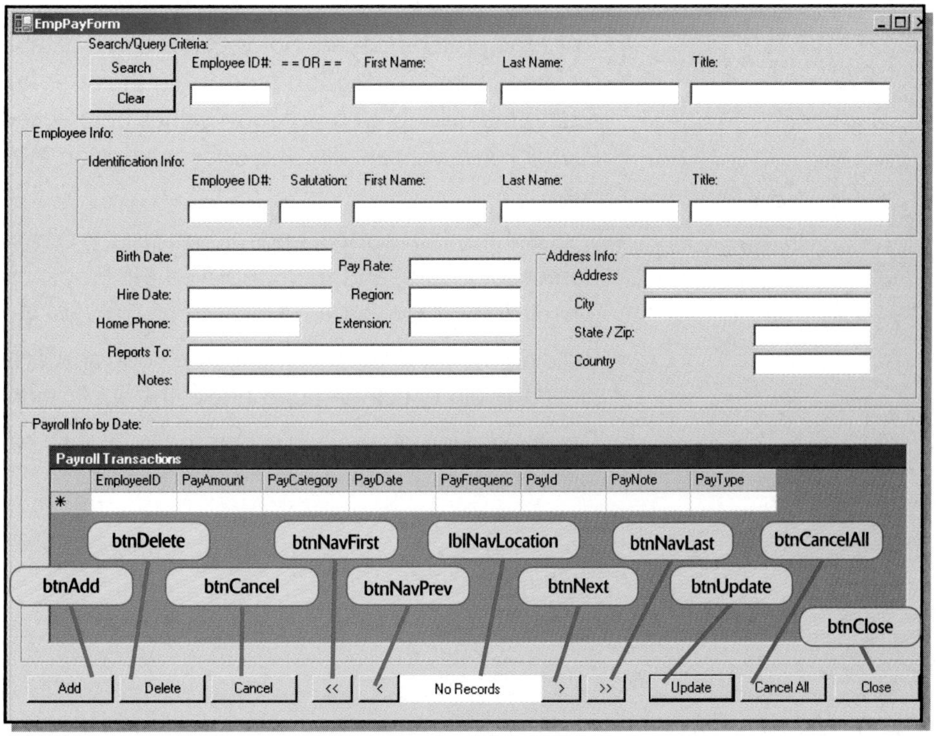

SUMMARY AND EXERCISES

SUMMARY

- Changing the project's startup object to Sub Main instructs the program to begin running code within the Sub Main code module rather than in hard-coded form used during the form development and testing process.

- Modifying the main menu on the homepage enabled users to reach the Employee Payroll Form.

- Since users may need to quickly locate payroll records for a single employee or a group of employees, a new search feature was added that allows the use of the % wildcard character.

- Using SQL statements that are created dynamically, searches are performed that have records from related tables based on the current selection criteria. This populates a grid control with payroll transactions for the current EmployeeID.

- To finish the Employee Payroll Form, a Close button was added.

- Color properties were used within the Employee Payroll Form to change its appearance.

- Since the preferences are not yet stored in a database, they will be retained in the ComboBox controls on the User Preferences form. By setting the color preference form values before viewing the Employee Payroll Form, we can alter the color settings on the Employee Payroll Form.

- Tested the splash screen, Login form, User Preferences form, and homepage menu, and then displayed the Employee Payroll Form, the Payroll Transaction System Help screen, and the Help About form.

- Building the application compiles the code and creates an executable file in the bin directory found under the application folder.

- Double-clicking on the exe program file proves that it is working without errors.

SKILLS

Add a Close button to the form (p. 10-14)

Add a Search group box to the EmpPayForm (p. 10-7)

Add code behind the Search button (p. 10-11)

Add code to the Clear button to empty search criteria (p. 10-13)

Add programming logic the populate the form controls (p. 10-12)

Add the User Preferences form to the sequence of forms loaded in the Sub Main procedure (p. 10-17)

Build the application so it can be distributed to another workstation (p. 10-19)

Change the project startup object from the EmpPayForm to the PayTransCommon Module (p. 10-4)

Create a PublicVariablesAndConstants module for code (p. 10-10)

Modify the EmpPayForm properties for background color and label text color based on the settings in the User Preferences form (p. 10-16)

Test the application (p. 10-18)

STUDY QUESTIONS

MULTIPLE CHOICE

1. Which code correctly closes a form and is found behind a form Close button?
a. Me.Close
b. Close.Me
c. Unload Me
d. Me Unload

2. When you build an application, the executable file is placed into what folder?
a. the same folder as the rest of the application code
b. a folder named Build
c. a folder named Bin under the application folder
d. a folder named Executable

3. Which of the following examples would you type in the Title field on the EmpPayForm object to retrieve all records that start with "Sales"?
a. Sales%
b. Sales*
c. %Sales
d. both a and c

4. When deploying an application, what does a user's workstation need to do to run the executable (*.exe*) program, assuming that the user has never run a Visual Basic .NET application before?
a. install the Visual Basic .NET SDK
b. just run the executable file (*.exe*)
c. install the Visual Basic .NET SDK and the executable (*.exe*) file, and a database if applicable
d. none of the above

5. When setting foreground colors for controls within a GroupBox control, we save a significant amount of coding because we
a. do not have to address each label contained within the group box individually.
b. only have to address labels within the GroupBox control.
c. only have to address TextBox controls.
d. have to address each label individually.

SHORT ANSWER

1. In order for users to run an application executable, exe file rather than in design mode, generated by Visual Basic .NET, what Microsoft software must they have previously installed?

2. It is often very convenient to copy and paste existing controls. This provides a consistent size and position for the controls. If the copied controls were data-bound to a data source, what data-related property must be set to None?

3. Where are public variables generally declared, and what scope do these variables have in the application?

4. What is the wildcard character used in this application, and why is it used?

5. What does it mean to concatenate strings, and what are the two equivalent examples provided in this project?

FILL IN THE BLANK

1. Changing the _____ object affects which form or code module is used when the application starts.

2. The _____ bindings property of a TextBox control determines what data field will populate the data-bound control.

3. The code statement _____ closes a form and is found behind the btnClose_Click event of a Close button.

4. To retrieve the background and foreground color values set in the User Preferences form ComboBox controls, we can check the _____ property of the label controls on that form.

5. When we build an application, the executable file is placed into a folder named _____ found under the application folder.

Glossary

About form A form that contains copyright information, the application name and version, and other information needed for support and additional help.

AcceptsTab When using a multiline TextBox control that has the AcceptsTab property set to True, Tab moves within the control. Press Ctrl + Tab⇆ to move to the next control in the tab index sequence.

Access keys Many users prefer to execute commands using the keyboard rather than mouse clicks. This is especially important in data entry activities and in situations where the keyboard is more efficient for end users (depending on their touch-typing skills). Access keys are identified by an underline. When you press the Alt key in conjunction with the access key, it invokes the option the same as if you had clicked it using the mouse.

Ampersand (&) An access key is an underlined character in the text of a menu, in a menu item, or on the label of a control such as a button. It enables the user to "click" a button by pressing the Alt key in combination with the access key. For example, if a button runs a procedure to print a form, and therefore its Text property is set to "Print," adding an ampersand before the letter P causes the letter P to be underlined in the button text at runtime. The user can run the command associated with the button by pressing Alt + P.

Assignment Variables enable you to store information for later use, and assignment is how you put information into variables.

Association An association is a straight line from an Actor or Use Case to another Actor or Use Case.

Autos window When you are debugging an application and stepping over a function call (F10), the Autos window displays the return value for that function and any functions that may be called by that function. To open the Autos window, you must be debugging; choose Debug | Windows | Autos.

BackColor property Returns or sets the background color of an object. For example, a form could have a background color of blue and all controls would appear on top of a blue background. Gray is the preferred background color.

BackColor-Transparent Setting the BackColor property of the UserControl object to Transparent allows whatever is behind your control to be seen between the constituent controls on your UserControl surface. When the BackStyleproperty is set to Transparent, the BackColor and Picture properties of the UserControl are ignored.

BackgroundImage Gets or sets the background image displayed in the control. This option enables you to choose an image to display or tile in the background of the form. You can either type in the image path in the BackgroundImage field, or click the Ellipsis (. . .) button and navigate to the file's location.

Bin subdirectory Specifies the working directory of the program being debugged. In Visual Basic, the working directory is the directory the application is launched from \bin by default.

BorderStyle Returns or sets the border style for an object. The following two properties are available: 1 for FixedSingle or 0 for None.

Breakpoint A breakpoint tells the debugger that an application should break (pause execution) at a certain point or when a certain condition occurs. When a break occurs, your program and the debugger are said to be in break mode.

Build Output box This window displays status messages for various features in the integrated development environment (IDE). These include build errors that occur when a project is compiled.

Build type Displays the kind of project build desired and lists all of the available kinds of builds. Visual Basic .NET can create two types of executable files; one as a debug build and the other as a release build.

Button control A button can be clicked by using the mouse, the [Enter ←] key, or the [Spacebar] if the button has focus.

Calling chain The code moves back up the calling chain to the procedure that called the code that contains the error.

Case statement Executes one of several groups of statements depending on the value of an expression.

Catch Optional. Multiple Catch blocks are permitted. If an error occurs while processing the Try block, each Catch statement is examined in textual order to determine whether it handles the error.

CausesValidation The CausesValidation control property exists on every control and can determine whether a control will trigger the validating procedure event.

CharacterCasing CharacterCasing is used to set the letters typed in to upper or lower case format.

CheckBox control The CheckBox control is used when the application needs to provide the user with one or more choices that can be selected at the same time.

CheckedListBox control The CheckedListBox control enables you to group related check box options in a scrollable list control. The user can place a check mark next to one or more items.

Class Classes are templates that have methods and attributes names and type information, but no actual values. They are an abstract representation of something. Classes are made of fields, properties, methods, and events.

Click event Occurs when the user presses and then releases a mouse button over an object. It can also occur when the value of a control is changed.

Code view Displays the code window so you can write and edit code associated with the selected item.

Collection A collection is a special type of property that contains a set or list of information in a predefined order. A collection is a way of grouping a set of related items. Collections are used in Visual Basic to keep track of many things, such as the loaded forms in your program (the Forms collection), or all the controls on a form (the Controls collection).

Color dialog box Enables the user to specify the desired color if one of the default values will not do.

ComboBox control A Combo Box control combines the features of a TextBox control and a ListBox control; users can enter information in the text box portion or select an item from the list box portion of the control.

Condition A condition can be any valid expression recognized by the debugger. It is usually evaluated as either True or False.

Configuration Manager Use this dialog box to create and edit solution build configurations and project configurations. Any changes you make to solution build configurations are reflected on the Configuration page of the Solution Property Pages dialog box. You can access the Configuration Manager from the Build menu, from the Solution Property Pages dialog box, or from the solution configuration drop-down on the main toolbar.

Connection A connection identifies the connection string and methods used to communicate with a database.

Constants Some variables do not change value during the execution of a program. These are constants that appear many times in your code. If the program performs mathematical computations with the value of pi (3.14159. . .), this value is best represented with a constant named PIE.

Control A self-contained object that has properties and provides features.

Control alignment To standardize the layout of the user interface of your Windows application, you can position groups of controls with a single command. Open the form containing the controls you want to position in the Windows Forms Designer. Select the controls you want to align so that the first control you select is the primary control to which the others should be aligned. Choose Format | Align, and then choose one of the seven options.

Control statements Control statements are parts of a programming language that exist only to determine what other parts of the program get executed. The determination occurs because the value of some variable or other criteria allows the program to act differently depending on the situation.

Copyright Statement of ownership and rules about distribution of files and components and licensing information.

Custom colors Within the Color dialog box, the user can choose to create a custom color. Once a custom color is created, the user can select it from the bottom of the Color dialog box and click OK to set the Color property.

Database Databases enable us to create tables, views, and stored procedures (predefined queries) in a consistent manner. A database is a set of data related to a particular topic or purpose. A database contains tables and can also contain queries and table relationships as well as table and column validation criteria.

Dataset A dataset is the container that holds the data used by the form. A dataset can have one or more tables and a form can have one or more datasets.

Data adapter A bridge that links your database and connection to the dataset.

Data model A data model is called an entity relationship diagram (ERD) and is used to depict relationships from one table to another.

Data Form Wizard The Data Form Wizard is a productivity tool that enables you to create Windows forms with data-bound controls without having to write the program from scratch.

DateTimePicker control The DateTimePicker control enables the user to select a date and time, and to display that date and time in the specified format. It returns a single date and time selected by the user.

Debugging Once you have created your application and resolved the build errors, you must correct any logical errors that keep your application or stored procedures from running correctly. You can do this with the development environment integrated debugging functions. These enable you to stop at procedure locations, inspect memory and register values, change variables, observe message traffic, and get a close look at how your code works or does not work.

Default item (ComboBox) The selected item in the combo box. The ComboBox control appears in two parts. The top part is a text box that enables the user to type a list item; the bottom part is a list box that displays a list from which the user can select one item.

Define Custom Colors button Within the Color dialog box, the user can create a custom color. Click the Define Custom Color button and then click in the Color Selection area to update the Hue, Sat, and Lum fields. You must click in the vertical bar at the right to select the exact color desired. This will update the Red, Green, and Blue values. The RGB color codes displayed in the Color field will be inserted when you close the Color dialog box. The decimal values displayed to the right of each slider range from 0 (no color) to 255 (maximum color).

Deployment The primary purpose of deployment is to install files on a target computer. The deployment tools in Visual Studio enable you to control where and how those files will be installed.

Design mode When the application is under construction and we can add controls and set properties.

Distribution When distributing your application, you need to determine what files are needed in your setup. The files you include depend on the components used in the application, the data source used for the application, and the options you want available to end users.

Encapsulation Encapsulation means that a group of related properties, methods, and other items are treated as a single unit or object.

Error Handler The Error Handler is where you handle errors when they occur.

Error Provider The Error Provider can be used to provide a visual cue of a user input error.

Events Events are notifications an object receives from or transmits to other objects or applications. Events allow objects to perform actions whenever a specific occurrence takes place.

Exception case Contains information about the error that occurred.

Executable A compiled version of project program code. A Windows-based application that can run outside the development environment. An executable file has an *.exe* extension.

Expression A combination of keywords, operators, variables, and constants that yields a string, number, or object. An expression can be used to perform a calculation, manipulate characters, or test data—for example, X=2.

Finally Optional. A Finally block is always executed when execution leaves any part of the Try statement.

Font Lists the available fonts.

Font dialog box Use the Text Tool Font dialog box to change the font, style, or size of the cursor font. Changes are applied to the text displayed in the Text area.

Font Size Lists the available point sizes for the specified font.

Font Style Lists the available styles for the specified font.

Foreign key A foreign key is a column or combination of columns whose values match the primary key of some other table.

ForeColor property Returns or sets the foreground color of an object. For example, the foreground color of a label is usually black to create a contrast to the gray background. You might set the foreground color to red to draw attention to a message. For example, if a required field is not filled in, you could create a label with red letters in a central location on a form, with the message text dynamically set—for example, "Employee Last Name is required."

Form—AcceptButton Optional property that sets AcceptButton=True.

Form—CancelButton Optional property that sets CancelButton=True.

Form icon Designates the picture that represents the form in the taskbar as well as the icon that is displayed next to the application control menu located on the left side of the title bar of the form.

FormatCurrency FormatCurrency is a specialized formatting command for easily and quickly generating output in a currency format.

FormatDateTime FormatDateTime returns a string formatted in a specified date and time format.

Form A collection of controls that is displayed when the program runs.

Form Load event Occurs when a form is loaded. For a startup form, it occurs when an application starts as the result of a Load statement or as the result of a reference to an unloaded form's properties or controls. Typically, you use a Load event procedure to include initialization code for a form-for example, code that specifies default settings for controls, indicates contents to be loaded into ComboBox or ListBox controls, and initializes form-level variables.

Form—MaximizeBox False value removes the Maximize button from the form at runtime.

Form—MinimizeBox False value removes the Minimize button from the form at runtime.

Form—ShowDialog() Forms and dialog boxes are either modal or modeless. A modal form or dialog box must be closed or hidden before you can continue working with the rest of the application. Dialog boxes that display important messages should always be modal. The About dialog box in Visual Studio is an example of a modal dialog box. A message box is a modal form you can use. Modeless forms let you shift the focus between the form and another form without having to close the initial form. The user can continue to work elsewhere in any application while the form is displayed. Modeless forms are harder to program, because users can access them in an unpredictable order. You have to keep the state of the application consistent no matter what the user does. Often, tool windows are shown in a modeless fashion. The Find dialog box, accessible from the Edit menu in Visual Studio, is an example of a modeless dialog box. Use modeless forms to display frequently used commands or information.

GroupBox control Displays a frame around a group of controls with or without a caption. Use a GroupBox control to logically group a collection of controls on a form. The typical use for a group box is to contain several radio buttons.

Hide Returns or sets a value that determines whether the object is hidden.

Icon An image associated with the application and displayed in the taskbar, or an application control at the left end of the title bar of a form. This is set in the project properties.

IDE The Visual Studio .NET Interactive Development Environment (IDE) is the command center console where you create applications and programs for business, education, and personal use.

If statement The If statement is one of the most useful control structures. It enables you to evaluate a sequence of statements if a condition is true and evaluate a different sequence of statements if it is not true. When a multiple-line If Then Else statement is encountered, the condition is tested. If the condition is True, the statements following Then are executed. If the condition is False, each ElseIf statement is evaluated in order. When a True ElseIf condition is found, the statements immediately following the associated Then are executed. If no ElseIf condition evaluates to True, or if there are no ElseIf statements, the statements following Else are executed. After executing the statements following Then, ElseIf, or Else, execution continues with the statement following EndIf.

ImageAlign—Left Aligns the image to the top left of the label.

Immediate mode The Immediate mode of the Command window is used for debugging purposes such as evaluating expressions, executing statements, printing variable values, and so forth. It enables you to enter expressions to be evaluated or executed by the development language during debugging. In some cases, you can change the value of variables.

Inheritance Inheritance describes the ability to create new classes based on an existing class. The new class inherits all the properties and methods and events of the base class, and can be customized with additional properties and methods. Inheritance enables you to write and debug a class once, and then reuse that code over and over as the basis of new classes.

Inherits Causes the current class or interface to inherit the attributes, fields, properties, methods, and events from another class or interface.

InputBox statement The InputBox statement displays a prompt in a dialog box, waits for the user to input text or click a button, and then returns a string containing the contents of the text box.

Instance Any one of a set of objects sharing the same class. For example, multiple instances of a Form class share the same code and are loaded with the same controls with which the Form class was designed. During runtime, the individual properties of controls on each instance can be set to different values.

Instantiate To create an instance of a class; that is, to allocate and initialize an object's data structures in memory.

Intrinsic controls Tools you can use. Some intrinsic controls include PictureBox, Label, Textbox, Group (Frame), Checkbox, Option Button, Combo box, List box, HScrollBar, VScrollBar, Timer, DriveListBox, DirListBox, FileListBox, Shape, Line, Image, and Data.

IsMDIContainer In Visual Basic 6.0, multiple-document interface (MDI) applications were created by adding an MDI form to a project and setting the MDI Child property of any child forms. In Visual Basic .NET, any form can be made an MDI parent by setting the IsMDIContainer property to true.

Label Within code, this character appears at the end of the line and is often reached using a Goto statement. An example of a label within code would be My_Error_Handler: The Colon character is an indicator of a label within a code statement.

Label control A Label control is a graphical control you can use to display text that a user cannot change directly. The Label control is a container for static text. It is often used to provide a caption that appears next to a text box or other type of control. It is also used to provide a read-only view of data.

Line continuation character A single line of Visual Basic .NET code can be as many as 1,023 characters long, but for readability purposes, you are advised not to type beyond the width of the code window. By using the underscore (_) character, you can split a Visual Basic .NET statement onto more than one line.

ListBox control The ListBox control enables you to display a list of items that the user can select by clicking. A ListBox control can provide single or multiple selections using the SelectionMode property. The ListBox also provides the MultiColumn property to display items in columns instead of in a straight vertical list. This allows the control to display more visible items and prevents the need for the user to scroll to an item.

Local variable If a variable is declared within a procedure, it is considered a local variable and only the code in the specific procedure has access to that variable. Local variables, declared within procedures with the Dim or Private statement, exist for as long as the procedures in which they were declared.

Location Sets the location of the label in pixels.

Logical errors Conditions that cause the program to produce the wrong results. Logical errors are the most common and most difficult to correct; many of the debugging tools help us diagnose and correct them.

MainMenu control The Windows Forms MainMenu control displays a menu at runtime. If you add this component in the Windows Forms Designer, the Menu Designer enables you to visually set up the structure of the main menu. The MainMenu control enables you to create and maintain menus in your forms. With the tool you can add, change, and delete menu items; reorder them; and set up access keys. There are properties to help customize menus, and you can use event procedures to invoke the menu commands when they are selected at runtime.

MaxLength Indicates the maximum length of the text the user can type into a control. Commonly found in the ComboBbox or TextBox controls.

MDI parent form The foundation of an MDI application is the MDI parent form. This is the form that contains the MDI child windows, which are the "subwindows" wherein the user interacts with the MDI application. Creating an MDI parent form is easy, both in the Windows Forms Designer and programmatically.

Menu Designer A Visual Basic .NET tool that enables you to create structured menus and context menus. To add menus using the Menu Designer, you need to have either a MainMenu or ContextMenu control added to your form. With either of these controls added (and selected within the control tray at the bottom of the Windows Forms Designer), you will see the text "Type Here" or "Context Menu" just below the caption bar of the form. Clicking this text and typing will create a menu item whose Text property is specified by the name you type. Additionally, by right-clicking the Menu Designer, you can insert new menu items, add a separator to the menu you are designing, or open the Name Editor (which enables you to modify the Name property of the menu items you are creating).

Menu–Separator Visual Basic .NET enables you to insert a gray line called a separator above the currently selected menu item. To add a separator, select a menu subitem, then right-click and choose Insert Separator. In Windows, most of the menus include separators to group similar processes. For instance, under the File menu, New, Open, and Close are all file commands and should be grouped together. Grouping menu items is not a perfect science and can vary by individual and organizational preferences.

MessageBox class The MessageBox class provides a way to display simple dialog boxes that show a message and/or ask the user to make a choice from a fixed set of options.

Method A member function of an exposed object that performs some action on the object. Methods represent actions that an object can perform. For example, a Car object could have StartEngine, Drive, and Stop methods.

MonthCalendar control Visual Basic .NET provides an extremely useful MonthCalendar control that enables the user to select a date (or range of dates) using a friendly user interface. You can limit the dates and times that can be selected by setting the MinDate and MaxDate properties.

MsgBox Displays a message. The MessageBox class is preferred in Visual Basic .NET.

Multi-line property A multi-line text box enables you to display more than one line of text in the control. If the WordWrap property is set to True, text entered into the multi-line text box is wrapped to the next line in the control. If the WordWrap property is set to False, text entered into the multi-line text box control will be displayed on the same line until a new-line character is entered. You can add scroll bars to a text box using the ScrollBars property to display horizontal and/or vertical scroll bars. This enables the user to scroll through text that extends beyond the dimensions of the control. Note: This property is set to False by default for all derived classes, with the exception of the RichTextBox control.

Object (1) A combination of code and data that can be treated as a unit-for example, a control, form, or application. A class defines each object. (2) An object is an instance of a class that combines data with procedures.

PasswordChar Indicates the character used to mask characters in a single-line TextBox control used to enter passwords.

PictureBox control A PictureBox control can display a graphic from a bitmap, icon, or metafile, as well as enhanced metafile, JPEG, or GIF files. It clips the graphic if the control isn't large enough to display the entire image.

Pointer control If you click to select a control from the Toolbox, the mouse pointer symbol will change to a plus sign (+). This is intended to prepare you to draw the control. If you change your mind and need the mouse pointer reset to normal, and the capability to click to select an existing control on the form to set properties, select the Pointer control in the Toolbox.

Primary key A primary key is a column or combination of columns that uniquely identifies a row in a table. It cannot allow null values and must always have a unique index.

Project A collection of related files.

Project startup object By default, the first form in your application is designated as the project startup object. When your application starts running, this form is displayed (so the first code to execute is the code in the Form_Initialize event for that form). If you want to display a different form when your application starts, you must change the startup object.

Property A named attribute of an object. Properties define object characteristics such as size, color, and screen location, or the state of an object, such as enabled or disabled.

RadioButton control A RadioButton control displays an option that can be turned on or off. Radio buttons are rarely used singly. Instead, they are grouped to provide a set of mutually exclusive options. Within a group, only one radio button can be selected at a time.

ReadOnly The ReadOnly property of a TextBox control prevents editing of text contained within the control.

Run dialog box Provides a place for you to type the location and file name of the program you want to run. If you are not sure of the program's location or file name, click Browse. You can make a temporary network connection by typing the path to a shared computer. You can also connect to the Internet by typing the address (URL) of the site you want to open. You can activate the Run dialog box by choosing Start | Run.

Runtime When the application is processing code using a compiled (*.exe*) version of the program.

Runtime errors Conditions that occur only after you run the program (hence "runtime"). A user may enter data out of the expected range of input, or a file may unexpectedly reach an end-of-file (EOF) condition. Runtime errors could also be misspellings, in which you incorrectly name a table or column and receive an error only when you attempt to use that table or column.

Scope Defines the visibility of a variable, procedure, or object. For example, a variable declared as Public is visible to all procedures in all modules. Variables declared in procedures are visible only within the procedure and lose their value between calls unless they are declared Static.

SelectedIndexChanged event A property provided by Visual Basic .NET when a combo box selection is made. The Selected Index property returns an integer value that corresponds to the selected list item. You can programmatically change the selected item by changing the Selected Index value in code. The corresponding item in the list will appear in the text portion of the combo box. If no item is selected, the Selected Index value is -1. If the first item in the list is selected, then the Selected Index value is 0. This indicates which item you selected from the list.

Server Explorer Visual Basic .NET can provide robust data storage using a database and provide forms that can update the database easily using the Server Explorer. This tool creates a link between a programming project and the database.

ShowDialog method In Visual Basic .NET, the Show Dialog method is used to display a form modally; the Show method is used to display a form nonmodally. A form shown modally must be closed before any other activity can be done in the application. It is often used to present a message to the user that you want to make sure he or she sees. The user then simply clicks an OK button and the form is closed. An About box is an example of form that is shown modally.

Size Mode Auto Size—Allows the image to be stretched if the form is resized.

Solution Explorer A collection of related projects.

Splash screen If you need to execute a lengthy procedure on startup, such as loading a large amount of data from a database or loading several large bitmaps, you might want to display a splash screen on startup. A splash screen usually displays information such as the name of the application, copyright information, and a simple bitmap. The screen that appears when you start Visual Basic is a splash screen.

Standard naming conventions Establishing standard naming conventions for controls helps identify the type of control being used and the associated properties available.

StartPosition Start the form centered from the parent form.

Statement A syntactically complete unit that expresses one kind of action, declaration, or definition. A statement generally occupies a single line, although you can use a colon (:) to include more than one statement on a line. You can also use a line-continuation character (_) to continue a single logical line onto a second physical line.

Structured error handling Structured error handling uses the Try, Catch, and Finally statements.

Switchboard form A form that provides a few buttons to simplify the screen for the user by reducing potential decisions for using an application.

Syntax checking A feature that checks your code for correct syntax. If the syntax checking feature is enabled, a message is displayed when you enter code that contains a syntax error and the suspect code is highlighted.

Syntax errors Conditions where a keyword or variable is misspelled; the code editor points out these conditions visually by underlining the syntax in question with a jagged blue line. These errors are the easiest to spot; you cannot run the program until all syntax errors are identified and corrected.

System.IO foundation class (Stream Reader)
The System.IO Namespace class enables you to read and write characters to and from streams or files, using specific encoding to convert characters to and from bytes. It includes a pair of classes, StreamReader and StreamWriter, which enable you to read or write a sequential stream of characters to or from a file.

TextAlign Indicates how text is aligned in the TextBox control, using a HorizontalAlignment value of Center, Left, or Right.

TextBox control A TextBox control, sometimes called an edit field or edit control, display information entered in Design-time.

Try Marks the beginning of a structured error handling routine that includes Try and the End Try statement.

UML UML is a system of notation for how concepts, automated processes, human interactions, and associations can be represented. With UML you use standard notation for defining various human and application activities.

Unload event In Visual Basic 6.0, the Unload event had a Cancel argument; in Visual Basic .NET, it is replaced by the Closed event, which does not have a Cancel argument. If you need to cancel during unloading, use the Closing event instead. To unload a form is to remove it from memory and no longer display the form.

Unstructured error handling Unstructured error handlers use the On Error Goto statement.

Use Case A Use Case is a process.

Use Case diagram A diagram used to describe the main processes in a system and the interactions between the processes (use cases) and external systems or individuals.

Validated Occurs when the control is finished performing its validation logic.

Validating Occurs when the control is validating user input (for example, when the control loses focus).

Visible Returns or sets a value indicating whether an object is visible or hidden.

Watch window You can use the Watch window to evaluate variables and expressions and keep the results. You can also use the Watch window to edit the value of a variable or register. To open the Watch window, the debugger must be running or in break mode. Choose Debug | Windows | Watch.

Window state Sets or returns the state of the window. The following are the three window state settings: vsWindowStateNormal 0 (window is normal), vsWindowStateMinimize 1 (window is minimized), and vsWindowStateMaximize 2 (window is maximized).

Windows Application project A project template designed to create applications using the user interface common to all Windows operating systems.

Index

T

Tab Order command (View menu), VB 7-42

Tab Order wizard, VB 7-42–43

tab order, VB 6-10

TabIndex property, VB 6-10

table relationships, VB 9-17–21
  parent/child, VB 10-10

TargetSite property, VB 8-16

templates, VB 9-13
  adding forms from, VB 5-13–14
  classes, VB 1-11
  Windows Application project, VB 1-5

terminology
  debugging-related, VB 3-5
  error-related, VB 3-13
  form controls and properties, VB 1-5, VB 4-3–4
  menu-related, VB 5-3–4, VB 5-16–17, VB 5-27
  multiple forms and events, VB 4-3–4
  programming-oriented, VB 2-4–6

Test Connection button, VB 9-9

testing
  applications, VB 10-16–17
  ButtonDemo form, VB 6-19
  code, VB 2-6, VB 2-16–17
  forms, VB 9-22–24
  HelpDeskTracker form, VB 6-33–35
  Login project, VB-10–11
  Pay Transaction System project, VB 1-14–15
  programs, VB 5-36–40
  software, VB 2-12–13
  Textbox Demo form, VB 6-14
  User Preferences form, VB 2-18–19

text
  alignment, VB 5-4
  buttons, VB 6-15, VB 6-22
  form labels, VB 5-9
  menu labels, VB 5-4
  text boxes, VB 6-9

color
  label text, VB 10-14–15
  Text/Foreground color combo box, 6-17–18

TextBox property, VB 9-29

Text property, VB-5
  &Close, VB 5-10
  ComboBox controls, VB 6-28
  forms, VB 5-6, VB 5-9
  GroupBox controls, VB 9-27–37
  ListBox control, VB 6-32
  switchboard, VB 6-6

Text Tool Font dialog box, VB 5-3

Text/Foreground Color combo box, VB 2-17

TextAlign property, VB 6-9, VB 6-15, VB 6-22

TextBox controls, VB 1-5, VB 5-7, VB 6-8–14, VB 10-8–9
  alignment of text, VB 6-9
  properties, VB 6-9, VB 6-24, VB 9-28–35
  Multi-line, VB 5-4, VB 6-30
  request number label, VB 6-23–24
  Textbox Demo form, VB 6-9–14
    adding controls, VB 10–12
    adding code to controls, VB 12–13
    testing, VB 6-14

This Imports System.IO statements, VB 5-11

ThreeState property, VB 6-22

time. *See* Date/Time

title bar, VB 1-8

TodayDate property, VB 6-26

TodayDateSet property, VB 6-26

Toolbars
  Debug, VB 3-10–11, VB 1-15
  saving with, VB-11

Toolbox, VB-9
  Button control, VB 6-7
  coded stored, VB 7-11
  double-clicking objects, VB 1-11
  Pointer control, VB 6-29

tools
  Debug menu, VB 3-10–11
  deployment, VB 3-5

Menu Designer, VB 5-4
Windows Forms Designer, VB 5-4

Tools menu, Debug, Run, VB-5

ToolTipOn property, VB 7-4

ToolTips
  properties, VB 7-3
  using with controls, VB 7-3–5

top-level menus, VB 5-19

TopIndex control property, VB 6-32

tracking values, VB 3-17–18

Transparent value, VB 5-8

Try code, VB 8-15

txtMulti-lineTextbox control, VB 6-11

txtNotes control, VB 6-30

TxtPassword control, VB 6-12

TxtRequestNumber control, VB 6-24

txtUpperCase control properties, VB 6-12

typing errors, VB 1-12, VB 3-13, VB 9-40

U

"Under Construction" message, VB 5-31–36, 40

underscore/line-continuation character (_), VB 2-6, VB 7-44

Unified Modeling Language (UML), VB-2–3

Unload event, VB 4-4

unstructured error handling, VB 8-11–13

user input
  errors, VB 8-17
  validating, VB 8-3

user interface objects, VB 1-11

user preferences, color, VB 10-15

User Preferences form
  adding to sequence of forms loaded in Sub Main procedure, VB 10-15–16
  creating, VB 1-7–8
  testing, VB 2-18–19

User Preferences Form, VB 5-30–31, VB 10-14–15

User Preferences screen,
  invoking, VB 5-36–40
UserControl object, VB 5-3
UserPreferences_Load, VB 2-15

V

valid commands, line feeds,
  VB 7-7
Validated property, VB 8-3
Validating property, VB 8-3
validation of user input, VB 8-3
validation routines, VB 8-3–6
values
  adding to ComboBox
    controls, VB 1-13
  arguments, VB 2-19
  assigning, VB 7-19, VB 10-11
  changing at runtime,
    VB 3-21–22
  CheckBox control, VB 6-22
  checking for, VB 7-31
  comparison by Visual Basic,
    VB 7-34
  current, watch objects,
    VB 3-19
  default, VB 2-15
  deleting, DataBindings Text
    property, VB 10-8
  FlatStyle button control,
    VB 6-15
  Foreign key, VB 9-17
  Form property, VB 5-6
  Homepage form properties,
    VB 4-7
  Label property, VB 4-13
  MaxDate, VB 6-24
  PictureBox property, VB 4-12
  property, Version Info, VB 5-16
  query, VB 10-12
  selecting, VB 1-12
  splash screen form properties,
    VB 4-10
  step, VB 7-37–39
  Transparent, VB 5-8
  using entered, VB 10-9
variable conversion functions,
  VB 7-8–9
Variable watches, creating,
  VB 3-17–18

variables
  assigning values, VB 7-19
  Boolean, VB 7-8
  changing properties, at
    runtime, VB 3-21–22
  counter, VB 7-37
  declaration statements for,
    VB 2-8
  declaring, VB 7-7
  examining, VB 3-23
  integer-type, Count, VB 7-38
  integrating, VB 7-5–10
  local, VB 7-14–15
  naming prefixes for, VB 7-6
  naming, VB 7-6, VB 7-10
  reinitializing, VB 7-33
  scope, VB 3-5
  setting lifetime, VB 7-19–20
  setting module-level,
    VB 7-15–17
  setting public, VB 7-17–19
  static, VB 7-20–22
  string-type, requestInfo, VB 7-7
  String, VB 2-17
  using scope with, VB 7-14
  using, VB 10-9–10
variables, VB 7-6
VB .NET. *See* Visual Basic .NET
verifying
  data connection setups,
    VB 9-9–11
  data type functions, VB 7-8–9
  property settings, VB 5-13–14,
    VB 5-16–18
version control systems, VB 1-7
Version Info property value,
  VB 5-16
View Code button, VB 4-2
View menu commands
  Code, VB 2-16
  Other Windows, Command
    Window, VB 3-22
  Properties, VB 5-24
  Properties Window, VB 2-9
  Tab Order, VB 7-42
viewing Autos window,
  VB 3-16–17
views
  Code, VB 2-5
  Design, VB 2-5

visibility of variables/
  procedures/objects, VB 3-5
Visible, VB 4-4
Visual Basic .NET
  exiting, VB-13
  interface, VB-4
    screen elements, VB-9–10
  launching, VB-5–6
  opening existing projects,
    VB-7–8
  programming terminology,
    VB-4–5
  running Login project,
    VB-10–11
  saving changes, VB-11–12
Visual Studio, executing
  commands, VB 3-22

W-X-Y-Z

warning messages, VB 2-18
Watch window, VB 3-5,
  VB 3-17–19, VB 3-23
When clause, VB 8-14
widening forms, VB 9-25–30
Width property, VB 1-9
wildcard character (%), VB 10-17
Window state, VB 4-4
windows
  Autos, VB 3-16–17
  closing designer windows,
    VB 7-9
  Property, VB-9–11
  Watch, VB 3-5, VB 3-17–19,
    VB 3-23
Windows (Debug menu option),
  VB 3-14
Windows Application project
  template, VB 1-5
Windows Form Color Dialog,
  VB 2-11
wizards
  Data Form, VB 9-4,
    VB 9-13–25
  Tab Order, VB 7-42–43
WordWrap property, VB 5-4,
  VB 6-9
writing code, VB 7-40

yellow highlighted text, VB 8-16